Praise for *Agile Game Dev*

"If you've ever felt that gaps exist between 'traditional software development' using Scrum and video game development using Scrum, this book is for you. Clinton effectively bridges those gaps by covering the adjustments necessary for disciplines, individual roles, and processes and project phases unique to game development, thoroughly supporting it with explicit examples and practical advice. Simply put, a must-read for game developers that are currently using or plan to implement Scrum or other agile processes within their company."

—*Jeff Lindsey, Producer, Longtail Studios*

"I wish Clinton Keith could go back and write this book 15 years ago—it would have helped me see things a lot differently. *Agile Game Development with SCRUM* is a one-stop-shop for game teams interested in using scrum techniques."

—*CJ Connoy, Game Producer, Treyarch*

"By the time you wake up and realize that you really need this book, your project will probably be too far gone. Dive into agile before it's too late and let Clinton be your guide. Tested under the fires of true game production, everyone involved in game development will gain from reading Clinton's wisdom."

—*Jason Della Rocca, Founder, Perimeter Partners, and former Executive Director of the International Game Developers Association*

"Clinton Keith has written an excellent book for both practitioners and students. He combines an in-depth analysis of the challenges of large scale game development with hands-on advice on the use of Scrum. His often funny anecdotes illustrate that this guy has really experienced the heat of large computer games projects."

—*Bendik Bygstad, Professor of Information Systems, The Norwegian School of IT*

"Clinton Keith combines his experience as both video game developer and agile practitioner to apply Scrum philosophy to the unique challenges of video game development. Clint clearly explains the philosophy behind Scrum, going beyond theory and sharing his experiences and stories about its successful application at living, breathing development studios."

—*Erik Theisz, Senior Producer, 38 Studios*

"Clinton has combined his extensive game and software development experiences with agile methodologies. The result is a thoughtful, clear, and, most importantly, realistic application of agile to game development."

—*Senta Jakobsen, Senior Development Director, DICE*

AGILE GAME DEVELOPMENT WITH SCRUM

The Addison-Wesley

Signature Series

Kent Beck, Mike Cohn, and Martin Fowler, Consulting Editors

Visit **informit.com/awss** for a complete list of available products.

The **Addison-Wesley Signature Series** provides readers with practical and authoritative information on the latest trends in modern technology for computer professionals. The series is based on one simple premise: Great books come from great authors. Books in the series are personally chosen by expert advisors, world-class authors in their own right. These experts are proud to put their signatures on the covers, and their signatures ensure that these thought leaders have worked closely with authors to define topic coverage, book scope, critical content, and overall uniqueness. The expert signatures also symbolize a promise to our readers: You are reading a future classic.

AGILE GAME DEVELOPMENT WITH SCRUM

CLINTON KEITH

Addison-Wesley

Upper Saddle River, NJ • Boston • Indianapolis • San Francisco
New York • Toronto • Montreal • London • Munich • Paris • Madrid
Capetown • Sydney • Tokyo • Singapore • Mexico City

The publisher offers excellent discounts on this book when ordered in quantity for bulk purchases or special sales, which may include electronic versions and/or custom covers and content particular to your business, training goals, marketing focus, and branding interests. For more information, please contact:

U.S. Corporate and Government Sales
(800) 382-3419
corpsales@pearsontechgroup.com

For sales outside the United States please contact:

International Sales
international@pearson.com

Visit us on the Web: informit.com/aw

Library of Congress Cataloging-in-Publication Data

Keith, Clinton.
Agile game development with Scrum / Clinton Keith.
p. cm.
Includes index.
ISBN 0-321-61852-1 (pbk. : alk. paper) 1. Computer games—Programming. 2. Agile software development. 3. Scrum (Computer software development) I. Title.
QA76.76.C672K45 2010
005.1—dc22

2010006513

ISBN-13: 978-0-321-61852-8
ISBN-10: 0-321-61852-1
Text printed in the United States on recycled paper at LCS Communications

5 17

To Sherry, Bryson, and Nathan—I love you with all of my heart.

Contents

Foreword

The insight that Scrum (indeed, agile software development in general) and game development were a near-perfect match was no surprise to Clinton Keith. As the CTO of his studio, he was a pioneer in the pairing of Scrum and game development. Though some were skeptical, Clint saw the possibilities, and as a result, he not only created the first game developed using Scrum but also helped his teams put the fun back into game development.

And why shouldn't game development be fun as well as profitable? It's true that the game industry is well known for aggressive deadlines and that teams are working with ambiguous requirements in a very fluid marketplace, but that is exactly the kind of environment where Scrum can help the most. Because Scrum is iterative and incremental and forces a team to put the game into a playable state at least every two to four weeks, the team members can see new features and scenarios develop right before their eyes.

In *Agile Game Development with Scrum*, Clint shares his experience and insights with us. He tells us everything we need to know to successfully use Scrum in the challenging field of game development. In doing so, he provides an introduction to agile and Scrum and tells us how they can help manage the increasing complexity facing most game development efforts. He explains how something as large and integrated as "AAA" console games can be developed incrementally. Along the way, Clint offers invaluable guidance on getting all of the specialists who are necessary on a game project to work together in an agile manner. He even delves into how to use Scrum when working with a publisher. In providing all of this guidance, Clint doesn't shy away from the challenges. Instead, he generously shares his advice so that we can perhaps avoid some of them.

There is little doubt in my mind that the book you are holding can have a profound effect on any game project and studio. Once introduced to and accustomed to Scrum, team members will not want to work any other way. They will have learned what Clint knew long ago—that Scrum is the best way to handle the complexity and uncertainty of game development.

—Mike Cohn
Cofounder, Scrum Alliance
and Agile Alliance

Foreword

Preface

This book was written for game developers who either are using agile methodologies or are curious about what it all means. It condenses much information from a number of fields of agile product development and applies it to the game industry's unique ecosystem. It's based on the experiences of dozens of studios that have shipped games using agile over the past six years.

If you are not in the game industry but curious about it or agile, you should enjoy this book. Since the book needs to communicate to every discipline, it doesn't get bogged down in the specifics of any one of them because, for example, artists need to understand the challenges and solutions faced by programmers for cross-discipline teams to work well.

As you can tell from the title, this book focuses on Scrum more than any other area of agile. Scrum is a discipline-agnostic framework to build an agile game development process. It doesn't have any defined art, design, or programming practices. It's a foundation that allows you and your teams to inspect every aspect of how you make games and adapt practices to do what works best.

How did agile and game development meet? For me, it started in 2002 at Sammy Studios. Like many studios, our path to agile came by way of impending disaster. Sammy Studios was founded in 2002 by a Japanese Pachinko manufacturing company. Their goal was to rapidly establish a dominant presence in the Western game industry. To that end, Sammy Studios was funded and authorized to do whatever was needed to achieve that goal.

As seasoned project managers, we quickly established a project management structure that included a license of Microsoft Project Server to help us manage all the necessary details for our flagship game project called Darkwatch.

The plan for Darkwatch was ambitious. It was meant to rival Halo as the preeminent first-person console shooter. At the time, we thought that as long as we had the resources and planning software, little could go wrong that we couldn't manage.

It didn't take long for many things to go wrong. Within a year we were six months behind schedule and slipping further every day. How was this happening?

- **Disciplines were working on separate plans:** Each discipline had goals that permitted them to work separately much of the time. For example, the animation technology was being developed according to a plan that called for many unique features to be developed before any were proven. This resulted in the animation programmer working on limbs that could be severed while the animators were still trying to make simple transitions work. Correcting these problems required major overhauls of the schedule on a regular basis.

- **The build was always broken:** It took exceptional effort to get the latest version of the game working. The Electronic Entertainment Expo (E3) demos took more than a month of debugging and hacking to produce a build that was acceptable. Even then, the game had to be run by a developer who had to frequently reboot the demo machine.
- **Estimates and schedules were always too optimistic:** Every scheduled item, from small tasks to major milestone deliverables, seemed to be late. Unanticipated work was either completed on personal time or put off for the future. This led to many nights and weekends of overtime work.
- **Management was constantly "putting out fires" and never had time to address the larger picture:** We managers selected one of the many problems to fix each week and organized large meetings that lasted most of a day in an attempt to solve it. Our list of problems grew faster than our ability to solve them. We never had the time to look to the future and guide the project.

The list goes on, and the problems continued to grow. Most problems were caused by our inability to foresee many of the project details necessary to justify our comprehensive plan's assumptions beyond even a month. The bottom line was that our planning methodology was wrong.

Eventually our Japanese parent company interceded with major staff changes. The message was clear: Since management was given every possible resource we wanted, any problems were our own fault, and we were given short notice to correct them. Not only our jobs but also the existence of the studio hung in the balance.

It was in these desperate times that I began researching alternative project management methods. Agile practices such as Scrum and Extreme Programming (XP) were not unknown to us. The original CTO of Sammy had us try XP, and a project lead was experimenting with some Scrum practices. After reading a book about Scrum (Schwaber and Beedle 2002), I became convinced that it could be used in our environment.

Upon discovering Scrum, we felt that we had found a framework to leverage the talent and passion of game development teams. It was challenging. The rules of Scrum were biased toward teams of programmers creating IT projects. Some things didn't work.

This began an endless series of discoveries about what *agile* meant and what worked for game developers. I began speaking about agile game development in 2005. This was around the time that studios were developing titles for Xbox 360 and PlayStation 3. Teams of more than 100 people were becoming the norm, and project failures cost in the tens of millions. Unfortunately, many took the agile message too far and perceived it as a silver bullet.

In 2008, after speaking with hundreds of developers at dozens of studios, I decided that I enjoyed helping game developers adopt agile enough to become a full-time independent coach. I now coach many studio teams a year and teach developers how to be ScrumMasters in public classes. My experiences working with and learning from these developers have led to this book.

Organization

Part I, "The Problem and the Solution," begins with the history of the game industry. How have the industry's products and methodologies for development changed? What has led us to bloated budgets, schedules that are never met, and project overtime death marches? It concludes with an overview of agile and how the problems of managing the development of games can benefit from agile's values.

Part II, "Scrum and Agile Planning," describes Scrum, its roles and practices, and how it's applied to game development. It describes how a game's vision, features, and progress are communicated, planned, and iterated over the short and long term.

Part III, "Agile Game Development," describes how agile is used over the full course of a game development project, including where some of the Scrum practices can be supplemented with lean principles and kanban practices for production. It explores agile teams and how Scrum can be scaled to large staffs, which might be distributed across the globe. Part III concludes by examining how teams continuously improve their velocity by decreasing the time required to iterate on every aspect of building a game.

Part IV, "Agile Disciplines," explains how each of the widely diverse disciplines work together on an agile team. It describes the role of leadership for each discipline and how each one maps to Scrum roles.

Part V, "Getting Started," details the challenges and solutions of introducing agile practices to your studio and publisher. Overcoming cultural inertia and integrating agile principles into a studio's unique processes—without destroying the benefits—can take time, and there many challenges along the way. The chapters in this part are a guide to meeting these challenges.

Although this is a starting place for agile game development, it is by no means the end. There are great books about Scrum, Extreme Programming, lean, kanban, user stories, agile planning, and game development. These books will provide all the detail desired on the path of continual improvement.

Developers for iPhone, PC, and massively multiplayer online games use the practices described here. I share many stories based on my technical background, and indeed there are more existing practices for the agile programmer, but the book applies to the entire industry. There are stories and experiences shared from many people from every discipline, genre, and platform.

Acknowledgments

To my colleagues for sharing your stories, knowledge, and feedback over the years.

To my manuscript reviewers: Bendik Bygstad, CJ Connoy, Jeff Lindsey, Erik Theisz and all of 38 Studios, Jason Della Rocca, and Senta Jakobsen. Their level of detailed feedback was tremendous and added a great deal of value to the book.

This book took almost two years to write. During this time, I received much feedback and advice from those who downloaded draft chapters and helped steer the direction the book took: Bas Vodde, Chris Oltyan, Diogo Neves, George Somaru, Heather Maxwell Chandler, Jamie Briant, Julian Gollop, Karen Clark, Lia Siojo, Lyssa Clark Adkins, Martin Keywood, Paul Evans, Philip Borgnes, Robert Bacon, Ron Artigues, Rose Hunt, Scott Blinn, Sheldon Brown, Steve Sargent, Wanda Meloni, LaRae Brim, Keith Boesky, Aðalsteinn "Alli" Óttarsson, and Barbara Chamberlin. Extra thanks to Justin Woodward for all his artistic help and advice!

To Bruce Rennie, Michael Riccio, Rory McGuire, Stephane Etienne, Caroline Esmurdoc, Shelly Warmuth, Chris Ulm, and Alistair Doulin. I thank them for letting me use their words.

Many thanks to everyone from Pearson including Chris Guzikowski for his persistence, vision, and support seeing this book through; Chris Zahn for his patient editing; and Raina Chrobak, Molly Sharp, and Kim Wimpsett for the great production support.

To everyone at High Moon Studios and at my client studios for allowing me to work with and learn from them.

I'd like to acknowledge the inestimable debt to my mentor and friend Mike Cohn. Mike visited High Moon Studios as a coach. Seeing the impact of his teaching inspired me to want to do the same. I couldn't have taken this major step without his support and encouragement.

Finally, I can't thank my family enough for their loving support and encouragement.

About the Author

Clinton Keith is an independent agile coach and Certified Scrum Trainer who helps game developers and nongame developers alike adopt Scrum, Extreme Programming, kanban, and other agile practices to greatly improve their productivity, workplace, and product quality.

Over the course of 25 years, Clint has gone from programming avionics for advanced fighter jets and underwater robots to overseeing programming for hit video games such as Midtown Madness and Midnight Club. Clint has been a programmer, project director, CTO, and director of product development at several studios. Through a series of presentations and his popular blog, Clint introduced the video game industry to Scrum in 2005. As CTO, Clint helped High Moon Studios achieve a place on *IT Week Magazine*'s Top 50 Technology Innovators list in 2005 and 2006 and win several of San Diego Society for HR Management's Workplace Excellence Awards in 2005, 2006, and 2007.

For more information, visit www.ClintonKeith.com.

Part I

The Problem and the Solution

Chapter 1

The Crisis Facing Game Development

The pioneer days of video game development have all but disappeared. The sole programmer—who designed, programmed, and rendered the art on their own—has been replaced by armies of specialists. An industry that sold its goods in Ziploc bags now rakes in more cash than the Hollywood box office. As an industry, we've matured a bit.

However, in our rush to grow up, we've made some mistakes. We've inherited some discredited methodologies for making games from other industries. Like children wearing their parents' old clothes, we've frocked ourselves in ill-fitting practices. We've met uncertainty and complexity of our projects with planning tools and prescriptive practices that are more likely to leave a "pretty corpse" at the end of the project than a hit game on the shelves. We've created a monster that has removed much of the fun from making fun products. This monster eats the enthusiasm of extremely talented people who enter the game development industry with hopes of entertaining millions. Projects capped with months of overtime (aka **crunch**) feed it. A high proportion of developers are leaving the industry and taking years of experience with them. It doesn't need to be this way.

In this chapter, we'll look at the history of game development and how it has evolved from individuals making games every few months to multiyear projects that require more than 100 developers. We will see how the business model is headed down the wrong path. We will set the stage for why agile development methods are a way of changing the course that game development has taken over the past decade. The goals are to ensure that game development remains a viable business and to ensure that the creation of games is as fun as it should be.

> **NOTE**
> This chapter will use "AAA" arcade or console games as the main examples of cost, because they've been around the longest.

A Brief History of Game Development

In the beginning, video game development didn't require artists, designers, or even programmers. In the early seventies, games were dedicated boxes of components that were hardwired together by electrical engineers for a specific game. These games first showed up in arcades and later in home television consoles that played only one game, such as Pong.

As the technology progressed, game manufacturers discovered that new low-cost microprocessors offered a way to create more sophisticated games; programmable hardware platforms could run a variety of games rather than being hardwired for just one. This led to common motherboards for arcade machines and eventually to popular home consoles with cartridges.[1] The specific logic of each game moved from hardware to software. With this change, the game developers turned to programmers to implement games. Back then, a single programmer could create a game in a few months.

In 1965, Gordon Moore, the cofounder of Intel, defined a law that predicted that the number of transistors that could fit on a chip would continue to double every two years. His law has persevered for the past four decades (see Figure 1.1).

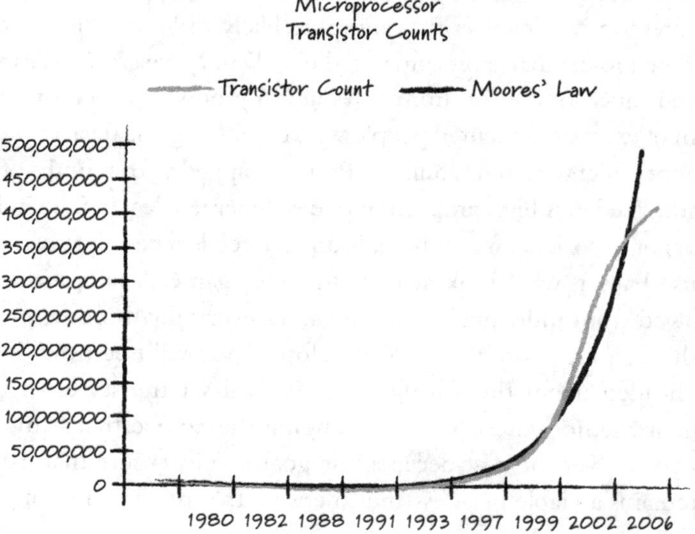

FIGURE 1.1 The number of transistors in PC microprocessors
Moore's law: www.intel.com/technology/mooreslaw/index.htm

1. Circa 1977 with the release of the Atari 2600 console

The home computer and console market have been driven by this law. Every several years a new generation of processors rolls off the fabrication lines, the performance of which dwarfs that of the previous generation. Consumers have an insatiable thirst for the features[2] this power provides, while developers rush to quench those thirsts with power-hungry applications. To game developers, the power and capability of home game consoles were doubling every two years—processor speeds increased, graphics power increased, and memory size increased—all at the pace predicted by Moore.

Each generation of hardware brought new capabilities and capacities. 3D rendering, CD-quality sound, and high-definition graphics bring greater realism and cost to each game. Memory and storage have increased as fast. Thirty years ago, the Atari 2600 had less than 1,000 bytes of memory and 4,000 bytes of cartridge space. Today a PlayStation 3 has 500,000 times the memory and 10,000,000 times the storage! Processor speeds and capabilities have grown just as dramatically.

Iterating on Arcade Games

The model first used to develop games was a good match for the hardware's capabilities and the market. In the golden age of the video arcade, during the late seventies and early eighties, games like Pac-Man, Asteroids, Space Invaders, and Defender were gold mines. A single $3,000 arcade machine could collect more than $1,000 in quarters per weekend. This new gold rush attracted quite a few prospectors. Many of these "wanna-be" arcade game creators went bankrupt in their rush to release games. A manufacturing run of 1,000 arcade machines required a considerable investment—an investment that was easily destroyed if the machines shipped with a poor game.

With millions of dollars of investment at stake, arcade game developers sought the best possible game software. Developing the game software was a tiny fraction of the overall cost, so it was highly effective to throw bad games out and try again—and again—before committing to manufacturing hardware dedicated to a game. As a result, game software development was highly iterative. Executives funded a game idea for a month of development. At the end of the month, they played the game and decided whether to fund another month, move to field-testing, or simply cancel the game.

Companies such as Atari field-tested a game idea by placing a mocked-up production machine in an arcade alongside other games. Several days later Atari would count the quarters in the machine and decide whether to mass-produce

2. Realistic physics, graphics, audio, and so on

it, tweak it, or cancel it outright. Some early prototypes, such as Pong, were so successful that their coin collection boxes overflowed and led to failure of the hardware even before the end of the field-test (Kent 2001)!

This iterative approach helped fuel the release of consistently high-quality games from companies like Atari. The market decline in the mid-eighties was caused by the increased proportion of inferior games released because of falling hardware costs. The cartridge-based home consoles allowed almost anyone to create and mass-produce games cheaply. The financial barrier of high-distribution cost disappeared, as did much of the disciplined iteration, which previously ensured only better games were released. When the market became flooded with poor-quality games, consumers spent their money elsewhere.

Early Methodologies

In the dawn of video game development, a single person working on a game didn't need much in the way of a "development methodology." A game could be quickly developed in mere months. As the video game hardware became more complex, the cost to create games rose. A lone programmer could no longer write a game that leveraged the full power of evolving consoles. Those lone programmers needed help. This help came increasingly from bigger project teams and specialists. For example, the increase in power in the graphics hardware allowed more detailed and colorful images on the screen; it created a canvas that needed true artists to exploit. Software and art production became the greater part of the cost of releasing a game to market.

Within a decade, instead of taking three or four people-months to create a game, a game might take thirty or forty people-months.

To reduce the increasing risk, many companies adopted **waterfall**-style methodologies used by other industries. Waterfall is forever associated with a famous 1970 paper by Winston Royce.[3] The waterfall methodology employed the idea of developing a large software project through a series of phases. Each phase led to a subsequent phase more expensive than the previous. The initial phases consisted of writing plans about how to build the software. The software was written in the middle phase. The final phase was integrating all the software components and testing the software. Each phase was intended to reduce risk before moving on to more expensive phases.

Many game development projects use a waterfall approach to development. Figure 1.2 shows typical waterfall phases for a game project.

---

3. http://en.wikipedia.org/wiki/Waterfall_model#CITEREFRoyce1970

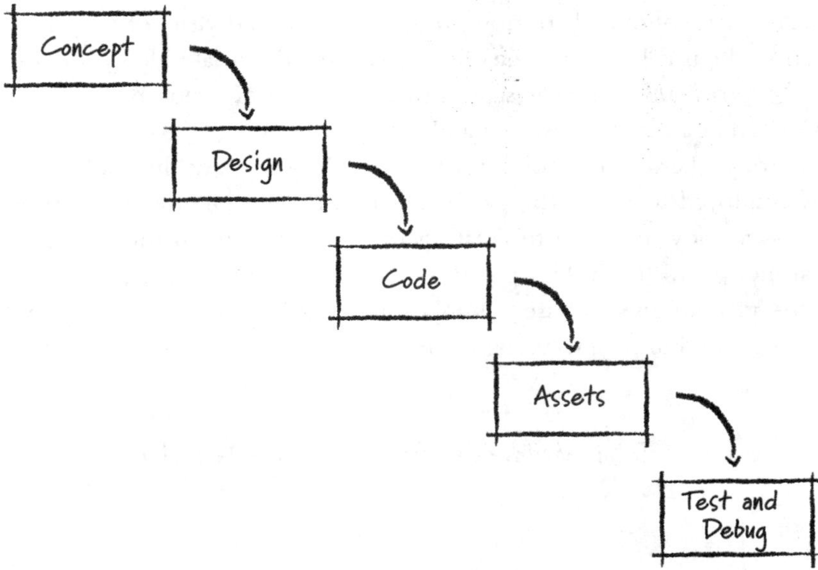

FIGURE 1.2 Waterfall game development

Waterfall describes a flow of phases; once design is done, a project moves to the analysis phase and so on. Royce described an iterative behavior in waterfall development, which allowed earlier phases to be revisited. Game development projects also employ this behavior, often returning to redesign a feature later in development when testing shows a problem. However, on a waterfall project, a majority of design is performed early in the project, and a majority of testing is performed late.

Ironically, Royce's famous paper illustrated how this process leads to project failure. In fact, he never used the term *waterfall*; unfortunately, the association stuck.

The Death of the Hit-or-Miss Model

In the early days of the game industry, a hit game could pull in tens of millions of dollars for a game maker. This was a fantastic return on investment for a few months of effort. Profits like these created a gold rush. Many people tried their hand at creating games with dreams of making millions. Unfortunately, a very small percentage of games made such profits. With the minimal cost of making games, however, game developers could afford to gamble on many new innovative titles in hopes of hitting the big time. One hit could pay for many failures. This is called the *hit-or-miss* publishing model.

Sales have continued to grow steadily over the 30 years of the industry's existence.[4] Figure 1.3 shows the sales growth for the total video game market from 1996 to 2008. This represents a steady growth of about 10% a year. Few markets can boast such consistent and steady growth.

Although hardware capabilities followed Moore's law, the tools and processes employed to create the games did not. By the nineties, small teams of people were now required to create games, and they often took longer than several months to finish. This raised the cost of creating games proportionally, and they've continued to rise, roughly following Moore's law. This growth of effort (measured in people-years) has grown to this day (see Figure 1.4).

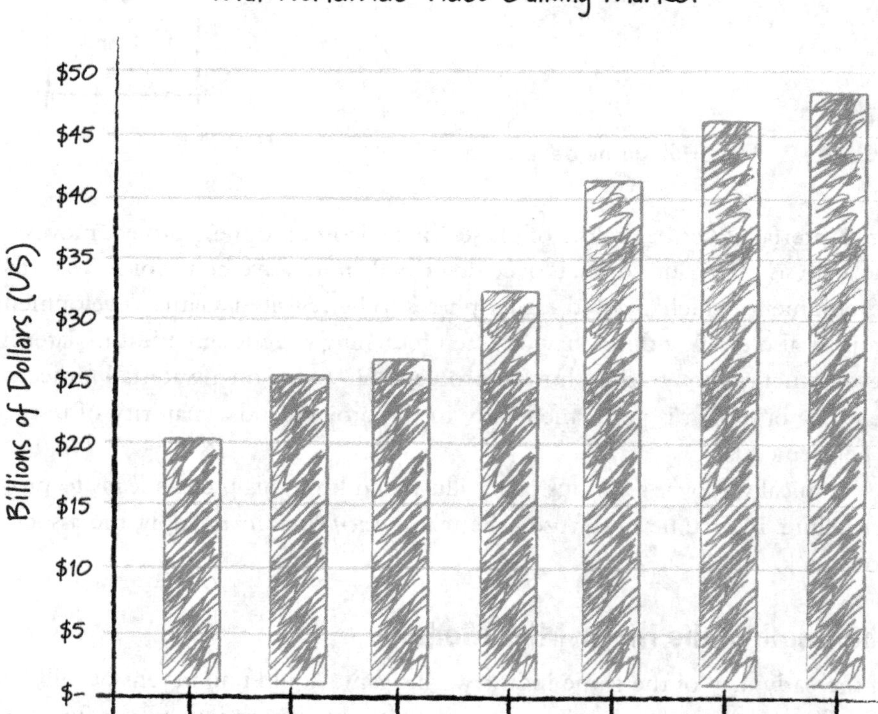

FIGURE 1.3 Market sales for video games
Source: Multiple, M2R, NPD, CEA, DFC

4. Except for the occasional market crashes every decade!

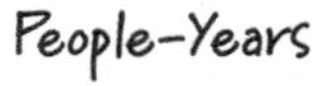

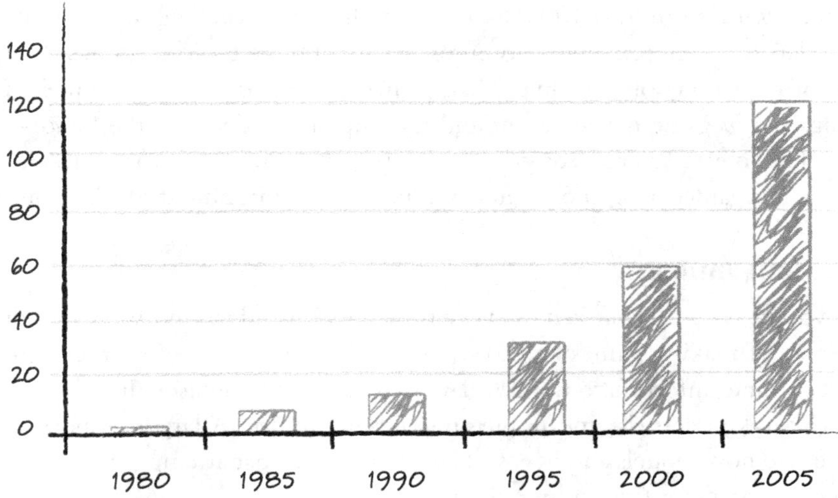

FIGURE 1.4 **People-years to make "AAA" games**
Electronic Entertainment Design and Research

The growth in effort to create a game has been much greater than the market's growth market. The number of games released each year hasn't diminished significantly, and the price of a game for the consumer has risen only 25% (adjusted for inflation).[5] This has greatly reduced the margin of the hit-or-miss model. Now a hit pays for fewer misses because the misses cost hundreds of times more than they did 30 years ago. If the trend continues, soon every major title released will have to be a hit just for a publisher to break even.

NOTE

According to Laramee (2005), of the games released to the market, only 20% will produce a significant profit.

PEOPLE-YEARS

It's almost impossible to compare the cost of making games through the decades. I use the phrases *people-years* and *people-months* to compare effort across time. "Ten people-years" equals the effort of five people for two years or ten people for one year.

5. Electronic Entertainment Design and Research

The Crisis

Projects with more than 100 developers, with costs exceeding tens of millions of dollars to develop, are now common. Many of these projects go over budget and/or fail to stay on schedule. Most games developed are not profitable. The rising cost of game development and the impending death of the hit-or-miss model has created a crisis for game development in three main areas: less innovation, less game value, and a deteriorating work environment for developers.

Less Innovation

We will never create hit games every time, so we need to find ways to reduce the cost of making games and to catch big "misses" long before they hit the market. One unfortunate trend today is to attempt to avoid failure by taking less risk. Taking less risk means pursuing less innovation. A larger proportion of games are now sequels and license-based "safe bets" that attempt to ride on the success of previous titles or popular movies.

Innovation is the engine of the game industry. We cannot afford to "throw out the baby with the bath water."

Less Value

Reducing cost has also led to providing less content for games. This reveals itself in the reduction in average gameplay time consumers are provided by today's games. In the eighties, a typical game often provided more than forty hours of gameplay. These days, games can often be completed in less than ten hours.

This reduction in value has had a significant impact on the market. Consumers are far less willing to pay $60 for a game that provides only ten hours of entertainment. As a result, the game rental and secondhand sales markets have blossomed (see Figure 1.5). Each rental represents the potential loss of a sale.

Deteriorating Work Environment

With predictability in schedules slipping and development costs skyrocketing, developers are bearing a greater burden. They are asked to work extended overtime hours in an effort to offset poor game development methods. Developers often work twelve hours a day seven days a week for months at a time to hit a critical date; lawsuits concerning excessive overtime are not uncommon (for example, see http://en.wikipedia.org/wiki/Ea_Spouse).

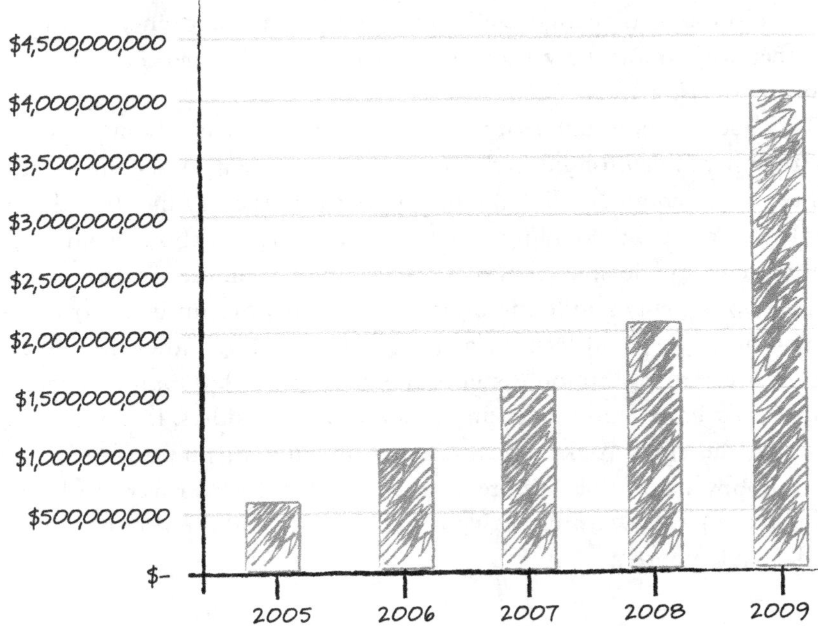

FIGURE 1.5 The growth of the used-games market
Source: M2Research

Talented developers are leaving the industry because they are faced with choosing between making games or having a life outside of work. The average developer leaves the industry before their ten-year anniversary.[6] This prevents the industry from building the experience and leadership necessary to provide innovative new methods to manage game development.

A Silver Lining

There is a silver lining. The market is forcing us to face reality. Other industries have faced a similar crisis and improved themselves.

6. www.igda.org/quality-life-white-paper-info

We need to transition as well. The game market is healthy. New gaming platforms such as the iPhone and online content distribution models, to name a few, offer new markets for smaller projects. The industry is still in its infancy and looks to change itself completely in the next ten years. It makes sense that we explore new ways for people to work together to overcome this growing crisis.

This book is about different ways to develop games. It's about ways people work together in environments that focus talent, creativity, and commitment in small teams. It's about "finding the fun" in our games every month—throwing out what isn't fun and doubling down on what is. It's not about avoiding plans but about creating flexible plans that react to what is on the screen.

This book applies agile methodologies, mainly Scrum but also Extreme Programming (XP) and lean, to game development. It shows how to apply agile practices to the unique environment of game development; these are practices that have been proven in numerous game studios. In doing this, we are setting the clock back to a time when making a game was more a passionate hobby than a job. We are also setting the clock forward to be ready for the new markets we are starting to see now, such as the iPhone and more downloadable content.

Additional Reading

Bagnall, B. 2005. *On the Edge: The Spectacular Rise and Fall of Commodore.* Winnipeg, Manitoba: Variant Press.

Cohen, S. 1984. *Zap: The Rise and Fall of Atari.* New York: McGraw-Hill.

Chapter 2

Agile Development

In the eighties, the backlash against waterfall methodologies was growing. Large defense and IT projects were failing with growing frequency. This led to numerous books and articles defining better practices. Some of these methodologies, such as evolutionary delivery, promoted incremental development of products using iterations. Each iteration contained a slice of all the phases of development instead of development being spread out over an entire waterfall cycle. The iterations could be as short as a week but included analysis, design, coding, integration, and testing within that time frame rather than spreading each of them out over years as they could be on a waterfall project.

Many emerging iterative and incremental methodologies were referred to as **lightweight methods** until 2001 when a group of experts gathered and decided to refer to them as **agile** methodologies. The result of this gathering was to create the "agile manifesto,"[1] which summarizes the values and principles of these lightweight methods.

The agile manifesto reads as follows:

> We are uncovering better ways of developing software by doing it and helping others do it.
>
> Through this work we have come to value:
>
> - **Individuals and interactions** over processes and tools
> - **Working software** over comprehensive documentation
> - **Customer collaboration** over contract negotiation
> - **Responding to change** over following a plan
>
> That is, while there is value in the items on the right, we value the items on the left more.

1. www.agilemanifesto.org

These simple values have enabled agile frameworks such as Scrum, Lean, and XP to share a common philosophy and principles. This book is about applying these frameworks, mainly Scrum, to game development.

In this chapter, we'll look at some of the typical problems that face game development projects, as illustrated by a hypothetical game postmortem. We'll see how agile helps meet the challenges faced by this game.

Why Projects Are Hard

This section uses the postmortems from game projects to help establish why projects are so hard. We'll begin by looking at a hypothetical but typical postmortem and then extrapolate from it the three most typical areas into which game project problems fall.

Learning from Postmortems

I've been a fan of *Game Developer Magazine* since it started publishing in 1994. My favorite articles are the postmortems of game projects. Not only do they show how different studios work, but they also show that none of us is facing such challenges alone. Some postmortems are brutally honest about the overwhelming challenges developers face. Reading these postmortems feels like passing a car wreck; you shouldn't look, but you do anyway.

These postmortems are a good starting place to reveal the reasons for adopting an agile framework for game development, so I've concocted a short postmortem based on a hypothetical game called Quintessential. It encompasses the more common issues seen in published postmortems and my own project experiences.

The Quintessential Postmortem

Quintessential is a sci-fi shooter released by Hypothetical Studios. Although the project tested the endurance of everyone—from quality assurance (QA) to publisher—it shipped to critical acclaim. This postmortem describes what went right with the development of the game and what went wrong.

What Went Right?

The things that went right had to do with the studio's culture and employees, the prototypes, and the license.

Studio Culture

Hypothetical Studios is a great place to work. The studio was founded by game development veterans who wanted to create the best possible environment in which to develop games. Everyone has their own office, a convenience for those late nights when you need a little peace and quiet. The kitchen is stocked with free beverages and snacks. Our game room has pool tables, foosball tables, and classic arcade machines for blowing off steam. No one works late alone. The entire team commits to working hard together. Hypothetical promotes teamwork. We're all "in it" together.

Talented Employees

Hypothetical Studios hires the best people for every discipline. Our programmers are top-notch; they are constantly exploring new areas of technology. Hypothetical doesn't rely on any middleware; we exert full control over every aspect of our engine. Our creative group has lofty goals and the talent to match.

Great Prototypes

The early prototypes of Quintessential demonstrated a great deal of promise for the game, and we were able to develop them very quickly. For example, we demonstrated a system that allowed every part of the visible world to be destroyed. Although this feature wasn't shipped with the game, it showed the capabilities of the technology early on.

Great License

Quintessential was based on the popular movie that was a summer blockbuster six months before the game shipped. This drove considerable interest in the game, especially considering that the DVD was released around the same time the game hit the shelves.

What Went Wrong?

The things that went wrong had to do with the ship date, the timing of going into production, when people were added to the project, and the technical challenges.

Unachievable Ship Date

Quintessential was supposed to ship simultaneously with the movie. Hypothetical, a small studio with only two projects, was under a great deal of pressure to meet the original ship date, but in the end, we were unable to do so. Part of the reason was that the game's features continued to change during development. These changes were not accounted for in the schedule, and they added time.

Going into Production Too Soon

The project was originally scheduled to start level production 12 months before the release date. Unfortunately, when the time arrived, we weren't far enough along with the game mechanics to lay out the levels properly. For example, the player was given a jet pack that allowed them to fly through the air after production started. This required us to add more vertical spaces than we had planned. Nonetheless, the schedule forced us into production on the originally scheduled date; launching the game on the same date as the movie was considered very important. As a result, many of the levels had to be reworked when the game mechanics were figured out.

Adding People Late to the Project

As we fell behind in production, the studio brought more people over from the other project to increase the pace. These new additions to the project team needed a lot of handholding to come up to speed, however. When they did come up to speed, they merely created more assets that had to be reworked later. In the final tally, merging the two project teams actually slowed us down.

Underestimating the Technical Challenges

The original destructible prototype showed so much promise that it was added to the design with few questions asked. It was going to be the killer feature that would make the game a hit. Unfortunately, the programmers discovered—too late—that the destructible system required a major overhaul to work on the Xbox 360 and PlayStation 3. We were forced to make the painful decision to drop the feature and replace all the destructible geometry in the production levels with the static geometry as originally planned.

Conclusion

We are proud of our efforts to produce a good game that is worthy of the license. Although we had some challenging times at the end of the project, that's the nature of making games. The lesson we learned is to plan a little better at the start of the project. Had we planned the destructible system a bit better, we could have delivered it in the final game on schedule.

The Problems

This postmortem tells a story familiar to many experienced developers. Why do projects start out so full of hope and end up in a spirit-numbing crunch of overtime and wasted effort? Is this the best way to make games? I hope not.

So, why do projects run into trouble? There are three major reasons: feature creep, overoptimistic schedules, and the challenges of production.

Feature Creep

Feature creep is the term given to features being added to a project after the original scope is defined. There are two main reasons for feature creep; the first is when the stakeholders see the game in progress and request new features. This is referred to as **emergent requirements**. The second is when the feature doesn't live up to its expectations so more work is added.

Feature creep isn't a bad thing unless the budget and/or schedule remain unchanged as work is added. It happens so gradually that management accepts it without much question. Why do they allow this? It's usually because they have little choice; troubled projects often agree to changes that the customer requests to avoid cancellation.

Opportunities to add value to the game are identified throughout the project, but with a tight schedule and workload, they either have to be ignored or have to be added at great peril to the deadline. Unfortunately, swapping out planned features for new ones that require the same amount of effort is not an option. Feature creep tends to expand the total scope.

Feature creep and change are inevitable. Have you ever gone back and read the original game design document for a game you just shipped? Often it seems that the title page is the only thing that doesn't change.

This is often the main problem with writing big designs up front (BDUF): The goal is to answer all questions about the game. In reality, we can't really know everything about a game at the start. Knowledge comes only when we have the controller in hand and are playing the game at a decent frame rate on the target machine. The only way to recognize fun is to play it.

In the early stages of the game, we have the greatest range of uncertainty. We may be certain that we're making a first-person shooter, but knowledge of exactly what types of weapons are best is lacking. We learn more when we can shoot characters in the game.

Figure 2.1 demonstrates how uncertainty diminishes over the phases of a game or feature's development. Uncertainty is highest at concept definition and slowly drops as a product or feature set is testable on the target machine.

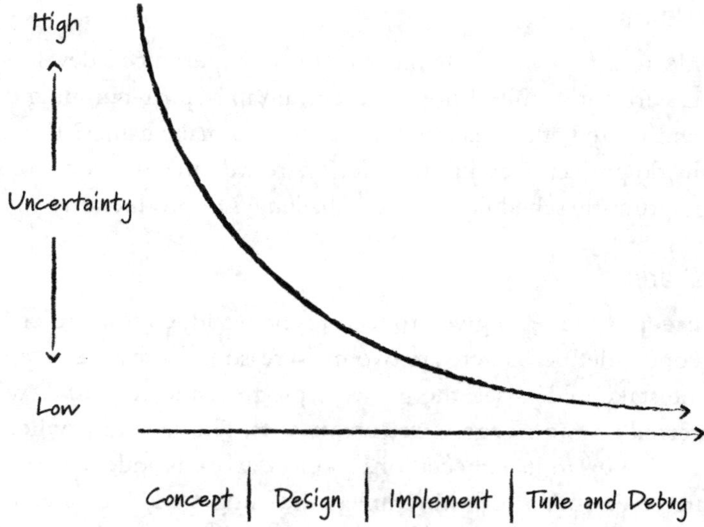

FIGURE 2.1 Reducing uncertainty

A waterfall project carries hundreds of uncertain features forward to the testing phases—called **alpha** and **beta**—just before shipping. An agile project eliminates the uncertainty in small iterations that include every part of development.

Overoptimistic Schedules

Task estimation is not an exact science. Even when we estimate simple things in daily life, such as running an errand at the store, unanticipated problems crop up and throw off our estimates. Traffic will jam, or the lines at the store will be long. The accuracy of estimates drops when more complex tasks are estimated, such as those for making games. Many things throw off the estimated time to complete a task:

- The difference in experience and productivity between two people who have a task assigned to them. Studies have shown that the range of productivity will vary by a factor of ten.
- How many other tasks a person is working on at a single time (multitasking).
- The stability of the build and tools used to complete the task.
- The iterative nature of a task: It's never certain how many iterations are going to be necessary for tuning and polishing a feature to "find the fun."

The Challenge of Production

The challenges for pre-production and production are quite different. **Pre-production** is the exploration of what the game is. The challenge of pre-production is to find the fun of the game that drives the goals of production. **Production** is the stage where the team builds a dozen or so hours of content, such as characters and levels. Production fleshes out the story and surroundings to leverage the mechanics created in pre-production. The challenge of production is to maximize efficiency, minimize waste, and create predictability.

Predictability is more important during production. Production represents a great deal of work. Dozens of characters and levels have to be built before a game is shipped. Production often accompanies a major staffing increase or engagement of an outsource company. Mass-producing assets such as characters and levels shouldn't start early. The game mechanics and asset budgets must be established to create proper assets on the first pass to avoid expensive rework.

Production should begin when the uncertainty about the game mechanics and the uncertainty of the technology and tools to make the game have been reduced. Figure 2.2 shows how a project should pass through the prototype, pre-production, and production phases based on the level of certainty about technical solutions, asset budgets, and quality and design knowledge.

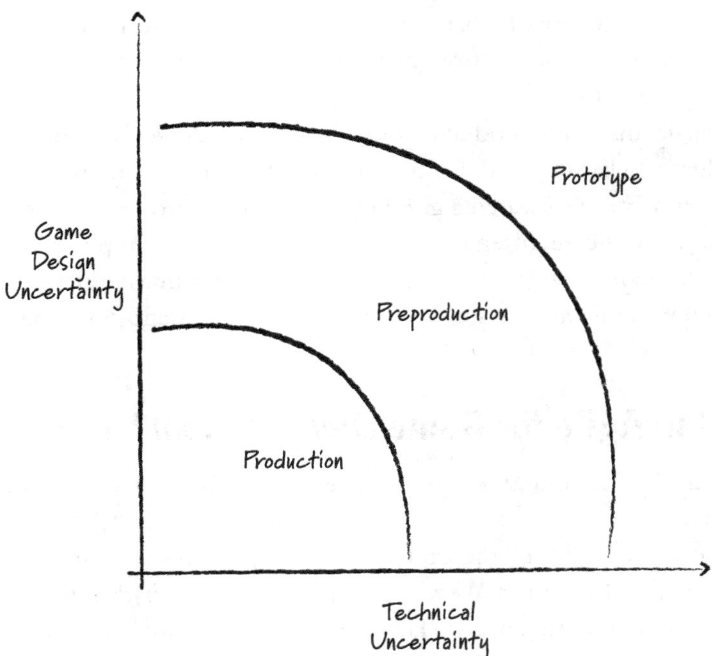

FIGURE 2.2 Uncertainty of design and technology

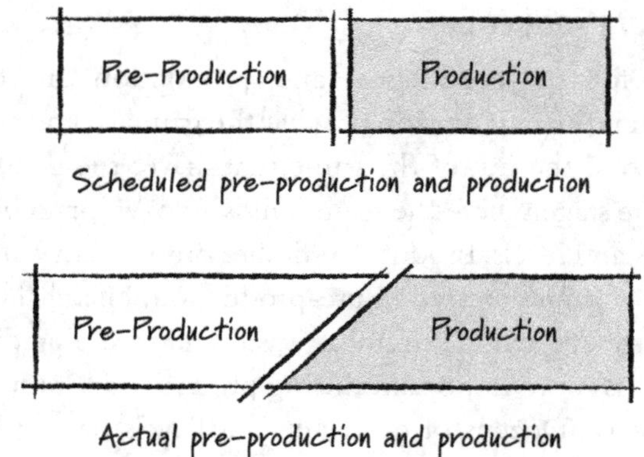

FIGURE 2.3 Scheduled vs. actual production transition

Most game projects cannot afford the luxury of entering production when they are ready, but pre-production is difficult to predict. The exploration of what is fun and the range of mechanics to mass-produce are difficult to schedule. When pre-production takes longer than expected, projects are often forced to enter production by the demands of a schedule. Figure 2.3 shows how the transition from pre-production to production should happen.

Some assets are ready for production earlier than others. Our knowledge of the budgets and quality of what the game should ship determines the timing of when an asset enters production. If these things are unknown, the asset should not be in production.

When teams enter production too soon, they do so without the proper knowledge of what to build. By the time the team discovers the true requirements, they may have created a good chunk of production assets based on false assumptions. If the requirements have changed—for example, removing the destructible geometry or adding the jet pack in Quintessential—then those assets need to be reworked. This creates a lot of wasted effort and time.

Why Use Agile for Game Development?

What is driving the industry toward agile? Primarily, market forces for higher quality and lower cost are driving us. As we saw in Chapter 1, "The Crisis Facing Game Development," the cost of creating games is growing much faster than the market for games. We're coming to a crossroads that will determine the future of the industry. Are we facing another fallout such as 1983, or will we discover new markets and new demographics of people we've never reached?

Knowledge Is Key

Imagine that after two years of effort, you have just shipped the gold master version of your game. The project was challenging; it was a genre new to the studio, so a lot of technology had to be created. It was the first title that the studio has shipped on the PlayStation 3. There were a lot of false starts and dead ends.

Now imagine that you and the entire project team could go back in time to the beginning of the project and start all over again. Would you do anything differently? Of course you would! You wouldn't repeat all the mistakes you made the first time. You would work far more effectively to reimplement code you knew would work or build levels you know are fun. With this increased knowledge, you would ship a better game far earlier.

This thought experiment demonstrates four things about knowledge:

- Its creation is something that occurs during the project.
- It has a great deal of value.
- Creating knowledge has a high cost.
- Knowledge is the greatest asset your studio can create.

A fundamental problem with the waterfall approach to games is that our crystal ball BDUFs are not entirely clear. As we develop a game, we are learning. We learn what plays well with the controller, what looks good on the target platform, and how to make the game run fast enough with enough artificial intelligence (AI) characters to make it challenging. We create knowledge every day.

This knowledge is impossible to fully embed in a BDUF or schedule. Game development is primarily about learning what to make and how to make it. It's about reducing uncertainty over time. Agile development focuses on building knowledge about value, cost, and schedule and adjusting the plan to match reality.

EXPERIENCE

"I've never subscribed to the style of documentation that attempts to predict the future, mostly because my crystal ball has long been out for repair. Having said this, I do end up writing a lot. I find it useful as a thinking tool. Trying to share an idea with a large team is difficult to do and even more so if that idea hasn't been fully thought through. Writing it down helps me to not only realize where the gaps are but also to work out the details. The result is clearer communication."

—Senta Jakobsen, COO, EA DICE

Cost and Quality

Let's take a quick look at the economics of the game market for "AAA" console or PC games. With a retail cost of $60, a game that sells half a million copies grosses $30 million. After licensing, distribution, marketing, and publishing costs are subtracted, about one-fourth of the gross sales, or $7.5 million, is left to pay for the development of a game. Many game development projects cost more than $7.5 million, and the largest majority of games don't approach sales of half a million units. Most games fail to break even!

Publishers and developers are trying to keep costs down on development by doing the following:

- Seeking opportunities to outsource asset creation and code development
- Relying on middleware[2] solutions
- Reducing the amount of content (releasing a game with eight hours of gameplay rather than sixteen)

Publishers are also trying to reduce the number of games that lose money for them by doing the following:

- Relying on a greater proportion of licensed properties such as movie-based games
- Relying more on sequels and older franchises that have been successful in the past
- Taking fewer chances on new ideas

These seem to be logical steps to take, but they also reduce the quality of games on the market.

Now let's look at how agile addresses quality and cost issues. We'll see how agile helps us "find the fun" and eliminate some of the most notorious sources of wasted work common to game development.

Finding the Fun First

A benefit of iterative development is to develop a product in small steps and incrementally add features that satisfy the customer in the fastest and most economical way. For video games, our customers are the people who purchase and play our games. A fun game is more appealing to players and results in more

---

2. **Middleware** is technology purchased from a vendor or another developer.

sales. "Find the fun" is the mantra of any iterative and incremental game development project. Fun is only found with the controller in your hand.

Figure 2.4 shows a notional representation of when the fun or value was discovered during a waterfall-developed game. Waterfall projects typically show minimal progress in finding the fun in the first two-thirds of the project. Except for occasional prototype or E3 demos, much of the work is spent executing to a plan and not demonstrating value. It's not until the end of the project—when all the pieces come together and the game is being tuned and debugged—that the project team has a clear idea of what the game is and can identify improvements. Unfortunately, the end of the project is the worst time for this to occur. The project is facing an impending deadline, and any significant change for the sake of increased value is often rejected out of consideration for the schedule.

QUESTION

How many times have you been in alpha or beta and wished for a few extra months to improve the game?

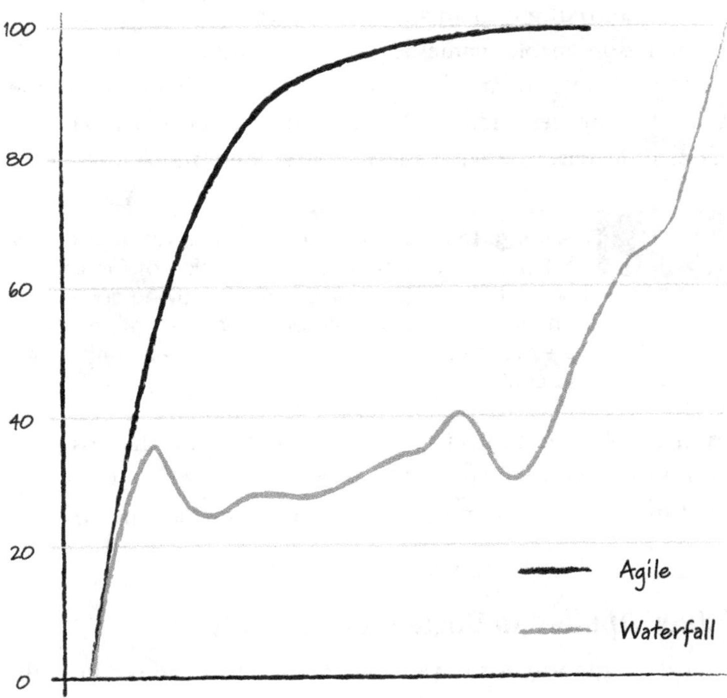

FIGURE 2.4 Finding the fun

The agile project value curve approaches development in a value-first approach. This happens when the project iterates on bringing features to a near-shippable state in a value-prioritized order. The publisher expects value to be demonstrated early unless the core idea is not good or the developers are not up to the task of making a great game. This enables the stakeholders and project team to avoid wasting years of effort and cost on projects that won't be fun. The "find the fun" mantra forces us to focus our efforts on making the game better every iteration. A game that is not fun must be questioned at every step.

Eliminating Waste

Agile practices focus the project on eliminating waste in many ways.

By "finding the fun" first, the project team finds the value early in the project rather than trying to retrofit it at the end. The same principle applies to the development of assets and technology within a game. Making changes at the end of a production cycle that affects every production asset is a lot more expensive than discovering the change before most of the assets are created. On the technology side, fixing a bug minutes after it is created can be magnitudes less expensive than fixing it in an alpha/beta phase.

Simple iteration enables game developers to explore more ideas. By delivering working software iteratively, a project can prove whether an idea is viable earlier in development. This makes it possible to enact the kill-gate model where a dozen ideas are launched and narrowed down until the best remain.

NOTE

A **kill-gate** model of development is where a number of prototypes are started with the intention of funding only one to completion. The prototypes are narrowed down as they demonstrate their value. The ones that are not proving their value are stopped at the "gate" and are "killed" rather than allowed to continue.

Iteration enables the project team to easily measure the cost of development and improve the efficiency of how groups of people work together. It creates a culture of continual improvement that can reduce the cost of developing games.

Agile Values Applied to Game Development

Let's look at the agile values from the agile manifesto and see how they apply to video game development.

Individuals and Interactions Over Processes and Tools

Our processes and tools to manage ever-growing projects have grown dramatically. Large teams have driven the creation of management hierarchies. Project schedules and design documents—which attempt to predict every requirement and task necessary to make a fun game—require expensive databases to manage. All of these are considered necessary to tackle the complexity that arises from having upward of 100 people working on a multiyear project.

Game development requires developers from widely different disciplines. Take, for example, a cutting-edge AI character who needs to walk around an environment and challenge the player in the game. The creation of this character requires the participation of animators, designers, character modelers, texture artists, programmers, and audio composers, among others.

It's important that these disciplines collaborate as much as possible to be effective. For example, it is important for an animator who discovers a bug in the animation technology to work with an animation programmer as quickly as possible. Processes and organization can add delay. In this example, the programmer may be working on a series of tasks that were assigned by a lead. This may prevent that programmer from helping the animator without permission from their lead. This leads to a chain of communication, as shown in Figure 2.5

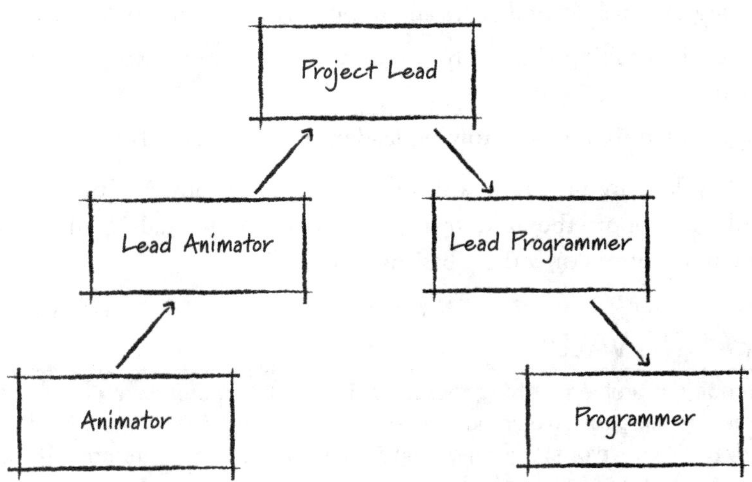

FIGURE 2.5 A chain of communication

The animator has to pass the request up through the chain of command; the request then has to make it back down to a programmer who can solve the problem. In this example, the request involves five people and four requests! This flow is prone to failure and delay.

So, what is happening in the big picture?

- More than 100 people from various disciplines on one team
- Thousands of unpredictable problems that can introduce wasted time and effort
- Inflexible plans and tools to manage people who can't predict and quickly react to these problems
- Hierarchies of management that can lead to further waste

Agile methodologies address these issues from the bottom up. One way is by promoting teams able to solve many of these problems on their own. They manage the smallest level of details but not the highest levels. They unburden leadership of the role of managing minor details. They enable leadership to focus on the big picture.

Teams start taking on larger problems as they discover they can take a small amount of ownership to solve the smallest problems. They begin asking for more ownership in other areas:

- In creating better team structures that can solve more problems by reducing external dependencies and improving focus on problem solving
- By identifying risks early and addressing them before they become problems
- By identifying and growing leaders among themselves

Agile values are preferences and not binary decisions. We still need process and tools to support the agile team, but having individuals solving problems with their colleagues on a daily basis is more valuable.

CREATING VALUE

"It is not just problem solving that agile helps—it also creates an environment of creating value that would not otherwise be created if the direct communication between developers was not there. An example is a programmer exposing some unrequested values of a feature of their own volition (and communicating this) because they better understood what the designer was trying to do—making a better product for it. This is some of the 'magic' that happens with the top game teams in the business."

—Scott Blinn, Vexigon, Inc.

Working Software Over Comprehensive Documentation

For game development, we'll use the following redefinition for the second value:

> Working game over comprehensive design

I've substituted *game* for *software* since a game is more than software.

Some form of design documentation is necessary. Publishers, licensors, and other stakeholders want a clear idea of the project goals and vision. Portfolio planning and franchise or licensing requirements may create constraints on the project. Communicating what is known about the project up front has great value.

> **NOTE**
>
> I've seen a game design document for a fantasy shooter game that contained details such as the number of bullets per magazine! How can we really know how many bullets per clip we should have in the design phase? Why do we need to plan for that detail before we have the knowledge of what we need? This is an example of the problem that detailed plans can create; they can create work that is not necessary. If all the assumptions about the weapon system were implemented before discovering what was fun about it, much of that work is wasted. If the project sticks to the detailed plan, then it won't be the best game possible.

Customer Collaboration Over Contract Negotiation

The typical game development contract has a series of defined milestones. Each milestone is associated with a specific date and features that need to be delivered on that date. If the developer delivers those features on schedule, they are paid for the milestone. Milestone payments are the lifeblood for most independent developers; they will do almost anything to avoid missing a milestone. This includes avoiding change that would improve the game if it threatens the milestone with additional work. Who can blame them? Many developers who miss a milestone payment miss payroll; that is a very bad thing for them to do. The contract is an impediment to change.

On the other side, a publisher doesn't have the full freedom to add features or change the milestone definition when they think the game would benefit from the change. The contract impedes working with the developer to fix the game.

Fixed-milestone deliverables have led to an adversarial relationship between developers and publishers. Both recognize the need for change to improve the game but lack the necessary level of trust to allow the change to occur.

Collaboration between developer and publisher should be valued more than a fixed contract. However, very few publishers allow a developer to work without a detailed contract. Outside our industry, many contracts in an agile environment follow the **time and materials** form, which is where the client pays for the cost of the last iteration. This style of contract requires greater trust between both parties. The client has to trust that the developer is spending money wisely. The developer has to trust that the client won't cancel the ongoing contract without good reason.

Although most Western publishers don't support this model, many have adopted flexible milestone definitions that allow some level of collaboration with developers every few months. As the use of agile spreads, we will see more collaborative business arrangements as trust is built through greater collaboration.

Responding to Change Over Following a Plan

Was there a detailed schedule on your last project? Did development follow that schedule? If development departed from the plan, was the detailed schedule updated to reflect the changes? The agile approach is to plan for what is known and to iterate against what is not known.

Expanding project teams and ever-increasing feature and hardware complexities have driven managers to turn to increasingly detailed planning. As we saw in Figure 2.1, defined processes are best applied when we have certainty about the technology required by a project and well-understood requirements we know will develop into a hit game. These two criteria are rarely seen. Not only do our platforms change frequently, but creating a fun, innovative game is always challenging.

What an Agile Project Looks Like

An agile project is composed of a series of iterations of development. Iterations are short intervals of time, usually two to four weeks, during which the game makes progress. Developers implement individual features that have value to customers every iteration. These features are called **user stories**. Iterations include every element of game development that takes place in an entire game project:

- Concept
- Design
- Coding
- Asset creation
- Debugging
- Optimizing
- Tuning and polishing

The game is reviewed at the end of every iteration, and the results influence the goals of future iterations. This is an example of using the "inspect and adapt" principle. Every four to eight iterations, the game is brought to a **release** state, which means that major goals are accomplished (like online gameplay) and the game is brought to a near-shippable level.

NOTE

Releases will be described in Chapter 3, "Scrum." User stories are described in Chapter 5, "User Stories."

The "inspect and adapt" principle is the cornerstone of agile practices. Teams and customers inspect the progress of a game every iteration and adapt the plan to address what is valuable and what is not. Teams inspect how they are working together every iteration and adapt their practices to improve their effectiveness.

NOTE

The first iterations of a project will often focus on building the minimum necessary infrastructure, if one does not exist, before any valuable gameplay is seen.

Agile projects don't avoid planning. They adopt planning practices that allow for change as the project is developed. In most waterfall projects, milestones lead the project toward the goal defined in the BDUF, as illustrated in Figure 2.6.

Once the project has achieved the goals foreseen in the BDUF, everyone realizes that they really want to be somewhere else. Unfortunately, as we've seen, the project is usually out of time and money here.

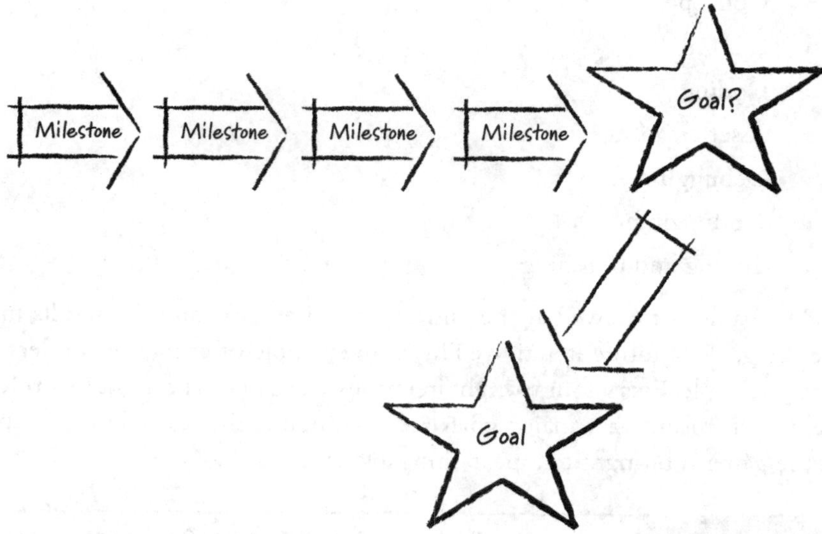

FIGURE 2.6 Milestone steps toward a goal

Agile projects also make steps toward a goal. However, using the "inspect and adapt" cycle, they achieve better results sooner through the ability to steer the plan toward a more desirable goal, as shown in Figure 2.7.

The constraints on the project sets limits on how much the goal can change. A driving game won't slowly morph into a golf game over time.

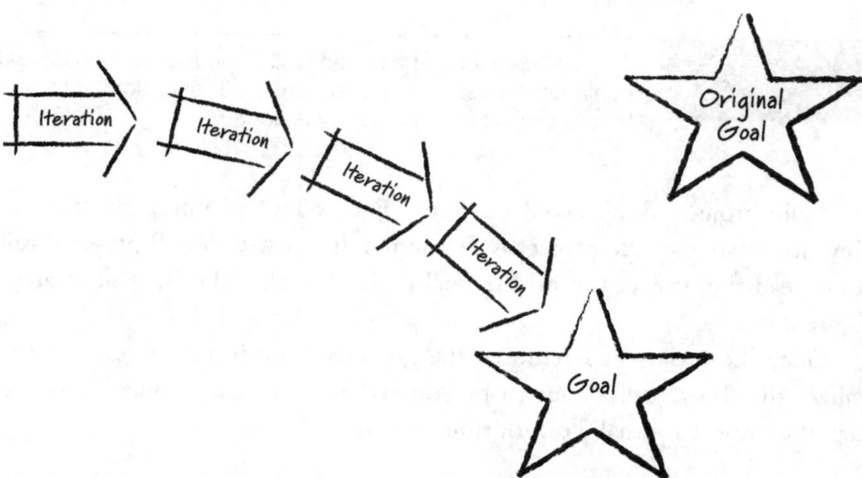

FIGURE 2.7 Iterations toward a goal

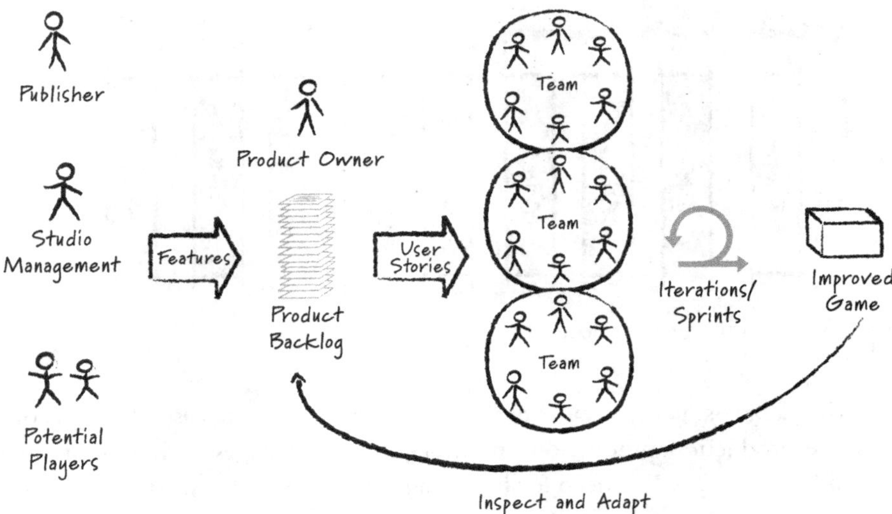

FIGURE 2.8 Agile development flow

Agile Development

Figure 2.8 shows the high-level flow of an agile game project.

Starting on the left, customers and stakeholders (see Chapter 3) identify features and other requirements (such as tools and infrastructure needs) for the game. These features are placed on a list called the **product backlog** (Chapter 3) that is prioritized by the product owner (Chapter 3). These product backlog items (PBIs) (Chapter 3) are expressed as user stories (Chapter 5) that communicate the value of each PBI to the customers and stakeholders. Small Scrum teams of developers (Chapter 3) commit to completing one or more user stories from the product backlog every iteration (or **sprint** in Scrum; see Chapter 4, "Sprints") and demonstrating them in an improved version of the game. A ScrumMaster (Chapter 3) assists each Scrum team, helping them remove impediments to progress and ensuring that they are following the agreed-upon process.

The Entire Project

Many agile developers outside the game industry ship versions of their products every several months. To do this, they use **releases**, which are sets of sprints, to produce shippable versions of their products.

Agile game projects use releases, but most don't ship a version of a game every three months. For them, releases are like milestone deliverables that bring the game to a "near-shippable" state (Chapter 6, "Agile Planning").

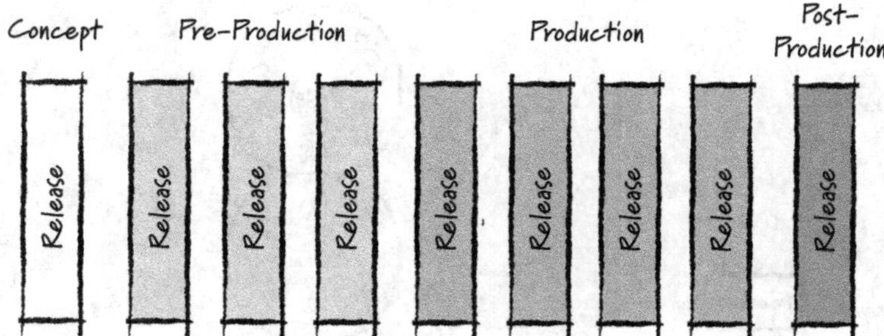

FIGURE 2.9 Agile project flow

Most larger-scale agile game projects execute a series of releases through concept, pre-production, production, and post-production stages of development, as shown in Figure 2.9. The need for these stages and how agile practices are modified for them are described in Chapter 7, "Video Game Project Planning."

The Challenge of Agile

The challenge of applying agile isn't in merely adopting the practices. The practices are simple. The real challenge arises in the collision between the culture of a studio, their publisher, and agile. Agile methodologies such as Scrum create transparency. Every deficiency that obstructs the best flow of work is singled out for examination. Rather than putting faith in a design document, a game needs to stand on its own merit every iteration.

Acting on transparency is the key to the success of applying an agile methodology. Scrum will merely show where and what the problems are. It is up to the individuals, teams, and leaders to solve those problems and thereby realize the benefits of Scrum. The remainder of this book addresses how agile is applied to game development. The next chapter will provide an overview of Scrum, which is the core set of practices for an agile game team.

Additional Reading

DeMarco, T., and T. Lister. 1985. Programmer performance and the effects of the workplace. *Proceedings of the 8th International Conference on Software Engineering in Washington, D.C.* Los Alamitos, CA: IEEE Computer Society Press.

Taylor, F. W. 1911. *The Principles of Scientific Management.* New York: Harper Bros.

Part II

Scrum and Agile Planning

Chapter 3

Scrum

In 1990, I was a member of the team developing the avionics test bed for an experimental fighter jet called the YF-23. This work required me to stay at a McDonnell Douglas facility in St. Louis, Missouri, for almost a year. Members of the team had gathered from all around the company to prepare the avionics for demonstration to the Air Force. We faced many imposing challenges—most caused because the various components of hardware and software had been separately developed, and they were resisting integration. The avionics were designed to survive destruction of up to half of their components and still perform their function. Unfortunately, the actual hardware could barely tolerate being installed. One key component, a fiber-optic communication interface, was so sensitive that 29 out of 30 initial boards produced failed before our final demonstration!

The team was led by a former F-14 pilot. He was an outstanding leader who didn't need to understand every detail of how each of us did our jobs. What he excelled at was removing obstacles from our paths.

We were guaranteed to see him every morning at the daily stand-up meeting. Scrum was largely unknown to the world in 1990, but F-14 pilots knew how to have a stand-up meeting. Each of us, in turn, told of our progress, what we were working on next, and what problems we were having.

Our pilot-lead had an interesting habit that I will never forget: He always trimmed his nails during this meeting. He focused on his nail clipper, but we knew he was listening. I didn't realize it at the time, but my inability to make eye contact with him forced me to speak to the group instead. If a discussion got too involved, he cut it short.

One day I reported that the McDonnell Douglas system administrator was not giving us access to a computer that he had promised to a week earlier. It was cutting into our efforts to test the avionics, and the administrator was being rude to the contractors. As soon as I said it, our lead's head snapped up. With a steady, steely glare he repeated what he heard me say. I verified that he had heard me right; the administrator was messing with his team.

Five minutes after the conclusion of the meeting, we heard our lead swearing at the top of his lungs at the administrator. They must have a class for F-14 pilots on the creative application of profanity. It was impressive to hear. It was even more impressive to realize that our pilot-lead had our back. He was our "wingman," and as Tom Cruise's character learned in *Top Gun*, you never leave your wingman.

We received access immediately and never had another problem with the administrator. It was a pivotal moment for the team. We had started the day as a collection of contractors from around the country. By noon, we were the team you didn't mess with. Did it affect our work? You bet. We didn't have any excuses not to solve our own problems with the dedication demonstrated by our lead.

Our lead demonstrated many of the values and practices of Scrum long before any of us had heard of it. Was he prescient? No, he was merely applying good practices known to many good leaders. Scrum does the same thing. Its practices derive from those who have worked in many high-performing organizations or teams for decades.

Scrum is a framework for creating complex products. It's not a process or a methodology; its practices aren't specific enough to tell programmers, artists, designers, producers, QA, and so on, how to do their jobs. A studio adopting Scrum merges its own practices into the Scrum framework to form its own methodology.

Scrum compels a studio to create an incremental and iterative development process with self-managing, cross-disciplined teams. The rules of Scrum are simple, but from these simple rules emerge vast improvements in how teams work together. They increase their productivity and enjoy their work more. It's like chess; from the simple rules of chess emerge complex tactics and strategy that take a lifetime to master. Scrum is also a never-ending pursuit for continual improvement, especially in the rapidly changing game development industry.

This chapter introduces Scrum. First, we have a rundown of Scrum and look at some of its components and practices in more detail. Next, we examine the various roles involved with Scrum. We finish up discussing customers and stakeholders and how Scrum scales.

The History of Scrum

Product development methods—from the industrial revolution through the information age—have undergone a slow evolution. It's an evolution of how people work together to create products.

The industrial revolution arose from the limitations of craftsmanship. The limited supply of craftspeople kept the supply of products low and their cost high. The assembly line transferred product creation to workers on the assembly line who were considered replaceable cogs performing only simple tasks. It removed the value of knowledge at every stage to a centralized few called **managers**.

With the introduction of the assembly line, everyone could afford a product like the Model T car. The cost in doing this was the loss of customization and variety that the craftsperson supplied.[1]

The weakness of Henry Ford's assembly line, which was optimized by Taylor (1911), was that it didn't leverage the knowledge and creativity of the people on the assembly line. Working in a factory became synonymous with the loss of humanity to the large machine of society that seemed to be emerging.[2]

Two world wars created demand for large amounts of material from a limited workforce. This drove innovation at the factory level. Millions of "Rosie the Riveters" had to be trained and made productive. This required more than mindless assembly-line workers. Leadership was required to train and guide this new workforce. Knowledge and skill at every level of the assembly line became recognized as a critical asset as valuable as the capital equipment in the factories themselves.

As the war ended, the soldiers returned to their jobs, and America found itself with the only intact industrial base. This led to a languid attitude toward the wartime lessons, many of which were forgotten in the factories. Additionally, the people who filled the roles in the factories of the departed soldiers (the "Rosie the Riveters" of America) left the factories and took much of the new knowledge tools with them.

Overseas the lessons were embraced. For example, as America occupied Japan, many of the industrial consultants who helped American industry ramp up production during the war were brought over to help Japan rebuild its devastated manufacturing industries. Companies such as Toyota merged some of these principles with their own. These companies were able to elevate productivity as American industry had done during the war.

These changes in Japan continued to restore the value of individuals in the workplace and decentralize many of the day-to-day decisions about quality and

1. Henry Ford's famous quote "Any customer can have a car painted any color that he wants so long as it is black" highlights this lack of variety of choice.
2. Read Orwell's novel *1984* to get a sense of this attitude toward the future.

efficiency. As a result, Toyota, and companies like it, has leveraged the lower cost and higher quality of its products to dominate the world automobile market.

In the mid-eighties, the differences in product development were researched and described in a groundbreaking article titled "The new new product development game" (Takeuchi and Nonaka 1986). This study described how some companies consistently and rapidly released new highly successful and innovative products into the market. What made these companies different was their process for developing products.

These companies didn't develop products using a traditional "relay-race" model of sequential development, such as the waterfall approach in the software industry. Instead, handpicked cross-discipline teams collaboratively iterated on the development of their products to a much higher degree. This approach to development was compared to the scrum formation of rugby teams that move the ball up and down the field together.

Scrum was first identified as a model for software development in the book *Wicked Problems, Righteous Solutions* (DeGrace and Stahl, 1990). This model was first applied at the Easel Corporation in the early nineties by Jeff Sutherland (2004) and Ken Schwaber at Advanced Development Methods. Then, Ken Schwaber and Mike Beedle (2002) teamed up to write a book, which popularized Scrum to a broad audience.

Although Sutherland and Schwaber were the first to use and define Scrum, Scrum integrates ideas from many sources. Teams meeting daily, owning the problem, putting the work to be done on a wall, and graphing the amount of work to be done are not novel ideas. What was novel about the earliest Scrum implementations was putting all of these ideas together.

The Big Picture

Figure 3.1 shows the major components of Scrum.

A game developed with Scrum makes progress in two- to four-week iterations, or **sprints**, using cross-discipline teams of six to ten people. At the start of a sprint, during the **sprint planning meeting**, the team selects a number of features from a prioritized list of them called the **product backlog**. Each feature on the product backlog is called a **product backlog item** (PBI). The team then estimates the tasks required to implement each PBI into a **sprint backlog**. Figure 3.2 shows a simple player jump feature and a sprint backlog of tasks to implement it.

The team only commits to features in a sprint that they judge to be achievable.

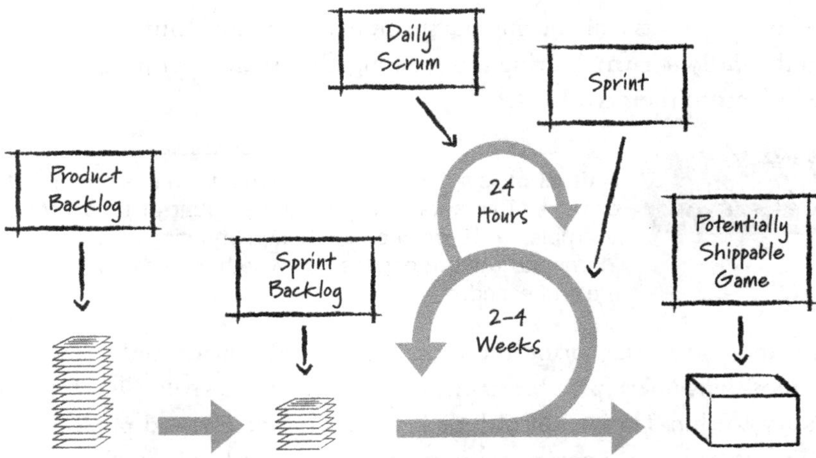

FIGURE 3.1 The big picture
Source: Mountain Goat Software

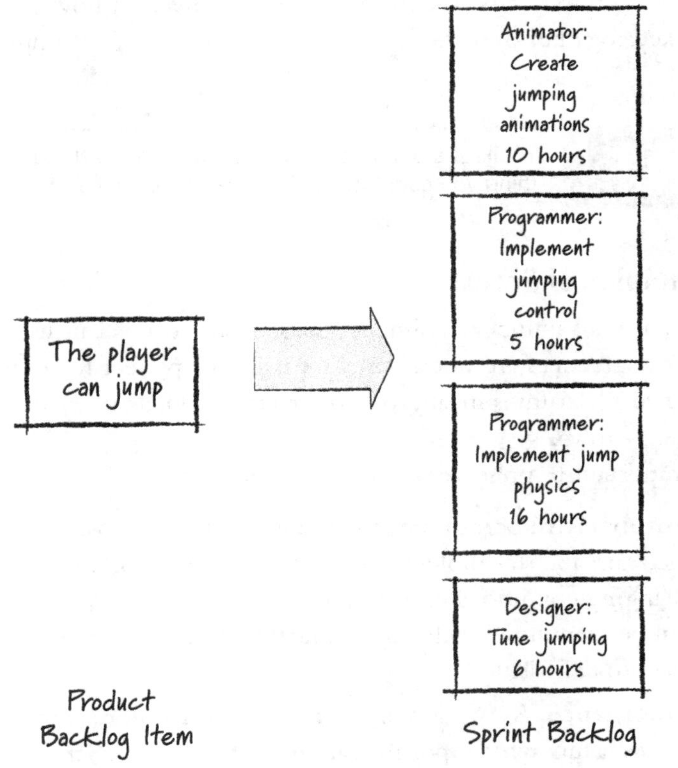

FIGURE 3.2 An example of breaking a PBI into tasks for the sprint backlog

The team meets daily during the sprint in a 15-minute timeboxed meeting called the **daily scrum**. During this meeting, they share their progress and any impediments to their work.

DEFINITION

A **timebox** is a fixed amount of time given to a meeting, task, or work. This sets a limit on the amount of time spent. For example, a 15-minute timeboxed meeting will end at the 15-minute mark regardless of whether all the agenda items are addressed.

By the end of the sprint, the team has created a **potentially shippable** version of the game: a playable game, which won't necessarily pass all the tests necessary to ship. The **stakeholders** (managers, directors, and publisher staff) of the game gather in a **sprint review meeting** to evaluate whether the goals of the sprint were met and to update the product backlog for the next sprint based on what they've learned.

One other practice is the **sprint retrospective**. This is a brief meeting held by the team following the sprint review to reflect on how effectively the team worked together over the last sprint and to find ways of improving their practices.

NOTE

Think of a potentially shippable version of the game as something you could run an informal focus test with.

The Principles of Scrum

Scrum has a small number of simple practices that teams can use to develop games. These practices are not all-encompassing or perfect for every product. As a framework, Scrum is meant to have practices added and changed as teams and products evolve.

It is important to preserve the principles of Scrum:

- **Empiricism:** Scrum uses an "inspect and adapt" cycle that enables the team and stakeholders to respond to emerging knowledge and changing conditions in real time using actual data. An example of this can be seen in the daily scrum practice, which enables the team to react to daily issues.
- **Emergence:** As we develop a game, we learn more about what makes it fun, what is possible, and how to create it. Scrum practices don't ban designs from being developed up front. They acknowledge

that we can't know everything about a game from the start. The sprint review and planning cycle is designed to maximize emergence of features as seen in a working game.

- **Timeboxing:** Scrum is iterative. It delivers value on a regular basis and enables stakeholders and developers to synchronize and micro-steer the project as value emerges. Sprints are an example of a time-boxed practice.
- **Prioritization:** Some features are more important to the stake-holders than others. Rather than approaching the development of a game by "implementing everything in the design document," Scrum projects develop features for a game based on their value to the player who will buy the game. The product backlog is an expression of this principle.
- **Self-organization:** Small, cross-discipline teams are empowered to organize their membership, manage their process, and create the best possible product within the timeboxes. They use the "inspect and adapt" cycle to continually improve how they work together, often through the sprint retrospective meeting.

By preserving these principles, Scrum teams can alter their practices and improve the benefits of Scrum.

Scrum Parts

In this section we look at some of the parts of Scrum identified in Figure 3.1 in detail as well as some additional practices.

The Product Backlog

The product backlog is a prioritized list of the requirements or features (called PBIs) for a game, a tool set, or the pipeline for making the game.

The following are examples of these requirements:

- Add a filtering function to the animation exporter.
- Add a particle effect to the game.
- Add online gameplay.

The product backlog is allowed to change after a sprint. PBIs that weren't anticipated are added. PBIs that are no longer necessary are removed, and the priorities are changed as necessary.

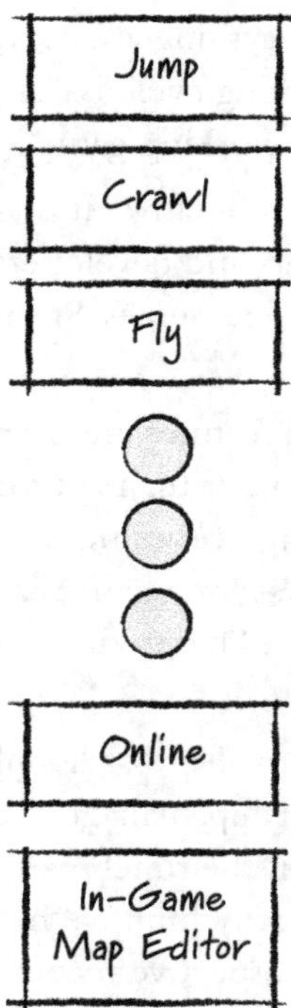

FIGURE 3.3 A backlog of features/PBIs

The value of each feature to the player is used to prioritize the backlog. The product backlog is not meant to be a detailed list of every feature we may need; that makes it too cumbersome to manipulate. Instead, the PBIs on the top of the list—in other words, the PBIs of highest value—are disaggregated, or broken down into small enough features for the team to work on over one sprint. Figure 3.3 demonstrates some PBIs for an example platform game.

Jump, *crawl*, and *fly* are the most valuable PBIs to implement right now and are at the top of the list. These PBIs are small enough to complete in a single sprint. PBIs such as *online* or *in-game map editor* are lower priority and are not disaggregated into smaller PBIs until the team is closer to implementing them.

Sprints

A Scrum-developed project makes progress in sprints. These iterations are the heartbeat of the project.

Sprints have a fixed duration (timebox) of two to four weeks. Teams commit to PBIs they can complete within the sprint. The overall objective of the sprint is called the **sprint goal**. A sprint goal is the overall theme of the sprint to which the team commits.

The sprint goal remains unchanged. At the end of the sprint, the team shows a new version of the game to the stakeholders, such as the publisher, which demonstrates the sprint goal.

DEFINITION A **stakeholder** is someone who has a stake in the outcome of the game project. These include people on the publishing side, other members of the project, and studio management.

Sprints produce vertical slices of functionality; they are like mini-projects themselves. A sprint contains design, coding, asset creation, tuning, debugging, and optimization—everything necessary to produce a potentially shippable game.

Many features require multiple sprints to develop. Sprints still need to demonstrate value at every review. Sometimes the customer wants to see some of the uncertainty or risk removed from the project as early as possible. Take, for example, a team delivering AI features: One of the most difficult challenges of AI behavior is navigation in a complex environment. The AI system has to identify obstacles that prevent an AI character from moving and calculate a path around them. With the addition of moving characters and objects, the problem can become intractable. Navigation is one the riskiest problems to solve for the entire game.

We want to solve the navigation problem as early as possible. Other related systems—such as character animation and physics—might not be mature enough to support the sprint goal of having a polished AI character walk through a complex environment. In this case, a sprint goal for the team could be to demonstrate simple capsules navigating a complex test environment. This goal doesn't demonstrate a complete feature, but it does represent value in reducing risk.

Does this remove all the risk associated with AI characters navigating complex environments? No. It addresses a big part of the problem. There still may be other problems that crop up when progress is made with the animation and physics. We want to minimize work built on assumptions. For example, the next sprint goal for the AI team could be to demonstrate the test capsule "climbing" stairs. Discovering that AI characters can't climb stairs during production could be a disaster if a number of levels and animations were built assuming it worked.

Releases

Releases are a set of sprints meant to bring a game with major new features to a near-shippable state. A typical release lasts between two to four months. The pace of releases is similar to those of milestones on a typical project.

Near-shippable state means "playable by potential buyers of the game but not necessarily ready to package with full content or pass all first-party requirements tests." On a two-year project, releases leading up to the shipped game should have a "magazine on downloadable demo quality." Games ship following the release that ensure first-party hardware (technical certification requirement [TCR] or technical requirements checklist [TRC]) or broad hardware compatibility tests are completed.

Releases establish longer-term goals for the team and stakeholders. They require an elevated level of polish and debugging that reduces a great deal of uncertainty about the work left to do to ship the game.

Releases start with a planning session that establishes major goals for the game. A release plan drives the goals for each sprint. Figure 3.4 shows how the release plan is a subset of features from the product backlog and how each sprint goal is a subset of the release plan.

NOTE Chapter 6, "Agile Planning," describes the release plan in detail.

Scrum Roles

Scrum gains much of its benefit from sprints and teams that make commitments to goals and own their work. There is a distinct separation in the roles and responsibilities between Scrum teams and the customers. Scrum teams and customers agree on goals, which satisfy clearly defined needs of the customer. Figure 3.5 shows the various roles described in this section.

The Scrum Team

A Scrum team consists of a ScrumMaster, a product owner, and a team of developers.

The **ScrumMaster** is responsible for educating the team about Scrum, ensuring the members follow the practices established for themselves. The ScrumMaster facilitates problem solving and runs interference for the team against the chickens (or invading pirates) when necessary (see the section "Chickens and Pigs" and the sidebar "Renaming Chickens and Pigs"). This was what our F-14 pilot did for us.

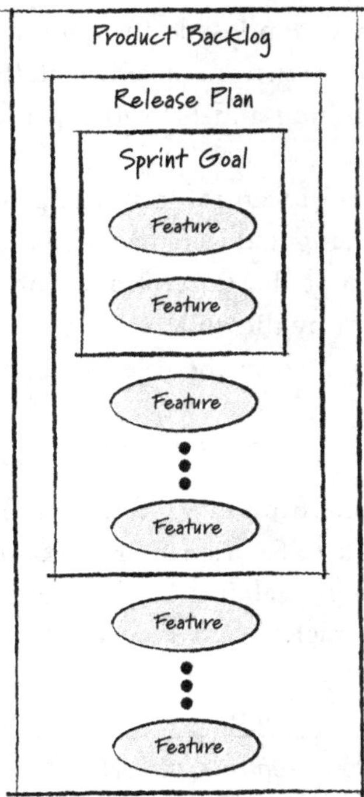

FIGURE 3.4 Subsets of planning

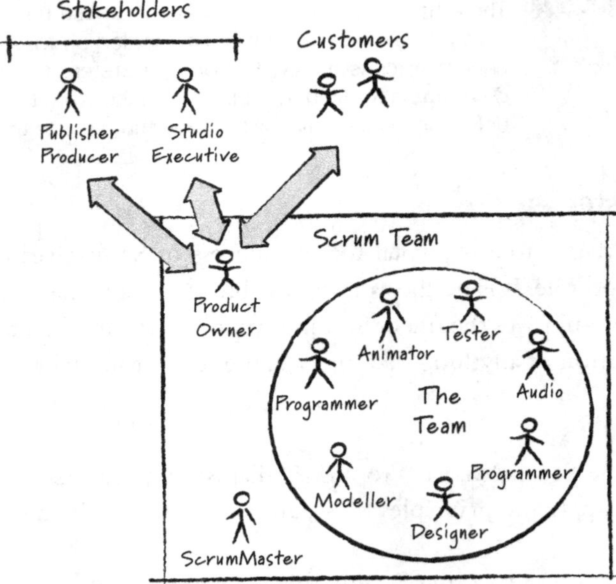

FIGURE 3.5 The Scrum roles

The **product owner** is responsible for communicating the vision of the game and maximizing the return on investment (ROI). The product owner maximizes ROI by establishing and prioritizing the desirable features in the product backlog.

The **team** delivers sets of features from the product backlog every sprint. Developers are self-organizing and self-managing; they determine how much work they can commit to at the start of a sprint and take responsibility to deliver the completed work by the end.

In coming sections, we'll cover the roles on a project that uses Scrum.

The Team

The team includes everyone from every discipline necessary to complete the goals that the team commits to for a sprint. For example, a team committing to a goal that required a walking, talking AI character should have animators, AI programmers, character modelers, and even QA to help the team ensure that the goal is done.

NOTE

The term ***teams*** often refers to everyone on a project. In the book, we'll call that group the **project staff**. Therefore, a project staff of eighty people might contain seven to nine teams.

TERMINOLOGY

There has been a lot of debate about these terms in the Scrum community. The community has settled on these terms for the benefit of consistency. Personally I prefer calling the team the **developers** to avoid multiple uses of the word ***team*** in the official definitions, but I'll stick with calling them the **team** for the book.

ScrumMaster

The ScrumMaster role is pivotal for the success of Scrum, yet it is the most misunderstood role. It is neither a traditional lead nor a management role. The ScrumMaster improves the use of Scrum through coaching, facilitation, and the rapid elimination of anything that distracts the team from delivering value.

Responsibilities

The job of the ScrumMaster is to ensure that Scrum is a success. The Scrum-Master must apply the principles of Scrum and deftly guide the team through the practices.

When a team starts using Scrum, they should rigorously apply a subset of Scrum practices "by the book." Over time, those practices gradually change as the team finds better ways of working together. The ScrumMaster's role is to ensure that the principles behind Scrum remain intact and that the team sticks to the practices they agree to follow.

NOTE

Chapter 16, "Launching Scrum," discusses such adoption strategies in greater detail.

The ScrumMaster is the conscience of the team in a sense; the principles of Scrum are inconvenient at times. For example, a team may be ignoring bugs or unpolished assets in their rush to deliver on a sprint. The ScrumMaster must remind them that each sprint delivers a vertical slice of the game and must not defer bug fixing or asset polishing to a future sprint.

One of the main responsibilities of the ScrumMaster is to nurture the sense of ownership within the team. Ownership has great value (see the sidebar "Ownership"). The ScrumMaster knows when to let teams occasionally falter and when to lend support. Much like a good parent, the ScrumMaster knows that protecting the team too much does not lead to growth and independence of thought and action.

The specific responsibilities of the ScrumMaster are as follows:

- Ensures impediments are addressed
- Monitors progress
- Facilitates planning, reviews, and retrospectives
- Encourages continual improvement
- Helps stakeholders and teams communicate

OWNERSHIP

A sense of ownership leads teams to solve impediments a bit faster than teams that take little control over their work. Ownership leads to more passion about their efforts. I've seen teams with a sense of ownership work overnight to implement something they felt strongly about. The goal, however, isn't to have teams work overnight but to engage in and enjoy the work. Making games should be a creative and fun process. If it isn't, how can we expect the game itself to be creative and fun?

Teams take ownership of their work during the sprint. This is an important feature of Scrum since it enables the team to truly commit to the work they estimated they could complete. Teams committed to their work far outperform teams that are not. If sprint goal changes are imposed on the team, they lose this sense of ownership and the commitment that comes with it.

Ensures Impediments Are Addressed

There is seldom a single event that causes a project to be late; there are usually many hundreds or thousands of problems. Losing just a couple of hours a day can extend the time required to finish a one-year project by several months!

Scrum refers to every problem that interferes with progress as an **impediment**. Impediments take various forms:

- Bugs that crash the game or tools
- Excessive or long meetings that don't produce results
- Constant distractions or interruptions from, for example, a frequently used intercom system
- Waiting for someone to finish something you need to make progress on your task

The list goes on. Scrum focuses the team on solving many of these impediments through the creation of cross-discipline teams and the daily scrum. A programmer who needs a test asset can turn to a team artist for help. A designer who shares the same sprint goal with a programmer finds that the programmer is easily motivated to help them solve a bug.

A cross-discipline team will rapidly solve most impediments identified throughout the day on their own. The ScrumMaster's role is to ensure that visibility of impediments is raised to the proper level so they are addressed.

Some impediments cannot be solved by the team. For example, if an animator needs a tool purchased, the team probably does not have the authority to issue a purchase order directly. Much like my former F-14 boss did, the ScrumMaster takes ownership of this problem and raises it to the necessary level for the purchase to be authorized. Without this daily support, the tool purchase could take weeks to resolve.

Sometimes impediments take time to be resolved. The ScrumMaster tracks these to ensure that they are not forgotten.

Monitors Progress

The ScrumMaster ensures that the team remains aware of how well they are performing against their goal. A Scrum team monitors its progress every day and projects progress against the goal. If the team is slipping behind, they must be aware of it as soon as possible.

Facilitates Planning, Reviews, and Retrospectives

The ScrumMaster ensures that all team meetings are prepared for and facilitated. Facilitating a meeting includes scheduling the time, preparing the space, and ensuring that the meeting occurs within the time limits to which everyone agreed.

Ensuring that a meeting runs well is a deep skill that ScrumMasters need to continually develop and help teams learn to execute well on their own.

Encourages Continual Improvement

The ScrumMaster encourages the team to seek ways to improve their performance as a team. This never ceases. Even with the most productive teams, the ScrumMaster encourages them to seek even a single percentage point of improvement. This promotes a culture of continuous improvement. Improvements could be as simple as moving desks closer to improve communication or as hard as requesting new technology that improves the efficiency of the production pipeline.

The ScrumMaster role is mainly a facilitative one. The ScrumMaster might recognize problems before the team and identify a favored solution, but they should never lead by implementing the solution. Instead, a ScrumMaster will help a team recognize problems and own the solution. This teaches them the invaluable skill of identifying and solving problems on their own. In many ways, the role of the ScrumMaster is to coach the team to eliminate the need for a ScrumMaster.

Helps Stakeholders and Teams Communicate

Stakeholders and development teams speak different languages. Stakeholders speak about return on investment, profit/loss calculations, sales projections, and budgets. Development teams talk about technology, gameplay, and artistic vision. This divide of language prevents real communication from occurring between the two groups. It's the job of the ScrumMaster to facilitate this communication, primarily through teaching the team the necessary amount of business language and focusing much of the communication bandwidth through the product backlog.

Attributes

A ScrumMaster's role on the team is compared to a sheepdog. They guide the team toward the goal by enforcing boundaries, chasing off predators, and giving the occasional bark. The role of a ScrumMaster requires a proper attitude. An overbearing sheepdog stresses out the flock. A passive sheepdog lets the predators in among them.

The ScrumMaster trusts the team. The ScrumMaster guides the team to do their best work through coaching and facilitation. The ScrumMaster role is not easy, but it is rewarding. A ScrumMaster has to be stubborn and persistent. Many issues facing a team require intervention at a personal level with people who may not want to change their behaviors. For example, take a manager of considerable authority and many years of experience in a command and control environment who does not believe self-organization works. This manager repeatedly interferes with a team in ways that distract the team by assigning new work in the middle of a sprint. The ScrumMaster needs to persistently remind the manager about the purpose of Scrum and the reciprocal commitments between the team and the stakeholders. This needs to be done in a way that does not offend and raise barriers. It's a coaching role. Not everyone can do it.

There is a formal course meant to introduce Scrum. This "Certified ScrumMaster Training Course" is an immersion in the practices and principles of Scrum given by a Scrum trainer who is certified by the Scrum Alliance.[3,4]

This course is highly recommended for anyone new to Scrum, and it will also benefit members of an experienced team by reinforcing the principles and practices of Scrum.

SHOULD THE SCRUMMASTER ALSO BE A MEMBER OF THE TEAM?

A ScrumMaster is usually not a developer on the team. A ScrumMaster can handle two to four teams before their role starts becoming a full-time job. It depends on how many organization impediments exist that the ScrumMaster needs to address. This limitation may mean that there are not enough ScrumMasters to go around.

NOTE

Sprint lengths are usually set between two to four weeks and don't change much. The best sprint length is discussed in Chapter 4, "Sprints."

3. www.ScrumAlliance.org
4. I also provide a Certified ScrumMaster (CSM) class specifically tailored for game development. Visit www.ClintonKeith.com for more details.

Teams often ask, "Should the ScrumMaster stay as a developer on the team?" I prefer that a ScrumMaster not be a developer on the team. The "ScrumMaster as a member of the team" role can cause some problems if any of the following occurs:

- They focus on their own tasks more than on the ScrumMaster role.
- They prioritize their own impediments over those of other teammates.
- The team assumes the role is a leadership one, but they defer ownership to the ScrumMaster.

Sometimes there is no choice but to have the ScrumMaster be recruited from the developers on the team. When this happens, everyone on the team needs to watch out for these problems.

WEARING THE SCRUMASTER HAT

Sometimes when a developer on the team takes on the role of the ScrumMaster, they carry a hat around with them. They don the hat when they are in the ScrumMaster role and take it off when they are in the developer role. It helps the team know who is speaking to them.

Product Owner

The product owner establishes and communicates the vision of the game and prioritizes its features.

The product owner is responsible for the following:

- Managing the ROI for the game
- Establishing a shared vision for the game among the customers and developers
- Knowing what to build and in what order
- Creating release plans and establishing delivery dates
- Supporting sprint planning and reviews
- Representing the customers, including the player who buys the game

Most video game projects have one true release to get things right. Most of our games can't slowly grow their feature sets and a market simultaneously like other products. This requires great vision; it makes the role of a product owner on an agile video game project critical.

Manages the ROI

The product owner is responsible for ensuring that the investment in the game is returned with a profit. This requires the product owner to know what the market wants, even years in advance of the release.

The product owner is responsible for other metrics of a project's success. These include the performance of the game on the target platforms, the final cost of the game, and the ship date. Forecasts, such as average game rankings and profit/loss (P&L) calculations, can be applied, but these are marketing projections that can't guide projects very well. The product owner creates a bridge between marketing, sales, and the Scrum team by demonstrating the emerging game and collaborating on the direction the game is heading.

Creates a Shared Vision

The product owner is a single voice for the vision that is shared with the team. They ignite creativity and ownership with the team and collaborate with them as the vision evolves with the emerging game.

Having a shared vision is critical for the success of any game. Lacking vision, a large team of developers will go off in separate directions, creating a Frankenstein game of parts that don't mesh. We've all seen these games—the ones that have beautiful art but no great gameplay, the games that have a great mechanic but too many performance problems to be playable, or the games that have dozens of mechanics but not one of them done well.

Sharing a project vision is not easy. It was easier when a game had a few less-specialized developers, but many games being developed today require a small army of specialists. Large development teams allow people to become isolated by discipline. This isolation creates further barriers to a shared vision; programmers sitting together start to see a game project as a computer science project. Artists produce art that satisfy other artists. Designers create baroque control schemes that only other designers can appreciate. Each group focuses on the challenges for their own discipline and loses sight of the business side.

The product owner's role in creating the vision for a video game project is comparable to the role played by key visionaries such as Shigeru Miyamoto,[5]

5. Creator of Donkey Kong, Mario, Zelda, and so on

Will Wright,[6] Tim Schafer,[7] Warren Spector,[8] and Sid Meier[9] on their projects. A product owner represents the ultimate customer during development: the player. The product owner has to foresee what the market will embrace up to three years in advance. They have to know the mind and emotional responses of the player.

Owns the Product Backlog

The product owner owns the product backlog and determines the order of features on the backlog. This order reflects the order of when those features are developed.

The product owner usually cannot manage a product backlog alone. The backlog may have features that require a technical, artistic, or design understanding to create or prioritize. Some features support the efforts of sales and marketing to help promote the game, such as in-game advertisements. The product owner needs to work with the various customers and stakeholders of the game to understand all of their needs.

Manages Releases

The product owner manages the releases and calls for release plans and the delivery date. The product owner revises the release plan based on changes to the goals or the progress from the teams during sprints. The product owner guides the various release activities. We'll cover these activities in more detail in Chapter 6.

Sprint Planning and Review

The product owner has the following major duties during a sprint:

- Establishing and updating the features on the backlog and their priorities
- Participating in sprint planning
- Participating in the sprint review and accepting or rejecting the results of the sprints

Figure 3.6 summarizes the role of the product owner regarding the product backlog and sprints.

6. Creator of The Sims and Spore
7. Creator of Full Throttle and Physchonauts
8. Creator of Deus Ex
9. Creator of the Civilization series

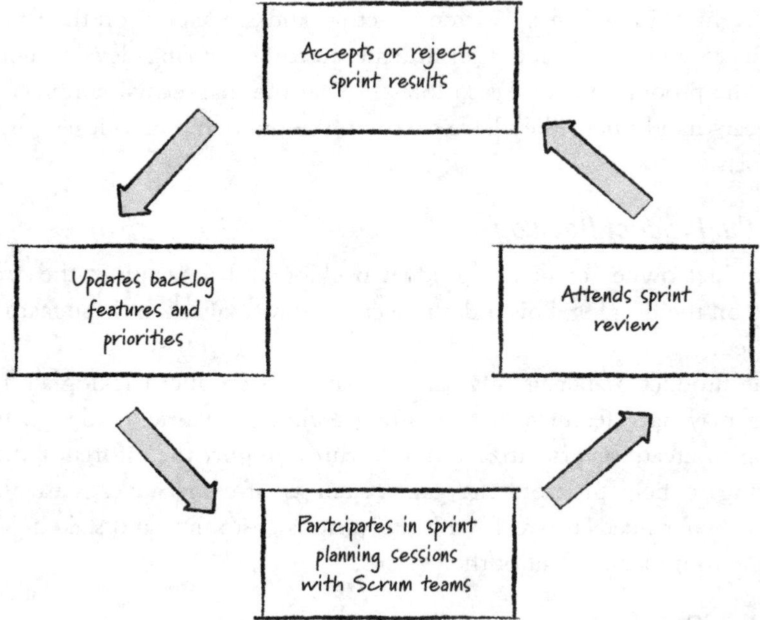

FIGURE 3.6 The product owner role

Customers and Stakeholders

The relationship of customers and stakeholders to the Scrum team is important. They define many of the items on the backlog. They work with the product owner to help prioritize the backlog. Although the product owner is a member of a Scrum team, the product owner is considered the "lead customer." This person determines the priority of features on the backlog. The product owner provides a service to the team by being the one voice of all the customers and stakeholders.

The ultimate customer is the player who will buy the game. Although the player doesn't directly define the requirements of the game, all stakeholders represent them. The stakeholders are people outside the team that have a stake in the game being made.

The following are some common stakeholder roles:

- **Publisher-producer:** The publisher-producer communicates the progress and goals between publisher and the studio. One of the main values of this role is to ensure that both sides have the same vision about the game and that there is transparency about the progress of a game.

- **Marketing:** Marketing provides input on the relative importance of features in the backlog and, by understanding the backlog, more effectively communicates the key features of the game to the market.
- **Studio leadership:** Studio art, design, and technology leadership help the product owner prioritize work, especially with respect to cost and risk of feature development. For example, as a former chief technical officer, my role was to work with the product owner and the project staff to address areas of technical risk through the product backlog.

Each of these stakeholders can introduce feature requests to the product backlog. For example, when I was a CTO, I was mostly concerned with the technical risk in implementing various features in the game and the pipeline. As a result, I introduced requirements that helped the team gain knowledge about risk or helped everyone understand the cost of implementing a feature.

NOTE

Many agile books will combine the roles of stakeholders and customers into the customer role. However, with many games taking years to develop that are externally financed, the distinction is important to game developers. Stakeholders are the proxies for the true customers who do not have a voice to communicate their wants and needs about the game every sprint.

Chickens and Pigs

A book describing Scrum can't avoid telling the story about "the pig and the chicken," so here goes:

> Once upon a time, a pig and chicken were talking. "I have an idea," the chicken exclaimed, "let's open a restaurant; we'll call it Ham and Eggs." The pig thought about it for a moment and said, "No thanks...you'd only be involved, but I'd be committed."

This is how the labels of *pigs* and *chickens* got their start (see the sidebar "Renaming Pigs and Chickens"). **Pigs** are the members of a Scrum team who commit to the work in the sprint. **Chickens** are the customers and stakeholders outside the team who do not make the personal commitment to the work.

Chickens influence the direction of the project between sprints. Chickens and pigs discuss the goals of an upcoming sprint and prioritize the product backlog. The pigs (teams) commit to implementing features. The chickens commit to allowing the team to achieve those goals without interference. This reciprocal commitment between the pigs and chickens enables Scrum to work. If the chickens are allowed to change a sprint goal, then it is not possible for the pigs to truly commit to it at the start of the sprint.

RENAMING PIGS AND CHICKENS

The distinction between the pig and chicken roles is important in Scrum. Companies that adopt Scrum are very conscious of the distinction when working out the practices. Some teams come up with new terms to replace the terms ***chicken*** and ***pig*** because no one enjoys being called those names.

A good example of replacement terms was coined by the developers at Swordfish Studios in the United Kingdom. They decided to refer to themselves as ***pirates*** and ***ninjas***.

These terms are more acceptable, but I was uncertain what they meant, so I asked them about it. "To us, pirates are the chickens; they invade, pillage, cause all sorts of mayhem, and then leave," I was told. "OK," I said, "that makes sense, but what about ninjas?" The reply was, "Oh, well we called ourselves ninjas because ninjas are cool."

As it turns out ninjas and pirates are natural enemies. An Internet meme has grown up around this.[10]

Scaling Scrum

Scrum teams have less than a dozen developers, but most game projects require more developers to create. Scrum supports these larger teams through scaling. This is done by having a number of Scrum teams work in parallel and coordinating their work through practices such as the scrum of scrums, which the book will address in great detail in Chapter 8, "Teams."

Summary

Scrum practices and roles are simple and easy to start using. So, why read an entire book dedicated to using agile practices, such as Scrum, for game development? The reason is that the practices previously described are only a starting point.

Scrum creates the opportunity for you to measure and question every practice you use to make games (inspect) and enables you to introduce change

10. http://en.wikipedia.org/wiki/Pirates_versus_Ninjas

to improve them (adapt). Scrum gives you empirical tools to measure the effectiveness of your team. These measurements give you feedback about the benefits and drawbacks of every change and enable you to enter the endless cycle of continually improving your practices. The challenge in adopting Scrum is to learn how and why it works and then modify your practices to leverage the transparency that Scrum creates.

The next chapter rounds out the basics of Scrum by detailing the activities involved in sprints. The remainder of the book addresses how game developers inspect and adapt the basic practices for developing their games.

Additional Reading

Schwaber, K. 2004. *Agile Project Management with Scrum*. Redmond, WA: Microsoft Press.

Takeuchi, H., Nonaka, I. 1986. The new new product development game, *Harvard Business Review*, pp. 137-146, January-February.

Chapter 4
Sprints

In the previous chapter, we introduced Scrum practices and roles. In this chapter, we'll go into more detail about sprints. We'll see how they are planned, how they are conducted on a day-to-day basis, and how the team and stakeholders review the progress at the end and reflect on how well they worked together. Finally, we'll see how sprints might fail to achieve their full goals and how the teams and stakeholders deal with that.

The Big Picture

Sprints have the following basic rules:

- They are timeboxed, usually between two to four weeks in length.
- The team commits to completing a sprint goal.
- No additions or changes are made by anyone outside the team.

Figure 4.1 shows the flow of meetings in a sprint.

The team and stakeholders establish a goal in the sprint planning meeting at the start of a sprint. The progress of the team's work is shared in the daily scrum meetings. At the end of the sprint, the team demonstrates their progress to the stakeholders in a sprint review meeting. Following the review, the team conducts a retrospective, where they discuss how the team worked together during the sprint and to seek improvements for the coming sprints.

Planning

At the start of a sprint, teams meet with the stakeholders of the project to plan the next sprint. Planning a sprint requires two meetings: the **sprint prioritization meeting** and the **sprint planning meeting**. The prioritization meeting

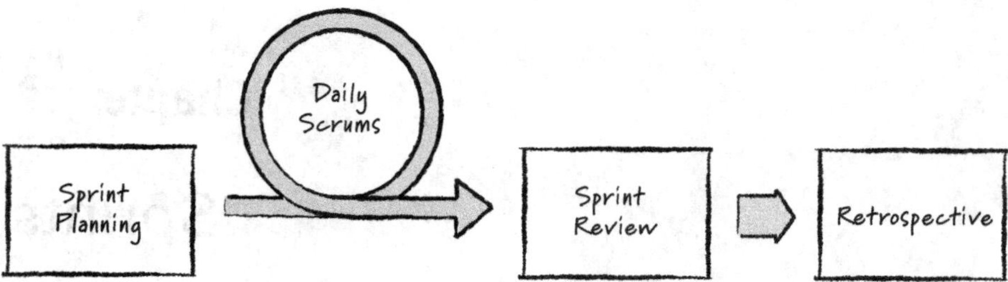

FIGURE 4.1 The flow of sprint meetings

prepares, or "grooms," the product backlog and identifies a potential sprint goal. The sprint planning meeting creates the sprint backlog that defines the work that the team commits to completing by the next sprint review.

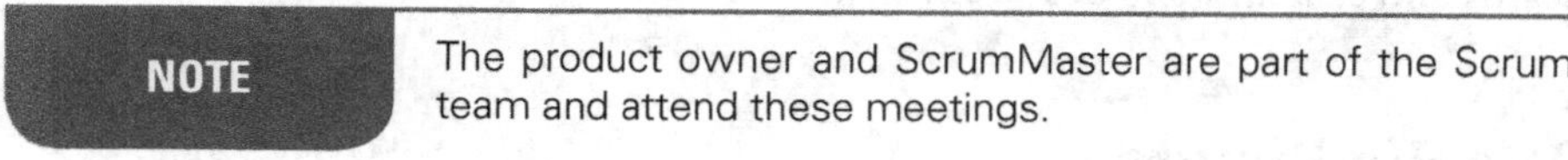
NOTE The product owner and ScrumMaster are part of the Scrum team and attend these meetings.

Sprint Prioritization

The goal of the sprint prioritization meeting is to review the high-priority items on the product backlog and to select a potential sprint goal. The meeting begins with the product owner describing the highest-priority features on the product backlog. The team needs to understand each PBI. This is the team's opportunity to raise any design (game design, technical, art, and so on) questions. For example, if a feature requires the main character to jump, there may be some questions about how the current animation and physics technology is applied. This discussion identifies design and high-level implementation details such as whether a physics-only, animation-only, or blended solution is best.

Sometimes high-priority PBIs on the product backlog are too large for a team to tackle in a single sprint. These features are broken down into smaller PBIs that are expected to fit.

The team next discusses the potential goal for the coming sprint. The team selects the top PBIs from the product backlog they think they might accomplish given the current composition of the team. It's best to end the prioritization meeting when approximately two sprints worth of PBIs have been discussed because some PBIs may not be accomplished by the team. For example, if a particular feature requires animation but no animators are on the team, then the team cannot commit to completing that feature unless they find one to join them.

Another reason to skip a particular PBI is because of a dependency from another team. For example, a feature that requires engine work to be completed first should be postponed if the engine team has not addressed that dependency. The organization of the product backlog and teams reflect the need to avoid such dependencies, but sometimes they do occur. We want to discuss enough PBIs during this meeting that the team has some leeway in which they choose to work on during the next meeting, all while working generally within product owner priorities.

At this point, the team hasn't committed to any work. They've identified the PBIs they may be able to complete, but until they've broken these PBIs down into individual estimated tasks—which they do in the planning meeting—they aren't yet ready to commit.

Sprint Planning

After identifying potential product backlog items for the sprint, the team breaks down the tasks from each PBI, one at a time, to build the sprint backlog. This occurs in the sprint planning meeting. The participants in this meeting include the entire team (including the ScrumMaster and product owner) and any domain expert who may be needed to answer questions or help the team estimate their work better (such as an online programmer, motion capture technician, and so on).

At the start of the meeting, the ScrumMaster helps the team identify constraints that might impact the team's ability to commit to the sprint goal. Here are some examples of these constraints:

- Holidays that reduce the amount of time available
- Team member commitments to work away from the team
- Potential impacts from other areas, such as the integration of a major engine change that has caused problems in the past

The team's ability to commit to work is based primarily on their past performance. This is best determined by examining what the team has been able to accomplish in past sprints. For example, if the team was able to finish an average of 400 hours of estimated work in the last few sprints, then it's probably a safe bet for them to commit to 400 hours of estimated work for the coming sprint. This becomes the limit of the sprint backlog, or task bucket, that they have to fill in the planning meeting.

NOTE The team doesn't track actual time spent; the team tracks the estimated time remaining to accomplish tasks. When first starting Scrum, actual time spent may be double that of the estimated time because the team isn't used to including debugging and tuning time. This is consistent across all tasks and so is predictable, but it will improve over time.

The team then discusses design and implementation details for every PBI that is potentially part of the sprint goal. The attendance of the product owner is important for this discussion since there are many subjective aspects to what needs to be implemented. For example, the team might want to discuss potential trade-offs on character motion that looks realistic vs. motion that is responsive to player input but more jarring in appearance.

The team then starts breaking the PBIs into tasks. Figure 4.2 shows the flow of how PBIs are taken from the product backlog and employed to build the sprint backlog.

The team starts creating a sprint backlog by taking the highest-priority PBI from the product backlog and breaking it into tasks. Everyone on the team is involved at first since design questions are raised. Once the requirements of the feature are agreed upon, the team starts writing individual tasks and estimating the amount of time each one takes to complete.

Task estimation takes place within discipline groups. For example, if the team has four programmers, they estimate the programming tasks together. If only one programmer is on the team, the programmer estimates all the programming tasks on their own.

Tasks are estimated in hours. The team estimate is in ideal time, which is the amount of time a task should take without interruption or any problems. This means that an eight-hour task is not the same as a one-day task. An eight-hour task usually takes more than one calendar day to accomplish. The reason is that our days are filled with interruptions, problems, and conversations that vary from day to day.

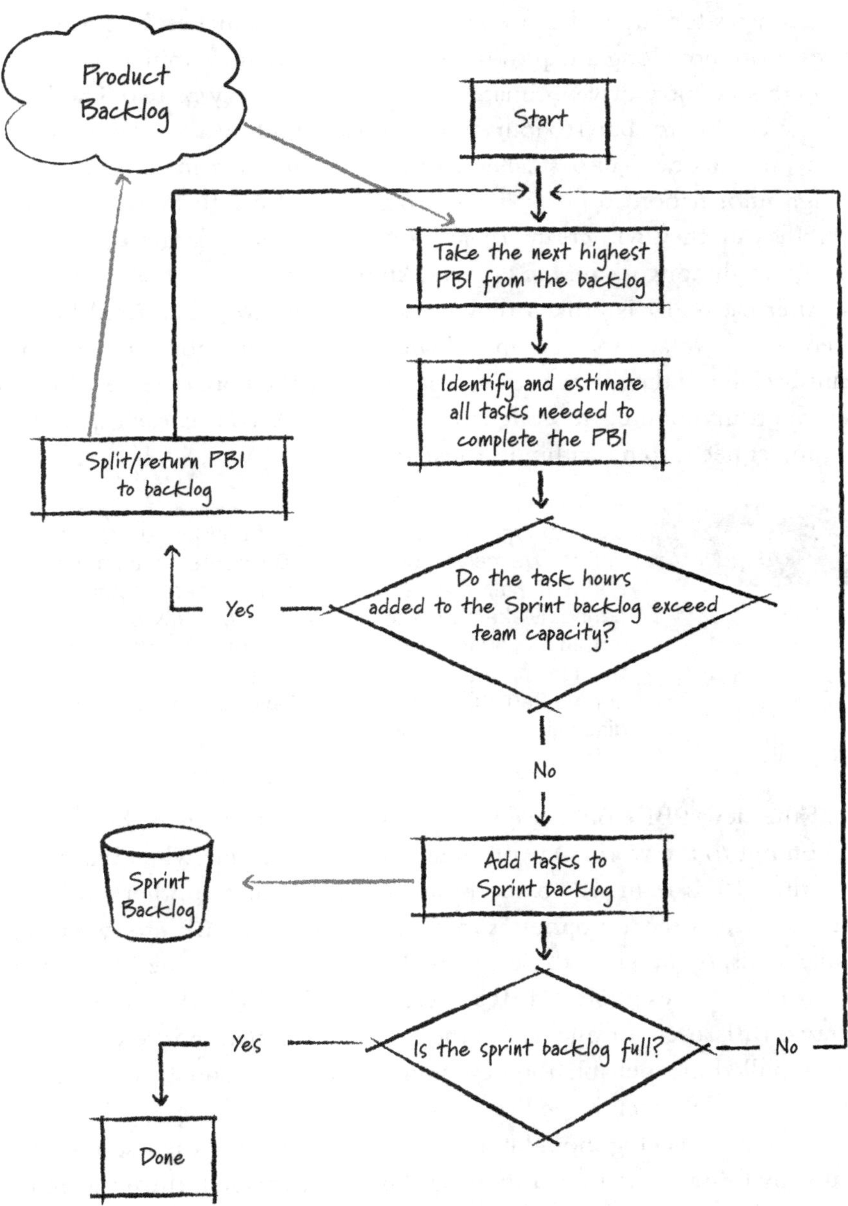

FIGURE 4.2 The flow of creating a sprint backlog

Estimates for large tasks are less accurate than estimates for small tasks. I can estimate how long a trip to the local store takes to within a few minutes, but a cross-country drive estimate might be off by a day or two. The limit of task size is arbitrary, but 16 hours is a reasonable limit as a size before it needs to be broken down into smaller tasks. Sometimes a team might not have enough information to break down a task larger than 16 hours into smaller tasks. Instead, they will create a placeholder task with a larger estimate until they are ready to work on the task and know more.

After each PBI is broken down into tasks, the total estimated hours are added up. This total is then compared with the remaining hours available in the sprint backlog. If the sprint backlog has room for the hours the new PBI adds, then the team commits to completing that PBI. Of course, each specialty on the project needs to be within its capacity.

NOTE

Even though we got 400 hours of combined work done last sprint, we can't commit to 400 hours of animations this sprint if half the team are programmers. Apply common sense. Make sure each discipline (specialty or skill group) is within its capacity, and use the amount of work done during the last sprint as a guide to what can be completed this sprint. Part III, "Agile Game Development," discusses the disciplines in more detail.

If the new PBI would overflow the sprint backlog, then the team does not commit to the work. One of three options is available when this happens. First, the PBI is returned to the product backlog, and another smaller PBI takes its place. A second option is to break the original PBI into two or more smaller PBIs. A subset of the original PBI might be identified that fits into the sprint. As an example, a PBI for creating a level could be broken down into two PBIs, each for one half of the level. A third option is to drop an item already pulled in to enable the new item to fit. The product owner can help the team decide which is the best solution.

The sprint backlog should not be completely filled to the last hour. There are usually forgotten tasks that show up during the sprint. If the hours remaining are small (a day or two worth of work), then the team doesn't have to worry about adding another feature to bring the remaining hours down to zero. A few hours of additional polishing work is never hard to find!

HOW TO ESTIMATE YOUR FIRST SPRINT

While planning a sprint, the team considers the amount of work accomplished over previous sprints to judge the approximate number of hours they commit to in the coming sprint. A natural question that comes up is, "How do we estimate our capacity for our first sprint?" I recommend that the team aim for one-third fewer hours than they initially estimate. The reason for this is that teams new to Scrum underestimate the effort to create potentially shippable features at first. This includes time for bug fixing and polishing, activities not traditionally included in waterfall task estimates.

If the team runs out of work during the sprint, they conduct a mini-planning meeting and pick another PBI or two to fit into the remainder of the sprint. They'll have a better feel for and be able to more accurately measure the work they can commit to with every successive sprint.

Length

What is the ideal length of a sprint? Sprints typically last two to four weeks, but many factors influence this:

- The frequency of customer feedback and change
- The experience level of the team
- The time overhead for planning and reviews
- The ability to plan the entire sprint
- The intensity of the team over the sprint

Over the course of a project, these factors will change, and the length of a sprint may change as well.

Customer Feedback

The duration of a sprint depends on the amount of time the stakeholders can go without seeing progress and providing direction on the game. Some core mechanics require frequent feedback in the early stages of development, so a shorter sprint is required to be sure the game is headed in the right direction. For example, the motion of the character, behavior of the camera, and layout of the controls may require frequent feedback. Some teams don't need such a rapid cycle of feedback (such as production teams), so a longer sprint is more appropriate for them.

The team must not have the goal changed within the sprint. If four weeks is unbearably long for stakeholders to wait for a review, then they need a shorter sprint.

Team Experience

Teams new to game development, agile, or working together should start with shorter sprints. This enables them to iterate on the practices and learn how to develop more iteratively and incrementally. Teams new to Scrum should be discouraged from practicing longer sprints because they tend to approach a sprint like a mini-waterfall project (see the top part of Figure 4.3). They'll spend a couple of days exclusively in design, spend a few weeks creating code and assets, and finally integrate, test, and tune during the last few days of the sprint and end up crunching at the end of the sprint to reach the finish line. This doesn't give them the opportunity to achieve the best possible result because there is little time left to iterate and polish their work.

Experienced teams will perform these activities more in parallel, designing, coding, creating assets, testing, and debugging every day. Working this way creates better results and enables the team to iterate more during the sprint and increase the value of their work.

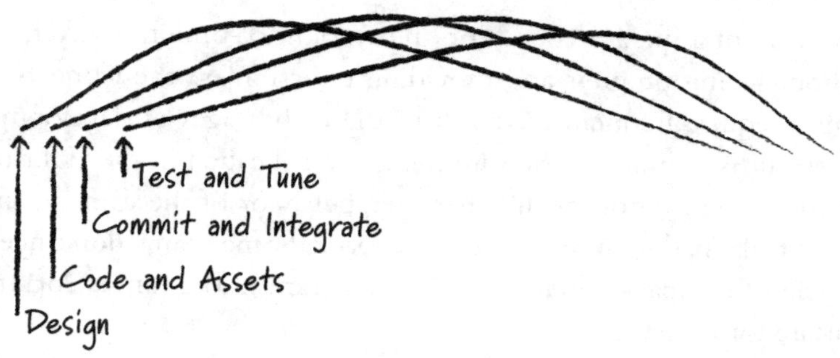

FIGURE 4.3 Sequential vs. parallel development models

Planning and Review Overhead

Shorter sprints often require a larger portion of a team's time for planning and review meetings. Review and planning usually require a good portion of a day regardless of the length of the sprint. Even though planning for a shorter sprint may take less time, the remainder of the day following the meeting is never 100% effective. Imagine that you had a sprint that lasted one week. You'd probably spend one day that week in review and planning. That's 20% of the team's time spent in planning!

> **PLAN TO PARTY**
>
> Allow the team to have a little celebration between sprints. Don't disrupt the cycle of the sprint for it. Set a little time aside as part of the sprint for people to play the game and relax. Besides, game developers don't need much excuse for a party!

Ability to Plan the Sprint

If the team is uncertain about how to achieve the sprint goal or if experimentation or prototypes need to be done, then the sprint should be shorter. Uncertainty implies that the work eventually required for the sprint might be significantly different from what was anticipated at the start. If this is the case, it's better to change direction after two weeks than four.

> **PROTOTYPE SPRINTING**
>
> Some prototype teams have chosen extremely short sprint times of days!

Balanced Intensity

Sometimes four weeks is too long for a sprint because it leads to a low-intensity mini-design phase up front and a high-intensity debug mini-crunch phase at the end. Although the mini-crunch phase isn't going to kill anyone, it's not the most efficient way to work.

> **CHOOSING A SPRINT DURATION**
>
> On my last team, a two-week sprint felt too short. It was as though the review was too soon to "do anything too challenging." A four-week sprint was too long to create a sense of urgency. We compromised and chose a three-week sprint because "it felt right."

When Is the Sprint Too Long?

A product owner usually limits a sprint's length to four weeks as the longest amount of time they let pass to direct the goals of the game. Some may argue that some technical areas (such as engine or pipeline development) cannot achieve any significant progress in as little as four weeks. The need for longer sprints to show value usually indicates that the technical practices need to improve. Any development practice that can't demonstrate progress at least once a month should be addressed. Interim goals should demonstrate a reduction in risk and have value. For example, if a team is implementing the infrastructure for online gameplay, they might demonstrate simple object messaging across a local area network after the first sprint. The longer a team goes without proving or disproving architectural assumptions, the greater the potential waste.

NOTE We'll discuss this in more detail in Chapter 10, "Agile Technology." Hold on to your tomatoes!

Who Selects the Sprint Duration and When?

The stakeholders and the Scrum team need to determine the duration of a sprint. If there is a disagreement, the product owner has the final say. The length of the sprint must be changed only between sprints, and it shouldn't be changed too frequently. Frequent changes to the length of sprints are disruptive. It takes some time for the team to adjust to the rhythm and pace of a particular sprint length and refine their ability to estimate the appropriate sprint backlog.

Tracking Progress

During a sprint, the team needs to share information about their progress and identify any impediments to their sprint goal. The team needs to have the proper information to make the best decisions. They need easy access to the sprint backlog of tasks. They need to understand where they stand in terms of achieving their goals. They need to recognize as early as possible when they won't achieve their goal.

Scrum has a number of low-tech practices and artifacts for providing this information to teams. Task cards, burndown charts, task boards, and war rooms have proven their value for tracking progress throughout the sprint. This section describes these in detail.

Task Cards

Tasks can be recorded and tracked in many ways. The most useful form to store tasks are on 3-by-5 index cards, called **task cards**. These cards have many advantages that no tool can match. The major benefit is that they enable everyone on the team to participate in task creation and management. The task card enables easy customization using various color cards and markings. For example, a cinematics team decided to categorize the order of asset creation tasks by using stamps with pictures of fruit to help them better prioritize their tasks. The "low-hanging" fruit were picked off the board first. Try doing that as easily with a tool!

Burndown Chart

During the planning meeting, the team commits to accomplishing the sprint goal based on the sum of the estimated tasks expected to complete it. The team updates the estimate of work remaining daily to help them track progress toward their goal. The team plots this day-to-day measurement on a graph, called a **burndown chart** (see Figure 4.4). The burndown chart is a tool for the team to use to gauge how well their efforts are leading to achieving their goal by the end of the sprint.

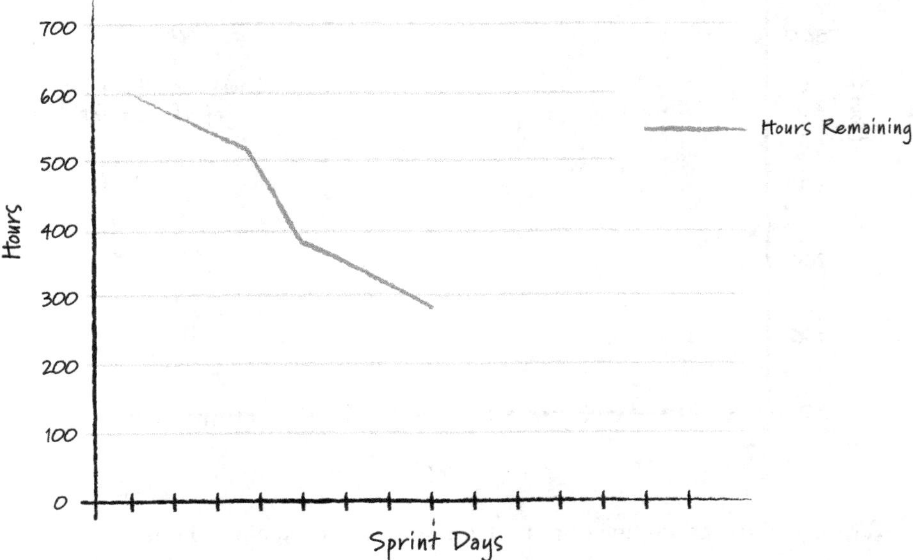

FIGURE 4.4 An example burndown chart

Daily Sprint Backlog Trend

As described in the planning section, tasks are estimated in actual "ideal" hours of work. An ideal hour is an hour of work accomplished without interruptions, bugs, tool problems, questions, coffee breaks, friends on the phone, and so on. We're lucky if we accomplish four ideal hours of work per eight-hour workday with all this competition for our time and attention.

The burndown chart tracks ideal hours remaining to accomplish the sprint goal. The rate that ideal hours decrease per day is called the **burndown trend**. Measuring this trend is a powerful tool for Scrum teams.

The burndown trend is for the team to track their progress toward accomplishing the sprint goal. Figure 4.5 shows the burndown chart of a team a little more than halfway through their sprint. Using this chart, the team, in midsprint, projects their trend (the dotted line) to the end of the sprint. The trend line is a warning that the team is falling behind and won't achieve their goal.

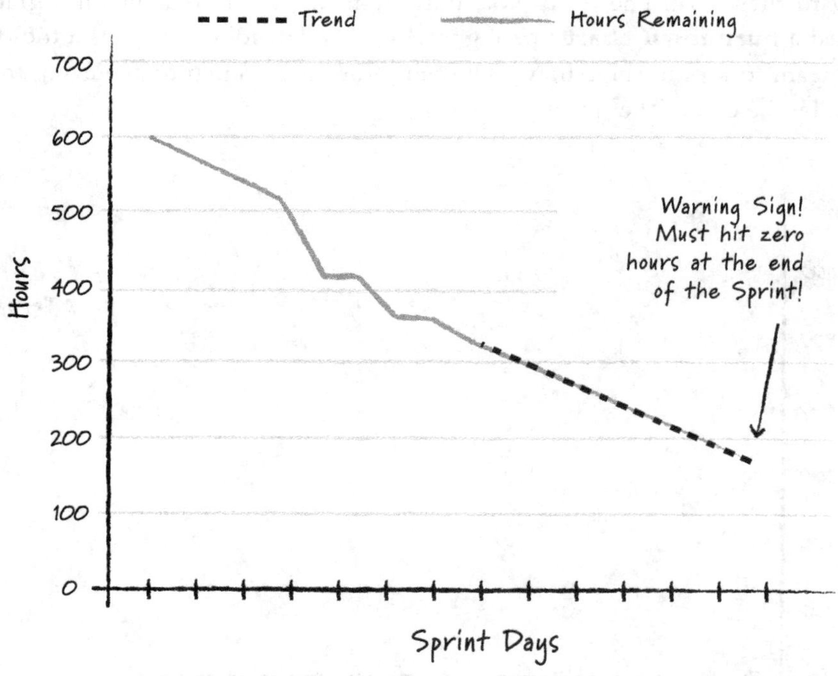

FIGURE 4.5 Projecting the sprint backlog rate by adding a trend line

NOTE The sprint backlog trend is a valuable empirical tool for examining the impact of any change that the team makes to how they work.

Some teams will draw an ideal line of progress from estimated hours remaining at the start of the sprint to zero hours on the last day. Figure 4.6 shows this trend line. This shows the team how far they are above the ideal projection of remaining time.

It's important for the team to understand that the goal isn't to have their burndown line match the ideal line. The goal is to use the burndown to show how they are progressing daily.

NOTE We'll discuss the options available when the team is running out of time later in this chapter.

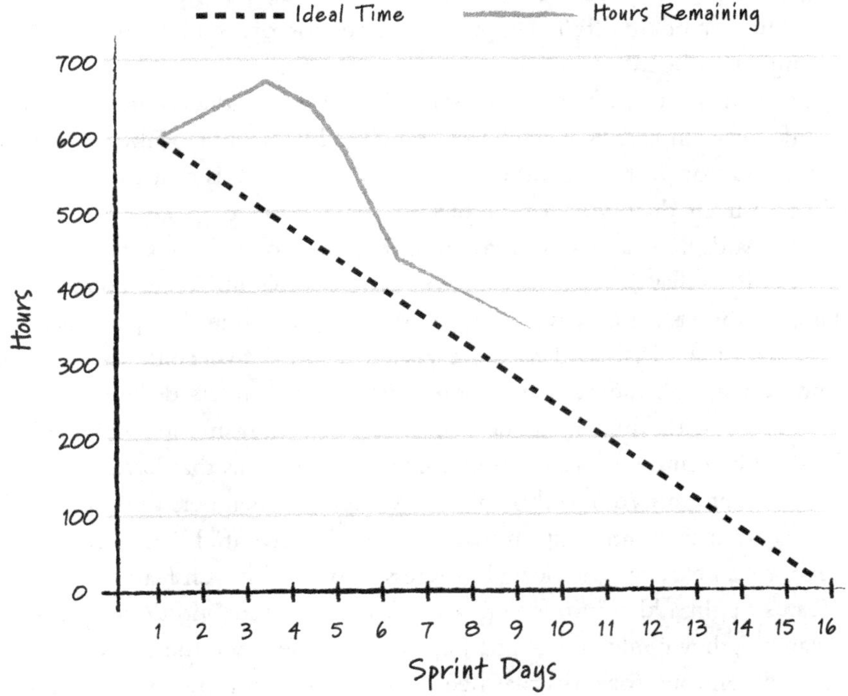

FIGURE 4.6 An ideal trend line

BURNDOWN CHARTS ARE NOT NEW

Long before I learned about Scrum, I encountered the power of burndown charts. When our team entered alpha, the publisher threw a couple dozen testers on the project, and all of us fixed bugs.

Once a week, we triaged the bug database to prioritize the bug "backlog." We tracked the total bug count and used a "burndown chart" to measure bug resolution velocity, bug discovery velocity, and the projected "zero bug" date that we were trying to reach. All I had to do was fix bugs and achieve the best possible resolution velocity.

Does this sound familiar? It's no coincidence that many of the Scrum practices reflect these practices. Given clear goals, discrete tasks, and an empirical measurement of progress toward a goal, teams achieve a high level of focus and effectiveness.

Task Board

A **task board** displays the goal, burndown chart, and tasks for a sprint. The team gathers around it daily and pulls the work that they need to accomplish from it. The task board often occupies a large section of a wall. Figure 4.7 shows an example task board.

Task cards move from the "not started" column to the "done" column as the work for each card is started and completed. A benefit of this movement, with the addition of the burndown chart on the board, is that the task board provides an immediate view of the progress of the sprint.

Task boards have at least four columns. The first column contains the prioritized list of PBIs that the team has committed to completing. The second column contains all the tasks that have yet to be started. Following the sprint planning meeting, all of the PBIs and tasks are placed in these two columns. The third column contains all the tasks in progress. As team members decide what they will "work on next," they move the associated task card from the second column to the third column. The last column contains all the tasks that have been completed. Cards are moved into this column when team members finish tasks.

Tasks are usually lined up in rows with their associated PBIs. This enables the team to quickly see the overall progress of work for each feature.

Teams might add columns to task boards to represent additional task states. For example, they could add a "pending" column, between the in-progress and completed columns, for tasks that need external approval before being moved to the "tasks completed" column. For example, tasks to complete models or animations that require aesthetic approval from an art director are placed in a pending column.

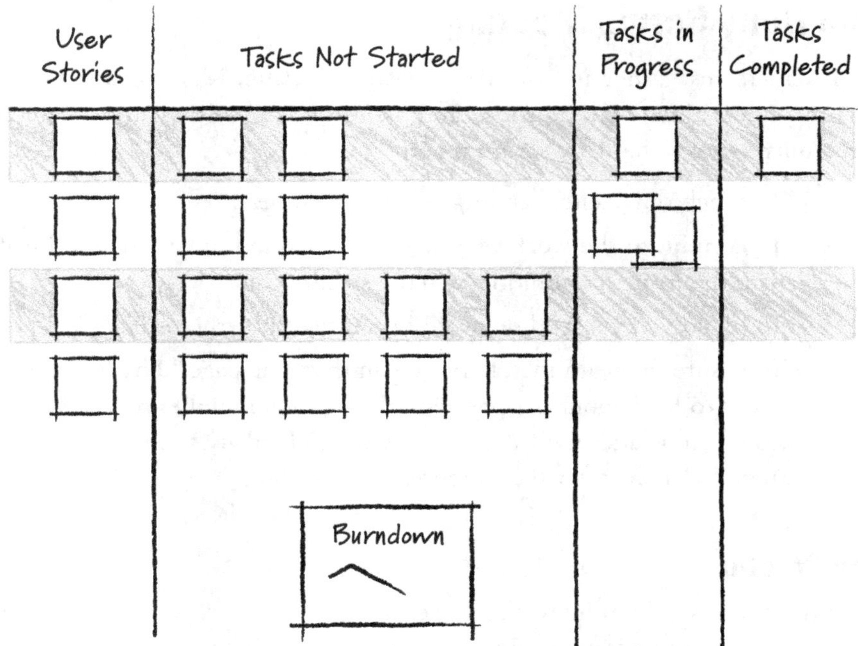

FIGURE 4.7 An example task board

TASK BOARDS AND GROCERY STORES

Scrum practices were not merely derived from practices used to develop past products. Sometimes they came from unusual sources. The use of the practices that guide task boards was influenced by observing how the grocers restocked shelves daily!

War Room

Many agile teams set aside a small space or room called the **war room.** The war room is where the team has their daily scrum meetings and where the tasks board is displayed. A war room is an austere place. Chairs or other furniture for people to sit on during the daily scrum are not allowed. Depending on the wall space, a half dozen teams can share a war room.

Some teams prefer to have the task board in their local team area and have their daily scrum meetings there.

The Daily Scrum Meeting

Each day, teams gather for the daily scrum meeting. Many teams new to Scrum underestimate the purpose and value of the daily scrum. There are three purposes for the daily scrum meeting:

- To synchronize effort among all team members.
- To commit to the work to be accomplished in the next day and reaffirm the team's commitment to the sprint goal.
- To identify any impediments to be addressed by the team.
- To ensure the team members are "on the same page." The full team needs to hear about the problems facing each member so that solutions can be addressed after the meeting. The daily scrum enables them to micro-steer their progress toward their goal together.

The Practice

A daily scrum is a 15-minute timeboxed meeting that every member of the team attends. No one is allowed to sit down in the meeting, which reinforces the idea that this is a quick huddle and not an open-ended laboriously long meeting. Daily scrums get to the point.

As the team gathers in a circle, each member of the team answers these three questions:

- **"What have I done since the previous daily scrum?"** This should relate to anything done for the sprint goal or what may have impeded progress (for example, "I spent the entire day trying to get the game to run on my PC!").
- **"What am I going to accomplish between now and the next daily scrum?"** Each team member describes what they plan to accomplish by the next daily scrum. If there is any work not related to the goal, the team member should mention it (for example, "I need to interview a candidate this afternoon").
- **"What are the problems or impediments slowing me down?"** Impediments are anything that gets in the way of delivering what was promised during the previous daily scrum (for example, "It takes two hours to bake assets for the PS3").

The daily scrum is not for solving problems. It's the ScrumMaster's job to ensure that all side conversations are kept to a minimum so that the daily scrum doesn't become protracted and ineffective. Solving problems is part of what occurs throughout the entire day.

The daily scrum is probably the most frequently modified Scrum practice, so this definition of the practice is just a starting point. As a team takes more ownership of how they work, they are free to modify the practice as long as the purpose of the meeting (status, commitment, and improvement) remains intact. For example, some teams will answer the questions one member at a time, while others will address the progress of each PBI.

Sprint Reviews

The sprint review occurs on the last day of the sprint. The review brings the team and stakeholders together to play the game and discuss the work accomplished. During the review, the product owner accepts or declines the results of the sprint. If the results for a particular feature are declined, then the product owner decides whether it returns to the product backlog or is deleted.

Sprint reviews should be structured to enable the best level of communication between the stakeholders and the teams. This is the opportunity for the stakeholders to inspect the game and communicate with the Scrum team. If this communication doesn't occur, the project can go off in directions that won't return the best results for the stakeholders.

For larger projects, with more than one Scrum team, reviews can take place with each team, with groups of teams, or as a single large review. Scrum team reviews enable a more informal conversation between the team and the stakeholders. They help communicate the progress of the game more directly. A large single review has the benefit of unifying vision and shared purpose across all the teams. This section describes some possible formats for each type of review.

NOTE Chapter 8, "Teams," will describe using Scrum on large projects.

Projects and teams are encouraged to vary their review formats, possibly combining elements of each approach for what works best for the teams and stakeholders.

Single-Team Reviews

Team sprint reviews take place with each of the Scrum teams on the project. The stakeholders visit the team area and review the sprint results. This creates a casual and comfortable environment for the review.

The meeting starts with a member of the team explaining the sprint goal and the overall results. If any of the PBIs were dropped, the reasons are discussed here. Then one or more team members play the game and demonstrate where each goal has been achieved. The controller is often passed to a customer to play.

There are numerous benefits from team reviews:

- It fosters high-bandwidth communication between the customer and the team. Individual team members and stakeholders directly communicate in depth, which creates an improved vision for the game.
- It enables more hands-on time for the stakeholders.

However, there are some drawbacks to small reviews:

- If other people on the project want to see the team reviews, it creates a roaming crowd that moves around a studio. This might interfere with some of the benefits previously listed.
- It inhibits cross-team collaboration. Teams might see their work as isolated products, which creates integration issues (among other problems).
- The review, for a large game made up of a dozen Scrum teams, is very time-consuming for the stakeholders.

Multiteam Reviews

A large sprint review meeting is held in an area that accommodates the entire project staff and all the stakeholders. This can require a large space. On projects with more than one team, one of the ScrumMasters or the lead product owner becomes the emcee and describes the results of the past sprint. These results include the overall goals and the major impediments of the sprint. The meeting is handed over, in turn, to a member of each team that contributed features. Each person describes their team's progress and shows an aspect of the build that demonstrates where the team added value.

> **NOTE**
>
> A **build** consists of the current executables and exported assets that make up the running game. The source code and assets for the current build are also considered part of the build as they are used to create it.

A Q&A session follows the presentations to allow comments about the game and discussion about its future direction. If the project staff is large (more than 50 people), then a smaller follow-up meeting may take place between the stakeholders, the leads, and the ScrumMasters. The reason for this meeting is that larger reviews inhibit some of the critical feedback and detailed conversations that need to occur. For example, conversations about the quality of animation across the entire game need to include the animation and technical leads for the project. In a large team setting, this conversation might be muted to avoid coming across as too critical of the animators when the problem could be caused by the animation technology.

The leads and ScrumMasters are strongly encouraged to discuss the results and decisions with their teams immediately following this meeting.

The benefits of a full project review are as follows:

- The entire project staff is able to see the progress of the entire game.
- Showing only one build encourages cross-team integration and improved build practices.
- The overhead in time for the stakeholders is minimized. The entire review should take place in an hour or two.

The drawbacks of a project review are as follows:

- The teams often require more time to prepare. Large reviews are often treated more as ceremonies rather than quick demonstrations for the customer.
- The one-on-one customer-to-developer communication that occurs in team reviews is diminished.

Publisher Stakeholders

One of the biggest challenges for game projects using Scrum is having the publisher's voice represented in the sprint reviews. We've all worked on games where the publisher ignores the progress for the first 80% of the project and then overwhelms the project with feedback during the last 20%, when the opportunities for change are at a minimum. If your project has a publisher, they must be included to avoid late course corrections.

If the publisher is thousands of miles distant, it's usually impossible to have a representative from them visit for every sprint review. This doesn't mean they cannot provide useful feedback, however. Every effort should be made to have the publisher play builds and have their feedback incorporated into the next sprint. We always demand that the publisher visit at least for release planning and reviews. These are just too critical to ignore.

NOTE

When a publisher is present during a review, it has a big impact on the project. Have them speak to all Scrum teams about the progress made. There is nothing like hearing feedback directly from the publisher!

Studio Stakeholders

Studio executives and managers need to attend reviews as well. Reviews provide a very concise and transparent view into the progress and challenges of a project.

Honest Feedback

It's critical that stakeholders provide honest feedback to the team. Too often, they see the progress but don't always insist that sprints need to deliver vertical slices of functionality. If the team has committed to delivering a character that walks and runs but has a few transition bugs, the stakeholders need to call them on it. Many stakeholders don't want to discourage teams by criticizing anything, especially when the team has worked hard and delivered value. However, allowing debt, such as bugs, to accumulate does the team a disservice later by creating further debt. Honesty is the best policy in reviews.

Retrospectives

Throughout the agile development of a game, we apply the "inspect and adapt" philosophy. We inspect the progress of the game and adapt our plans to the value of the emerging game. We inspect the progress of the team daily and adapt our tasks to maximize progress. This philosophy also applies to how team members work together and apply Scrum. This is one purpose of the sprint retrospective meeting.

The sprint retrospective meeting is possibly the most important, yet most neglected, practice. The goal of the meeting is to continually improve how the team creates value for the game. This is accomplished in the retrospective by identifying beneficial practices, stopping detrimental practices, and identifying new practices to be tried in the next sprint.

The retrospective is where much of the improvement of development practices occurs. Changes don't necessarily have to be large ones; a 1% improvement in the effectiveness of the team every sprint compounds into huge improvements over the long term.

The Meeting

The retrospective meeting occurs after the sprint review. The entire Scrum team attends. It's facilitated by the ScrumMaster and is a timeboxed meeting. The team selects a time limit for the meeting before it starts. Teams will select times from thirty minutes to three hours depending on how much needs to be addressed.

The following three questions are raised at the meeting:

- **"What things should we stop doing?"** The team identifies detrimental practices identified during the last sprint that they want to stop.
- **"What should we start doing?"** The team identifies practices that help them improve how they work together.
- **"What is working well that we should continue to do?"** The team identifies the beneficial practices that should be continued. Usually these are changes introduced at recent retrospectives.

It's up to the team whether they want to invite people from outside the team. If a team interacts with people outside the team during the sprint, then including these people in the retrospective is valuable.

A lot of discussion should occur during the retrospective. The ScrumMaster should facilitate these discussions to help keep the pace of the meeting within its timebox.

The purpose of the retrospective meeting is to identify changes in the ways the Scrum team works together, usually in the form of action items. The answers to the questions asked result in action items. These action items aren't always assigned to individuals during the meeting; it depends on the action item itself. The following are examples of answers to the question "What should we start doing?" and some potential actions that could result:

- **"Start having QA approve all tasks marked 'done,' if possible."** This doesn't require an action item; it is a working agreement for all of QA to adopt.

- **"Make sure Joe tests his animations before committing them."** Clearly, Joe has to follow up on his animation testing, but since this has to happen daily, there doesn't need to be a specific action item.
- **"Have the build server send an e-mail when the build is broken."** If the team has programmers who can implement this change, then they could implement it themselves. If not, this generates an action item to pass along this request to the team that maintains the build server.

Posting and Tracking Results

The ScrumMaster records all the answers given for each question. Following the retrospective, they post the results of the meeting in the team area and check off all the items on the list that have been fulfilled during the next sprint. Any items left unchecked from the last retrospective are discussed at the next retrospective. These items are either carried forward to the next sprint or removed from the list based on what the team decides.

Retrospectives help the team become more effective over time. Ignoring this critical practice prevents the benefits of agile adoption from being realized.

Sprint Failures

The goal of a sprint is to advance the value of a game within a fixed amount of time. The team meets with the stakeholders and negotiates to find a goal that they commit to achieve. The team then implements the code, assets, and behaviors. What could be simpler?

Sometimes things don't work out quite so simply. Unforeseen roadblocks slow progress. Stakeholders change their mind. Our process has to accommodate the vagaries of life and development.

Scrum handles these problems in a number of ways. Small and large impacts to the sprint are quickly exposed. The Scrum team addresses these and works with the stakeholders to react to the problems. Sometimes these problems can't be handled through daily fixes and result in the team failing to achieve the sprint goal. This section looks at what they are able to do when this occurs.

Sprint Interrupted

In the fall of 2007, following an unusually warm weekend, we woke up to a different world in San Diego. The southern sky was different; a horizontal column of dark orange sky fell across it like a wall. Blown from the east by a Santa Ana (desert) wind, it could only mean that there was a wildfire out of control again.

A quick check of the news assured me that the fire was distant and no immediate threat to our town, so I decided to head into work. The studio was like a ghost town; many employees had distant commutes, and they decided not to press their luck that day.

Shortly after lunch, our fortunes changed. The main fire had spawned a number of other fires, some of which were a direct threat to the studio and surrounding homes. This happened so suddenly that we found ourselves in an evacuation zone. I faced the imminent threat of being cut off from my family by closed roads, so I raced for the door.

On the way out, I was met by one of our ScrumMasters. Although he was just as determined to escape, he paused to ask, "What do you think this means to Friday's sprint review?" I initially thought he was joking, but his expression was one of concern. I had to admire the tenacity of his ScrumMaster training. I told him that all bets were off and wished him and his family the best of luck.

Fortunately, none of the studio employees lost their homes (or worse) this time around, and the studio was spared. People trickled back in over the next week, and the sprints resumed. The studio probably lost close to two weeks of work.

We discussed restarting a new sprint or finishing the remainder of the sprint in progress, but we decided to finish. Work picked up smoothly where we had left off, and we had a successful sprint.

Sprint Resets

One of the most drastic practices in Scrum is called the **sprint reset** (also called an **abnormal termination**). A sprint reset allows the team or the stakeholders to declare that the sprint goal needs to change or that the team is unable to complete that goal by the end of the sprint. When a sprint is reset, all of the incomplete PBIs are returned to the product backlog. Code and assets in development are regressed, and the team and stakeholders return to sprint planning.

Sprint resets are costly. Much of the work in progress is potentially lost. Resets should be rare. They must always lead to ways the stakeholders and team improve communication and their ability to plan.

When Teams Fail

Although you may not have wildfires and earthquakes, there are a few more common reasons for sprints to fail. The two main reasons are when the sprint goal changes or the team realizes it will not achieve its sprint goal because it has run out of time.

Goals Change

Imagine a team is working on their jump feature when the CEO runs in with an emergency; he's agreed to demonstrate an online feature in two weeks! This new feature is suddenly more important to him than any other feature. What does the team do?

First, the team does nothing. The ScrumMaster must intervene at this point. The first thing that the ScrumMaster does is separate the CEO from the team area and firmly remind them that interrupting a sprint has great costs. The CEO needs to understand the cost of a sprint reset. Next, the product owner is brought into the discussion. The three of them then discuss the feature in more detail. The product owner then brings in domain experts to discuss the feature if necessary. For example, if the CEO wants an online feature, an online programmer may be consulted.

If the group decides the online feature should be pursued (or if the CEO sticks to his guns), then a proper PBI encompassing the feature is written. The team best suited to accomplish this feature is gathered to perform a preliminary sprint planning session to evaluate the scope of this new feature and whether it could possibly be finished in a two-week sprint.

If the team determines that the goal cannot be accomplished, then the CEO must be told "no." Perhaps a smaller portion of the original feature is discussed, but the team must not commit to the work. If the team determines that it is possible to complete the feature within a new sprint, then the sprint is reset, and a new sprint is fully planned to deliver the online feature within two weeks.

OBJECTION: MY CEO DOESN'T TAKE "NO" AS AN ANSWER

There is a saying that "a dead ScrumMaster is a useless ScrumMaster" (Schwaber 2004). If you are fired for standing up to the CEO because he is not following the "Scrum rules," you aren't helping your team. Live to fight the battle another day and to influence stakeholders to do these things less often.

Running Out of Time

Estimating work for even a two-week sprint isn't 100% certain. Problems can blindside the team; tasks that seemed minimal can balloon into large challenges.

Sprint teams sometimes find themselves approaching the end of the sprint with too much work and not enough time left to accomplish it.

The first tool in evaluating the progress of a sprint is the burndown chart. As previously described, the burndown chart is a tool to monitor the work remaining. In some cases (see Figure 4.5), the burndown chart shows that the team will not hit zero hours by the end of the sprint. Projecting the burndown trend clearly shows this. The rules for a sprint are that teams must hit zero hours of work remaining by the end of the sprint and that the end date for a sprint must never change.

In this situation, the team then has one of three choices:

1. Work some overtime to make up the difference.
2. Negotiate with the product owner to remove one or more of the lower-priority PBIs or remove part of a PBI.
3. Request a sprint reset. Set a new sprint with more achievable goals.

The team explores the solution to the problem in this order; they committed to the work and should do their reasonable best to accomplish it. If the debt of work remaining exceeds what can be accomplished with a reasonable amount of effort, they should approach the product owner and request that some PBIs be dropped from their list of goals for the sprint. If the product owner agrees to drop some PBIs, they are usually one of the lower-priority ones. Dropping individual PBIs may not be possible if they are highly interrelated. In this case, the team and product owner should call for a sprint reset.

NOTE

For teams I have been on, we commit to work evenings during the week if we need to catch up, but we never work any weekend hours. After the sprint we will discuss the reasons for why this extra work was necessary and try to find ways to avoid it in the future. Chapter 14, "The Myths and Challenges of Scrum," will talk about overtime and crunch more.

The question is often raised about how much overtime the team should put in before they request that some of the work be dropped. There is no specific answer to this. Teams typically abhor dropping goals. They prefer to work some overtime but not crunch hours. Overtime should not be invoked very often. If teams experience overtime every sprint, they need to reduce the amount of work to which they are committing.

NOTE

This is a balancing act; as a customer and coach, I expect a team to not deliver all committed PBIs in perhaps one out of every five of their sprints. If the team never fails, I suspect that the team fears "overcommitment." If the failure rate is significantly higher, I suspect that the team is not taking their sprint commitments seriously enough. It's a fine line and one of the biggest challenges that ScrumMasters and coaches encounter with teams.

Whatever the cause, when teams need to drop PBIs during a sprint, the reasons should be discussed in the retrospective following the review.

Running Out of Work

Occasionally a team accomplishes their goal well before the end of the sprint. If it's a day or two away from the end of the sprint, the team can come up with useful work to fill the time; the team can usually identify enough housekeeping and polishing tasks. If they run out of work sooner than that, they can meet with the product owner to find a small PBI on the product backlog to estimate and complete.

NOTE

If teams encounter this problem a few times, I encourage them to commit to more work during the sprint planning meeting.

Summary

Sprints provide the heartbeat of iteration on an agile game project. They are a contract between the customer and the team to provide value demonstrated with a controller rather than promised in a document. However, a game project isn't made of a series of sprints that all look the same. We start many projects by iteratively exploring the possibility and end them by creating many assets to provide hours of entertainment. The next part of the book examines practices that help with longer development cycles, called **releases**, and how we plan in an agile way over the entire duration of the project.

Additional Reading

Derby, E., and D. Larsen. 2006. *Agile Retrospectives: Making Good Teams Great.* Raleigh, NC: Pragmatic Bookshelf.

Chapter 5

User Stories

Communication is one of the biggest challenges for developing games, and one of the largest communication problems is language. Stakeholders often speak the language of business. To them, cost and consumer value influence how they see the world and communicate.

Developers speak a different language. Their language pivots around their specialty. Programmers speak the language of math, code, and algorithms. Designers speak the language of pacing and reward. Artists speak the language of polygon color, texture, and lighting. These languages are not exclusive of one another, but they present communication challenges when everyone on the team needs to understand the same vision of the game.

The solution is for developers to speak the language of the stakeholders. We can't expect stakeholders to learn the language of development (although many stakeholders are often familiar with the jargon). As a business, the language of the customer must be the universal language of development. To this end, we need to be sure that the critical lines of communication between the stakeholders and developers—and even between developers of separate disciplines—are made and kept open using this universal language.

This is where user stories come in. A **user story** is a short description of a game, tool, or pipeline feature that has a clear value to a user. If the feature is a tool or pipeline change, the user can be a developer who uses the tool or pipeline to make the game.

Up to this point, we've used the terms *feature*, *requirement*, and *PBI* to define what is developed. This chapter introduces user stories as a replacement for all those terms and describes how good user stories are created.

A Fateful Meeting

I recall a certain meeting years ago on a game project called *Smuggler's Run*. Although I've attended hundreds of meetings like it, none other would change the focus and course of my career as this one did.

The purpose of the meeting was to review the work remaining to achieve the alpha milestone, which was two weeks away. Alpha was the cutoff date for incomplete features; features planned for but not fully implemented were to be cut from the game. You could sense how close alpha was. *Smuggler's Run* needed to be out for Christmas. It was also a launch title for the PlayStation 2. Everything rested on this game being on time. No one really wanted to be at this meeting; there was much to do, but the meeting was critical and, as the director of product development for the studio, I had to know whether we would achieve alpha.

All the leads attended. I had to keep an eye on the lead programmer and lead designer; they often clashed over the ideals of design and the feasibility of what our technology could accomplish. They approached their roles perfectly, and the natural tension between them benefitted the game. I just had to make sure it didn't go too far.

That day tested that tension. The lead designer had brought a big concern to the meeting. "When are the animals going to be added to the game?" he asked. The lead programmer didn't have a clue about this feature. So, the lead designer pulled out the game design document and pointed to a paragraph on page 97, which described the feature. The game was to have animals wandering about the levels in herds that avoided the player vehicles. The feature had been added to the game design document partway through the project, and the lead programmer had not read it.

The lead programmer didn't know whether to laugh or explode in anger. "How am I expected to know when a new paragraph was added to the design document?" he demanded. "I barely read it the first time!"

We spent some time calming everyone down and were finally able to discuss options for the feature. In the end, a simplified version of the feature was added. Rather than herds of animals avoiding the vehicles, lone animals wandered about ignoring the vehicles and, when hit, turned into tumbling rag dolls. As it turned out, this was a popular feature in the game. Players spent hours hunting down the entire populations of animals. Had this feature been more exploited, the game would have met with even more commercial success.[1]

As the project director, that meeting was a wake-up call about the issues of documentation and communication. I saw the futility of trying to know everything about a game up front and using monolithic documents to capture change and knowledge. This started my path to agile.

1. And the ire of animal rights groups everywhere

The *Smuggler's Run* game design document was well maintained by the designers, but it still failed in a few basic ways:

- **It failed to communicate the priority of features:** Each team member evaluated the priority of each feature on their own.
- **It failed to communicate changes to the rest of the team:** Few team members reread the document on a regular basis to keep up with the frequent changes.

The conversation that occurred two weeks before alpha was very fortuitous, but requirements that make it into the game shouldn't be left to chance. What we had was a failure to communicate. The information in the document was valuable, but the document itself was a poor medium for communicating change and priority.

This underscores some problems with traditional requirements gathering and tracking. What we need is a method that does the following:

- **Communicates the priority and value of the features:** The team needs to focus on delivering the highest-value features ahead of the lower-value ones.
- **Enables change and communication of change:** Change is going to occur, and discussions about those changes need to happen regularly and frequently.
- **Is a placeholder for future communication:** Documentation can't replace conversation.
- **Enables details to emerge as more information is learned:** It shouldn't require all design details up front or impose a great deal of effort to spread knowledge or change.
- **Enables continuing refinement of the work estimated for each feature as the team learns more:** Uncertain features can't have precise estimates. Accuracy can grow as the feature requirements are refined.

User stories were designed to address these needs. The rest of this chapter defines what they are and how they are used.

What Are User Stories?

User stories were created (Beck 2000) to express the value of features to a customer and elicit conversation. Identifying the value of individual features coupled with the benefit of agile development demonstrating value throughout a project is a powerful combination. User stories represent the requirements of the game from the point of view of the user, not the developer. They don't fully describe design details. Stories are placeholders for conversation about the details. User stories follow a template determined together by the team and stakeholders. Mike Cohn (2004) recommends the following:

> As a <user role>, I want <goal> [so that <reason>].

This template includes the following:

- **User role:** A customer of the game or a user of the pipeline who benefits from this story.
- **Goal:** The goal of the story. This is a feature or function in the game, tool, or pipeline.
- **Reason:** The benefit to the customer or user when this feature or function is used.

The last portion of the story template, "so that <reason>," is optional. It's often left out when the reason is apparent.

Examples of user stories follow:

> As a player, I want a player mute button so that I stop being distracted by some of the other players online.
>
> As an animator, I want to change animations directly in the game without restarting it so that I can iterate faster on animations.
>
> As a prop modeler, I want the exporter to check the naming conventions of the props to ensure that they are correct so a poorly named prop does not crash the game.
>
> As a player, I want to see my health level.[2]

Levels of Detail

Teams complete one or more user stories per sprint. These user stories have to be small enough to fit into a sprint. Had we used stories on *Smuggler's Run*, we may have had an initial story something like the following:

> As a player, I want to see herds of animals running around the environment so that it seems more realistic and alive.

2. It's apparent why I want to see my health level, so we don't need to state the reason.

As it increased in priority and approached implementation, it could have been disaggregated into smaller stories such as the following:

As an animal in the game, I want to run away from vehicles.

We don't want to break down every large feature into sprint-sized stories at the start of the project. That creates too many stories to be practically managed by the product owner. Instead, priority determines when features are broken down. Higher-priority stories are worked on sooner, so they are broken down into smaller stories in a planning meeting. User stories that are too large to be accomplished in a single sprint are called **epics**, such as the animal herd story. Sometimes a number of related user stories are gathered together in a **theme**. Themes are beneficial for aggregating user stories together for estimating.

NOTE Some projects have required an even higher level of scope than an epic and have introduced what they call the **saga**!

User stories, epics, and themes can be decomposed into smaller user stories. Figure 5.1 shows an example of an online epic broken down into smaller stories.

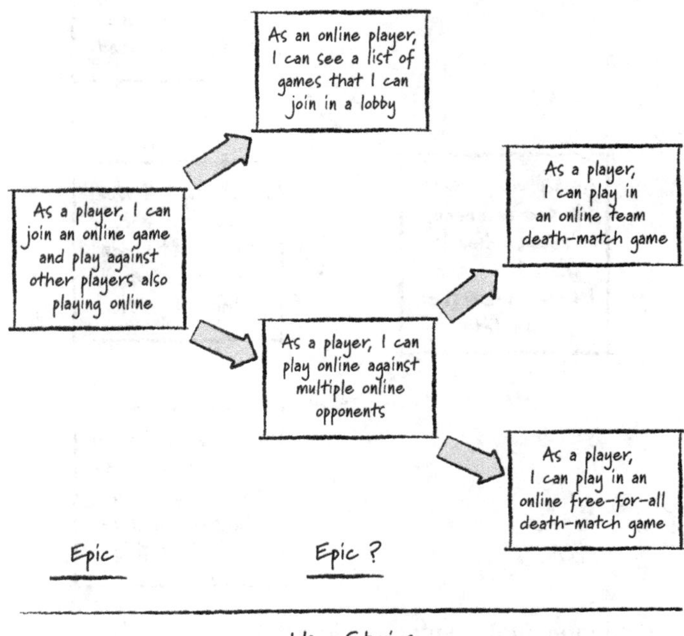

FIGURE 5.1 Breaking down an epic into smaller stories

In this example, the stakeholders identify the lobby and online game as two online epics. They break down the gameplay story further into death-match stories. This decomposition of stories occurs throughout the project. A product backlog can be considered as a hierarchy of user stories that change. Branches grow in detail or are pruned as we learn more about what is fun.

Conditions of Satisfaction

Sometimes we want to add some specific details to a small story.

Take the following example story:

> As a player, I want to shoot an enemy character and see it react so that I know when it is hit.

If this leaves a bit of uncertainty in the details, the stakeholders and team decompose the story into smaller stories, as shown in Figure 5.2, to add those details.

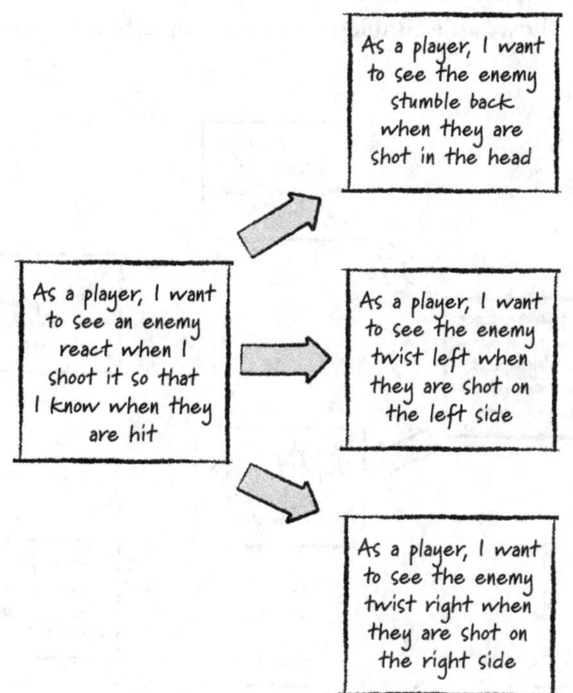

FIGURE 5.2 Disaggregating a story to add details

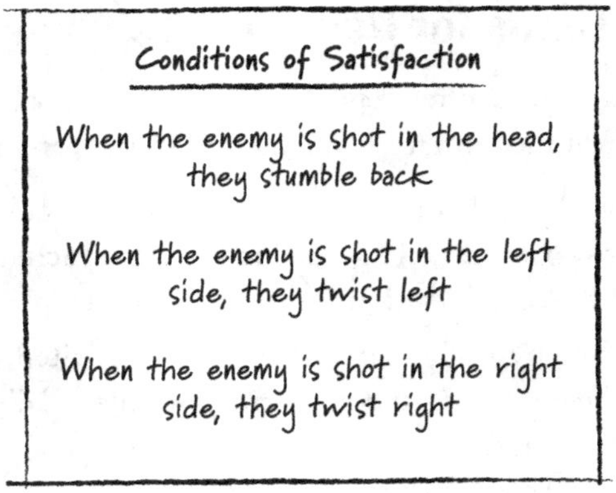

Conditions of Satisfaction

When the enemy is shot in the head, they stumble back

When the enemy is shot in the left side, they twist left

When the enemy is shot in the right side, they twist right

FIGURE 5.3 Adding details as conditions of satisfaction

However, if the initial story is small enough to fit in a sprint, then this decomposition is not necessary. Another approach is to list these substories as **conditions of satisfaction** (CoS), as shown in Figure 5.3.

This is a very powerful tool. CoS help the team understand the ultimate goal for every user story and avoid delivering the wrong feature at the sprint review.

CoS have to be testable. The team should verify whether the CoS are met by running the game and ensuring that behaviors described exist.

EXPERIENCE

"I really thought user stories worked well in the development of our game. It forced the designers to really think out what they wanted. On my last project, programmers worked closely with the designers on the conditions of satisfaction so that everyone knew what was expected. It was critical that the programmers found out as much detail as possible. It kept any creeping seat-of-the-pants design to the planning session where all the interested parties were present. Programmers debated the merits of some of the design decisions, and designers came to understand the technical effort involved. Programmers with design skills had an opportunity to get their input heard."

—Mike Riccio, lead programmer, High Moon Studios

Using Index Cards for User Stories

As with tasks, user stories are often represented in the form of a 3-by-5 index card. These cards are a great medium for handling user stories for a number of reasons:

- The size of the card constrains the amount of detail in a story. We don't want stories to be large documents that include every necessary design detail. A small card prevents this from happening.
- Cards can be physically manipulated (sorted, edited, replaced, and passed) by many hands in collaborative settings (daily scrums and planning meetings).
- The backside of the card is an ideal location and size for listing CoS. Once again, the constraint imposed by the size of the card prevents pages of CoS from being listed, which interferes with the story being negotiable.

INVEST in User Stories

What makes a good story? Mike Cohn and Bill Wake (2003) suggested the acronym INVEST, which stands for the following attributes of a good story:

- Independent
- Negotiable
- Valuable
- Estimatable
- Sized appropriately
- Testable

Independent

Stories should be independent from other stories in the order they are implemented. Dependencies create problems that make them hard to prioritize and estimate. For example, suppose we have the following two stories:

> As a player, when I shoot a door, it splinters into hundreds of pieces of wood.

> As a player, when I shoot a window, it shatters into hundreds of shards of glass.

If the technology for creating this effect does not exist, then the first of these stories to be implemented requires underlying technology to be developed as well. Because these stories appear almost identical, they should not have such a discrepancy of work to implement. The dependency inherent in the first story implemented does not make this possible. There are two solutions to this. The first is to combine these into one larger story:

> As a player, I want to shoot certain objects and have them break into many pieces.

The door and windows could be handled as two conditions of satisfaction. This works when the larger story fits within a sprint. If the aggregated story takes longer, we break the story into the one that creates the base technology:

> As a designer, I want to shoot certain objects and have them break into many pieces.

and into two others, which allow the window and door instances of this effect:

> As a player, when I shoot a door, it splinters into hundreds of pieces of wood.

> As a player, when I shoot a window, it shatters into hundreds of shards of glass.

These stories aren't truly independent because the first story must be completed before the others, but dependency is now clear, where it wasn't in the first place.

NOTE

One key difference to note is that the customer for the first story is the designer who uses the system to finish the second story. This enables the team implementing the first story to focus on the needs of the designer, including an interface to tune the system, which the player does not need. Beware of the "parts on the garage floor" problem described in Chapter 12, "Agile Design."

Negotiable

Stories are not contracts or detailed requirements. They are placeholders for conversation between the stakeholders and the team. A story that is too detailed and specific shortcuts those conversations by creating the illusion that all details are known and don't require any dialogue. For example, consider the story in Figure 5.4.

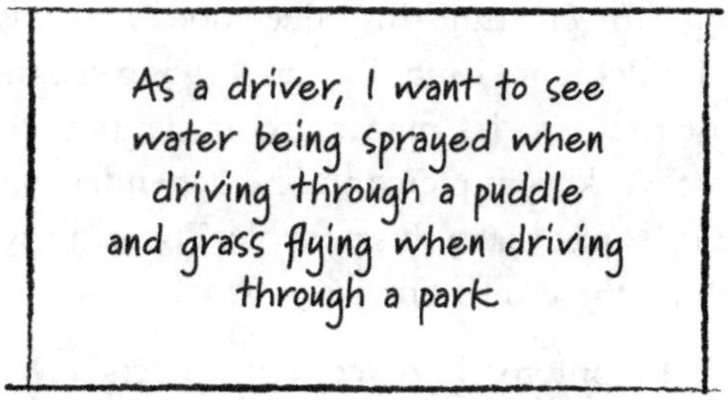

As a driver, I want to see water being sprayed when driving through a puddle and grass flying when driving through a park

FIGURE 5.4 A story that doesn't allow much negotiation

The detail in the story may not be as comprehensive as it implies. Did the customer forget about sound effects of the tires on these surfaces? Do they want more effects in the future? Would they like wheel friction to change depending on the surface? Figure 5.5 shows a better version of this story.

This story is a better placeholder for the conversation. It drives conversation. The requirements of the water spray and grass particles could be added as conditions of satisfaction on the backside of the card if the stakeholders want to ensure that these things are demonstrated.

NOTE

A missing requirement in an overly detailed story is more likely to lead to that requirement being overlooked by a team focused on fulfilling the "letter of the law." Negotiable stories serve the "spirit of the law" better.

HARNESS THE CREATIVITY OF TEAMS!

Negotiable stories raise questions on purpose. They enable anyone on the team to suggest ideas. Talk about being motivated when millions of people love a feature that you thought up!

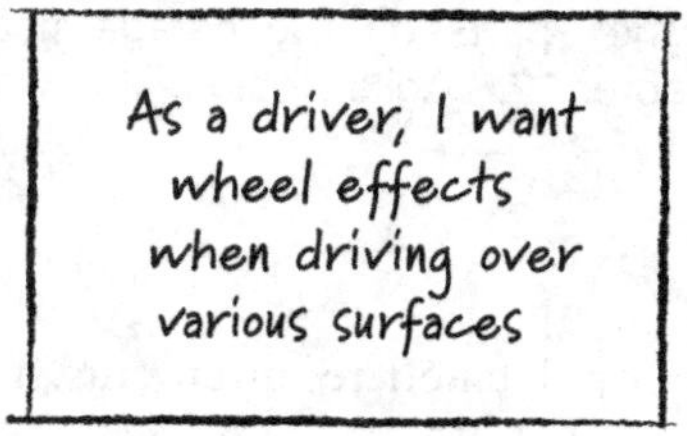

As a driver, I want wheel effects when driving over various surfaces

FIGURE 5.5 A more negotiable story

Valuable

Stories need to communicate value not only to the player but also to the team developing and marketing the game. The product owner adjusts the priority of user stories on the product backlog by judging their value. Stories not expressed in terms of value are difficult to prioritize. Consider the following story:

> Sort rigid bodies in the environment into islands of objects local to one another.

This story does not communicate value to the player or pipeline users, but it may be a story that has a great deal of value. In this example, a physics programmer may request that these changes be made so that the game runs at 30 frames per second (fps). If this is the case, the story can be written to express this value to the player:

> Sort rigid bodies in the environment into islands of objects local to one another so that we maintain 30 fps.

Note that the expression of the user role is missing in this story. The player and the developers all benefit from the game running at 30 fps, which is far more enjoyable than a game running at half that rate.

Estimatable

Stories need to be estimated. This requires knowledge about what we are building and how we are going to build it. If not enough is known or the scope of the story is too large, then we cannot estimate it well enough.

Sometimes stories push the boundaries of knowledge about what our technology can do or the level of effort required. For example, suppose the following story was introduced:

> As a player, I want to knock over stacks of boxes to block the AI players from approaching me and to allow me to escape tight situations.

This story could present a number of problems to the programmers:

- The physics engine might not support a stable stacking of objects.
- The AI navigation system may not "see" dynamic objects such as boxes in the environment.

Implementing this story may be simple or require months of effort. To mitigate this risk, a story is introduced to explore these risks. This story is time-boxed, or limited in the amount of effort spent on investigating these risks; we don't want to sign a blank check. This type of story is called a **spike**, and its purpose is to add knowledge about the cost of implementing the main story. After the spike, the product owner and the team should better understand the cost of implementing the full feature.

SPIKES

Spikes are important for video game development. Spikes are timeboxed stories. The reason for this importance is that spikes address areas of great uncertainty, and their only goal is to create knowledge that helps the product owner evaluate the cost of other stories. For example, the product owner may have a spike defined that says the following:

As a product owner, I want to see a mock-up video of how our fighting mechanic might look on an iPhone.

The product owner may only be willing to spend a sprint or less of the team's time investigating something. In this case, they want to know what a mechanic might look like on the iPhone before they develop the iPhone technology. At the end of the sprint, the team shares what they have learned so far. If the product owner decides to investigate further, they can create another spike.

Spikes are also called **tracer bullets**. In warfare, tracer bullets are special bullets that glow when they are fired from a machine gun. There is usually one tracer bullet every 10 or 20 normal bullets. These tracer bullets allow the gunner to see where the other bullets are headed. Spikes are called tracer bullets because they "show the way" for subsequent work, or they "show the way" not to go if it's a bad path to pursue.

Sized Appropriately

Stories need to eventually be made small enough to fit into a sprint when implemented. If they are too large, they are disaggregated.

A group of small stories can be combined into a larger story more easily managed as a theme. Examples of this are minor bug fixes and polishing tasks placed on the product backlog. We don't need to track and estimate small one-hour fixes within separate stories.

TIP

One trick teams do is to collect all their small polishing tasks into a single spike each sprint and dedicate a fixed and predictable amount of time polishing the game. Over time these tasks are included at the start of the sprint, and the spike becomes unnecessary.

Testable

The story should be written so that it is verified before the end of the sprint. Without this, the team cannot determine whether they satisfied the stakeholders. It's best to use the conditions of satisfaction on the back of the card to define those tests. Some stories require approval to check off.

Consider the following stories:

> The prototype shooting level is fun.
>
> The boss character model is complete.

Both of these stories are subject to interpretation. In this case, the team had a lead designer or lead artist to sign off on the level or model, respectively. The CoS should identify when these approvals are needed. Sometimes a team adds a column on the task board between the "in progress" and "done" columns called "needs verification." This is a holding stage for all the stories that are considered complete only when a lead signs off on them. If a team has many subjective stories or tasks, this is a good solution.

User Roles

Many games provide difficulty levels for the players who buy the game. They usually implement several levels of difficulty as a means of adding replayability and accommodating a range of player skills. The levels are differentiated by scaling challenges in the game such as the number of opponents and damage from weapons hits.

Games benefit from considering a broader range of players and placing more emphasis on their roles. As an example, consider the popular *Battlefield* games, which enable players to adopt specific roles. If you are not familiar with the games or the specialties, they are divided across these roles:

- **Assault specialist:** Is equipped with an assault weapon and grenades for close quarter combat
- **Sniper:** Carries a high-power sniper rifle and a targeting device used to call in precision strikes
- **Engineer:** Has a bazooka and mines and can repair vehicles
- **Special forces:** Carries a light automatic weapon and C4 explosives for sneaking around behind enemy lines disrupting opponents
- **Support:** Totes a heavy automatic weapon and a radio to call in mortar strikes

These specialties require different behavior from the player. It's difficult to insert these roles at the end of a project. They need to be developed in parallel during pre-production because they have an impact on level design and should be added before production starts.

User stories allow roles and their associated features to be clearly defined. A good method for differentiating roles is to use them in the story template. Instead of saying this:

> As a player, I want a bazooka so I can blow up tanks.

the story becomes this:

> As an engineer, I want a bazooka so I can blow up tanks.

What's the difference? It's mainly one of value and priority. For a generic player, the bazooka is one of a host of important weapons. However, for the engineer, the bazooka is probably the most valuable weapon because the engineer role exists to counteract tanks. There's nothing more gratifying than taking out a tank with a well-placed shot. The bazooka is useless for a sniper to carry because snipers maintain a distance from the fight that is greater than the bazooka's range and firing it leaves a trail of smoke that reveals the sniper's position.

Even if your game isn't going to use such specialties, there is a lot of value in brainstorming the various types of players early in development. Who is buying your game? Do you hope to attract casual and hardcore players to your game? If you do, it benefits you to identify the "casual player" role in some of your stories. It may lead to many small decisions such as offering an option to simplify the controls or adding more checkpoints so the casual gamer doesn't become frustrated.

User roles also apply to developers who use the pipeline and tools to make the game. Pipeline and tool stories have to express value as well as gameplay stories. This enables the product owner to better prioritize the order in which these stories are implemented. For example, if animation creation is a bottleneck for a project, the product owner elevates the priority of stories that address the animation pipeline. This is best accomplished by having those stories start with the phrase "As an animator...." Here's an example:

> As an animator, I want the animation exporter optimized so I can create and test more animations.

Defining Done

The team commits to completing a number of stories from the product backlog and demonstrates that these are done in the sprint review. However, defining what *done* means can be challenging. If the team assumes a feature only needs stand-in assets and the stakeholders think they'll see shippable-quality assets, the stakeholders will not be happy with the results. An agreement of what *done* means has to occur before each story is broken down into tasks.

There are standard and additional definitions of *done*. The standard definition of *done* applies to every story. For example, *done* might mean that every feature implemented runs on a development PC without any crash bugs. The following list is a collection of standard definitions of *done* that teams might adopt:

- The game runs on a development machine.
- The game runs on one or all target platforms.
- The game runs at a shippable or target frame rate.
- The assets all conform to naming and budget conventions.
- The game runs within the memory budget and has no memory leaks.

Teams expand the standard definition of *done* by improving their practices. This enables the team to continually improve their effectiveness. Each additional element in our definitions of *done* reduced debt carried forward. Debt represents work that must be done in the future before we ship a feature. Debt, or undone work, also represents risk. We don't want to discover shortly before we ship a game that a key feature causes the frame rate on the PlayStation 3 to drop to 10 fps; we may have built hundreds of assets based on the assumption that 30 fps is possible. The sooner we address debt, the less it costs to address it. Increasingly stringent definitions of *done* prevent debt.

NOTE It's useful to have the definitions of ***done*** posted for everyone to see and for the ScrumMaster to remind the team, during planning, what the standard definition of ***done*** is for every story.

Additional definitions of *done* are created for specific stories and defined in the CoS:

> As a designer, I want to have my character jump across a gap to determine whether the mechanic is fun.
>
> CoS: Poses will be used in place of any animation.

A LEXICON OF DONE

Some studios create a "lexicon of done" to label *done* definitions. These are useful for stories completed at various stages of feature development such as prototyping with stand-in assets or in production with polished assets. These labels are assigned to each story during planning to identify what the stakeholders are expecting from the story. Here are some examples:

- **Prototype done:** Demonstrates potential value. Assets are for demonstration purposes, and the game only runs on development PCs.
- **Pre-production done:** Demonstrates feature value and identifies areas that need to be polished before the feature is shippable. It runs on target debug platforms and lower than shippable frame rates.
- **Demo done:** Demonstrates demo quality (90% assets, not all TRC/TCR requirements). The target frame rate and hardware resource budgets are met.
- **Shippable done:** Ready to be shipped. It passes all TRC/TCR tests and has no memory leaks.

Collecting Stories

Collecting stories in the product backlog is an ongoing process that occurs throughout development. At the start of an agile project, the team and stakeholders collect enough stories to encompass all the major requirements (epics) known and enough detailed stories to enable the team to start iterating.

The collection of stories for an agile project isn't the sole responsibility of a few leads. Instead, there are many ways to gather stories including marketing studies and focus group questionnaires, but the most beneficial method for game developers is the story-gathering workshop.

The story-gathering workshop brings stakeholders and teams together to brainstorm user stories for the game. The product owner facilitates the workshop and invites everyone who can contribute ideas.

Attendees discuss the goals and constraints for the game. This is especially important if it's the first workshop. For example, if the title is to be tied to a license, then the customer who represents the licensor describes what is allowed in the game, such as not allowing a licensed car to catch fire. The publisher shares the major goals of the game including the product's position in their portfolio, release date options, and targeted demographics. User roles are explored. Domain experts discuss risks and opportunities. For example, the design leadership may identify areas of strength and weaknesses in the level design feature set related to delivering on requested mechanics.

NOTE Many of these points do not directly lead to the creation of stories right away but are placed in a "parking lot" of topics to be discussed in detail as time permits.

At the first workshop, the major epics are identified. An example of an initial summary of epics for a first-person shooter might resemble Figure 5.6.

The story-gathering workshop identifies enough detailed stories to fill the next release. This requires the product owner to identify story priorities and discuss the capacity and capabilities with the teams. For our first-person shooter project, the product owner identifies that the player control and artificial intelligence epics are the most valuable areas to focus on for the next three or so months. If the teams confirm that they have the necessary specialists to accomplish work in these areas, then the workshop focuses on breaking out stories sized appropriately. As the workshop drills down on smaller epics, then the subtrees become populated with stories that fit into sprints. Figure 5.7 shows some of the smaller epics identified for player control.

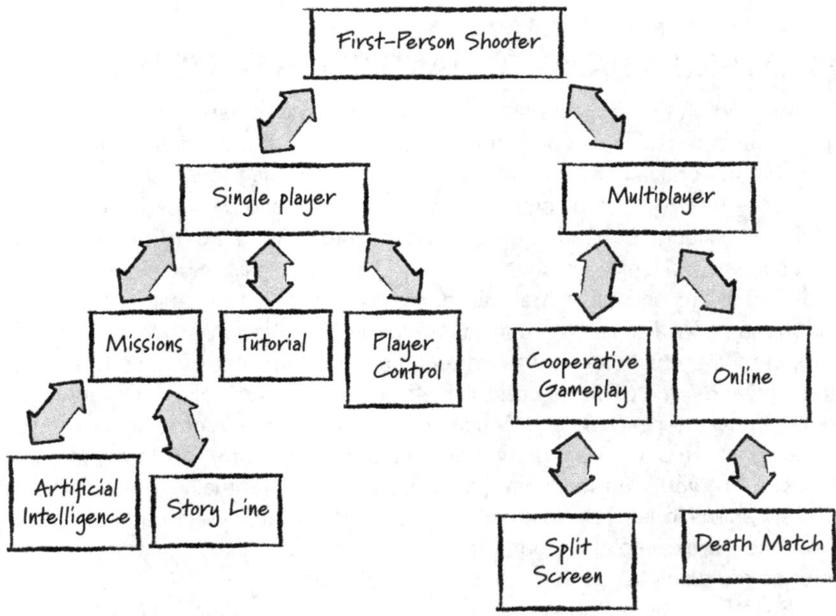

FIGURE 5.6 Identifying a hierarchy of epics is valuable in communicating the big picture.

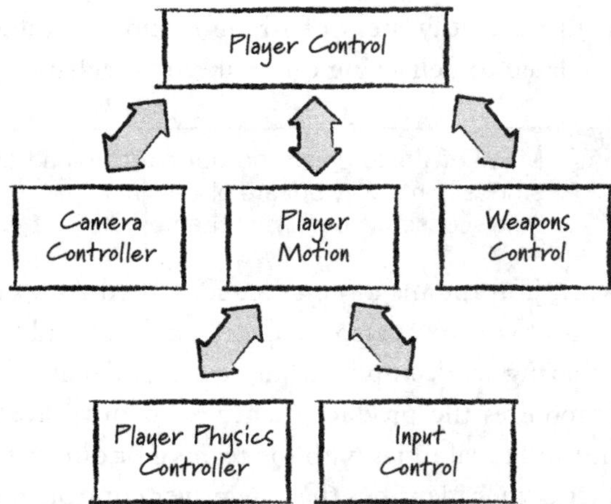

FIGURE 5.7 Smaller epics

The team and domain experts are critical in contributing their ideas here. If, for example, the physics engine causes problems with player controller development, they should discuss it in this meeting. This may lead to work that investigates the potential issues with physics.

PLANNING A HAND-TO-HAND COMBAT SYSTEM

I've worked on two projects that have included hand-to-hand combat. The first game was a sequel to a popular fighting game developed by another studio. The hardship the original project suffered—it took more than four grueling years to develop—was due to the complexity of its hand-to-hand combat system.

The challenge of hand-to-hand combat systems is to create a proper blend of responsive player control and smooth, seamless animation. The approach chosen for the original game was entirely physics based. Animations drove the motion until a collision occurred. The force of a collision then controlled the motion of the character. It was an ambitious system that promised flexibility and a great degree of player control. Unfortunately, it didn't allow for very good-looking character movement. Much of the contact between characters was resolved incorrectly. After wasting enormous amounts of effort trying to make this system work, the team reworked the system, eventually settling with an entirely animation-driven solution. The publisher wanted the sequel to implement the physical solution, but after several months of experiments, we could offer no good solution, and the project was abandoned.

Based on this previous experience, I had some opinions about the technical approach when I attended the story workshop for another game with a hand-to-hand combat system. The product owner introduced the feature and told us that the most important value of this feature was that it be fun and look good. The discussion eventually touched on a physics-driven solution. Given my experiences from the past project, I was able to give a detailed description of the problems this created. When the animators, programmers, and product owner heard this, they decided that the risk and cost potential did not justify the physics approach, and attention turned to an animation-driven solution.

This small example demonstrates how story workshops address the vision of each feature and the potential design impacts with a cross-discipline group. Too often projects don't discuss this impact, which leads to decisions that take the project down a bad path.

Advantages of User Stories

User stories have many advantages over the traditional practice of written requirements. This section emphasizes the face-to-face communication advantages and ease of comprehension.

Face-to-Face Communication

At the start of this chapter I told the story about a misunderstood feature in Smuggler's Run. This misunderstanding was driven mainly by a lack of ongoing communication between the designers and the rest of the team. User stories encourage an ongoing face-to-face conversation between separate disciplines that must happen for game development teams to be effective.

Consider the following requirement:

> As a player driving a vehicle, I want a rearview mirror to see behind my vehicle.

On the surface, this requirement seems clear. However, there may be a number of issues with delivering this function to the player:

- Do we show a mirror in the third-person camera view? Wouldn't a mirror floating above the vehicle look a little odd?
- If the AI opponents cheat by using "rubber banding" or other tricks to catch up with the player, wouldn't the mirror reveal these tricks?
- Does the second view of the environment reduce the overall rendering budget?

Many of us have seen issues like these crop up during implementation that impact the schedule by adding work not foreseen at the start of the project. By having these conversations at the start of every sprint, we create opportunities to address such issues when we know far more about the immediate value they provide.

Everyone Can Understand User Stories

Mike Cohn writes, "Because stories are terse and are always written to show customer or user value, they are always readily comprehensible by business-people and developers."[3] Consider an actual story I've seen:

> As a programmer, I want a checkbox in the audio objects menu to control the bLooping boolean flag.

Although this story follows the template, it fails to communicate value. It's a task, not a story. Does the programmer benefit from this change? Perhaps they don't have to write separate looping audio object code, but that is not communicated here. More than likely, the audio designers wanted looping sounds in the game. If this is the case, the story should be written as follows:

> As an audio designer, I want to set a looping flag on a sound object so that I control looping environmental sounds in the game.

This story represents real value that the product owner understands. Alternatively, we could have expressed the story in terms of the player. The average player does not understand looping sounds but certainly would miss the depth of the sound environment if the designers didn't include the capability to loop sounds in the background such as a babbling brook or the sounds of combat off in the distance.

WHAT HAPPENS TO THE DESIGN DOCUMENTS?

User stories collected on a product backlog are meant to replace much of the design documentation. However, external stakeholders, such as publishers, may demand to see design document in a traditional format, and many tools that manage product backlogs will output the backlog in a single document.

Personally, I would still maintain a technical design document that listed technical risks and strategies for handling those risks, but I would use that document to help prioritize the backlog, which is where all work done by the team originates.

---

3. Cohn, M. 2004. *User Stories Applied: For Agile Software Development*. Boston: Addison-Wesley. Reproduced by permission of Pearson Education, Inc.

Summary

This chapter has covered the creation of stories and explained how they clearly communicate intent between the stakeholders and developers. Stories encompass what have been called features, PBIs, and requirements. Now that we have this powerful tool, we'll examine how to use it for planning over the longer term.

Additional Reading

Cohn, Mike. 2004. *User Stories Applied.* Boston, MA: Addison-Wesley.

Chapter 6

Agile Planning

Agile planning is a commonly misunderstood part of agile project management. Many consider *agile planning* to be an oxymoron—that agile teams plan very little and iterate with no end in sight.

This chapter introduces what agile planning really is and corrects this misconception. It describes how user stories are prioritized and managed in the product backlog. It introduces the concept of separating the size of user stories from the time it takes to implement them so that teams and stakeholders can easily measure and forecast a project's progress. It then unites these ideas to describe releases, the longer iterations where major project goals are planned and managed.

Why Agile Planning?

> In preparing for battle I have always found that plans are useless, but planning is indispensable.
>
> —Dwight D. Eisenhower

Agile planning does not call for a complete plan up front but spreads the work of planning throughout the entire project. In fact, agile teams spend more time planning than traditional teams; it's just not concentrated at the start of a project.

Agile planning avoids the typical planning pitfalls—like those seen on Darkwatch—by the following means:

- **Deliver potentially shippable features in value-first order:** Features are built in the order of the value they add for the consumers who buy the game. Delivering the highest-value playable features ahead of lower-value ones drives the development of the game rather than a preset ordered list of work. This enables the true value of the game to emerge earlier, when we can make better decisions about its direction.

- **Plan by feature, which creates cross-discipline behavior:** Delivering features every sprint encourages separate disciplines to collaborate to produce results that matter to the stakeholders. Problems that impact one discipline impact the rest and are likely to be solved more quickly, rather than ignored for the sake of a schedule.
- **Avoid debt to allow better measurement of progress:** Sprints combine the full cycle of feature development. This reduces the debt of debugging, tuning, polishing, and optimization and makes the pace of development easier to forecast.
- **Plan continually:** Plans created at the start of a project are very good at telling us when the project has failed. Agile planning continually fine-tunes the course of the project to avoid pitfalls and to double down on valuable practices and features. They help teams find success.
- **Work with clear objectives:** The ongoing communication between the team and the stakeholders enables clear objectives to be created. Establishing a definition of *done* with the product owner enables the team to understand each sprint goal and accurately estimate the work required to achieve it.
- **Prioritize scope to control the budget and delivery date:** Many projects that run into trouble first choose to add people or slip the ship date. This is usually done because many key features are developed in parallel and need continuing development to produce any value. Sprints and releases implement features in order of value. This gives the project the option of meeting a ship date by allowing the stakeholders to draw the line and ship with a set of the highest-valued features.

The Product Backlog

The product backlog is a prioritized collection of user stories. Its goals are to do the following:

- Enable stories to be prioritized so that the team is always working on the most important features
- Support continual planning as the game emerges so the plan matches reality
- Improve forecasts so that the stakeholders make the best decisions about the project goals

This section describes these goals.

Prioritizing the Product Backlog

The product owner has the chance to prioritize the product backlog prior to the start of each sprint. It's done with the input of stakeholders, team members, and domain experts. The following guides help determine the priority of each story in the product backlog:

- **Value:** The value that a story adds for the player who buys the game is the main criteria in determining the priority of that story on the product backlog. By focusing the team's effort on adding the highest value every sprint, the product owner is generating the best possible ROI. They measure value using their own judgment, feedback from focus testing, and feedback from stakeholders. Value applies to the "nonfunctional requirements" as well. Tool and pipeline stories that improve productivity have a place in the product backlog because improving productivity also improves ROI.
- **Cost:** Cost is a key factor in the product owner's ROI calculation. Some highly desirable features might cost too much to implement. An example of this is implementing fully destructible geometry for a shooter. Although this feature may add a great deal of value to the game, the product owner must weigh its value against the cost of developing the technology and producing level assets that leverage it. Two equally valuable features are often prioritized by cost; the lowest-cost feature is given a higher priority.
- **Risk:** Risk implies uncertainty about value and cost. As a team refines its knowledge in these areas, the product backlog becomes a better tool for the product owner. Stories with higher risk are often prioritized higher to refine a product owner's understanding of value and cost. If they are not, then potentially valuable stories might be left at the bottom of the product backlog and potentially dropped because of schedule or budgetary limitations.
- **Knowledge:** Sometimes the product owner doesn't know the value, risk, or cost of a feature. They simply need more information. In this case, they could introduce a timeboxed story for a prototype or experiment to the product backlog. Such a timeboxed story, called a **spike**, limits how much time the team spends working on it and is intended to produce information alone. An example of this is a two-week

prototype to determine whether the physics engine supports destructible geometry. If this spike demonstrates that the cost and risk of implementing the system and tool set is not too great, the product owner is more likely to raise the priority of a story to develop the feature.

Continual Planning

The work done by a Scrum team is determined by the priority of stories on the product backlog and what the team is capable of accomplishing. Every sprint they take stories off the top of the product backlog and break them down into small tasks that they estimate in hours. For this to happen, each story they consider must be small enough to be accomplished in a single sprint and detailed enough to support task creation. Therefore, defining the details of the highest-priority stories is where most of the planning effort needs to take place.

Not every story on the product backlog should be small enough to fit into a sprint. If they were, then the product backlog might contain thousands of user stories, which is too cumbersome to maintain. Instead, the lower-priority stories are not broken down until the higher-priority stories are finished. This is an advantage because the lower-priority stories, which are more distant from implementation, are expected to change as the team and stakeholders learn more about what is possible and what is fun.

A useful metaphor for the product backlog is an iceberg (Cohn 2008), as shown in Figure 6.1. The highest-priority stories are represented by snowballs at the top of the iceberg, which are small enough to be completed in a single sprint. Below them are the lower-priority stories, or larger chunks of ice, called **epics**.

Everything above the waterline represents the work we want to complete in the current release. Each sprint sweeps off the snowballs (stories) from the top of the iceberg. The stakeholders and team break down the larger chucks of ice (epics) into snowballs for the next sprint.

Forecasting the Future

As we'll see in the next section, the size of user stories is estimated with units called **story points**. The rate at which teams implement the stories and remove them from the product backlog is measured in story points per sprint, called the **velocity**.

This isn't an abstract practice. It's the same method we use to calculate velocity in other areas of life. For example, imagine you plan to drive 3,000 miles across the United States in five days. This predicts an average velocity of

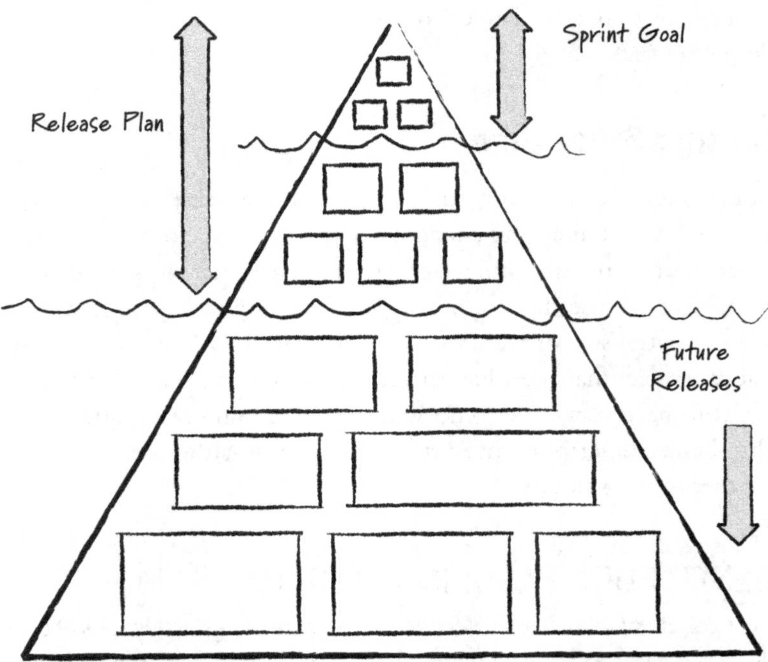

FIGURE 6.1 The product-planning iceberg

600 miles per day. You could use this velocity to forecast, even after the first day, whether you are on track to achieving your goal or not. If, after the first day or two, you discover that your actual velocity is 500 miles a day, you have a number of options available. You can adjust the number of days you plan to drive, alter your destination, or even try to adjust your driving habits (drive longer each day or drive faster). If you've placed all your faith in the plan and discover, at the end of the fifth day, that you're 500 miles short of your destination, your options are far more limited.

Agile planning uses frequent measurements of velocity to forecast the accomplishment of the goals of the project (either knowing what will be accomplished by a given date or when the project will achieve all given goals). This is in contrast to traditional project management practices that place more faith in a plan and are only able to reliably measure location near the end of the project, closer to the testing phase.

By measuring the story points accomplished each sprint, an agile project measures its velocity. The velocity is used to predict how much scope can be implemented by a specific date or to predict a date for a fixed amount of scope to be implemented.

Estimating Story Size

To measure the velocity of anything (a car driving or a ship sailing), you need to measure the size of something changing over the passage of time (such as miles driven per hour or nautical miles per day). Similarly, for measuring velocity on an agile project, we use the size of user stories completed per sprint.

Measuring the size of features has been a product management challenge for decades. Project managers have tried measures such as "lines of code," which turned out to have very little to do with the actual progress made on the project.[1] This section describes proven methods for estimating user story sizes to be used for measuring velocity.

A BENEFIT OF MEASURING VELOCITY

A major benefit of measuring velocity is to measure the effectiveness of change. Positive changes to practices improve velocity. For example, teams that collocate often see up to a 20% improvement in velocity. This is mainly because of the improvement of communication within the team. Most changes create smaller increases in velocity, but their impact accumulates and compounds over time. Without measuring velocity, many small changes might be overlooked.

How Much Effort Should We Spend Estimating?

How much time should we spend estimating stories? We could spend anywhere from a few minutes to a few hours. In a few minutes, we could discuss a broad outline and come up with a guess. In a few hours, we could break a story down into the detailed tasks required to implement it.

We want to spend our planning time wisely. One assumption of planning is that the more time we spend planning, the more accurate our plan becomes. This is, in fact, not true. Figure 6.2 shows that beyond a certain amount of effort, our accuracy decreases (Cohn 2006).

Planning provides an initial spike of accuracy with little effort spent. As more effort is spent, the accuracy of estimates actually starts to decline! This is surprising at first glance, but it makes sense. Say we spend an entire day estimating

1. In fact, it only led to more lines of code.

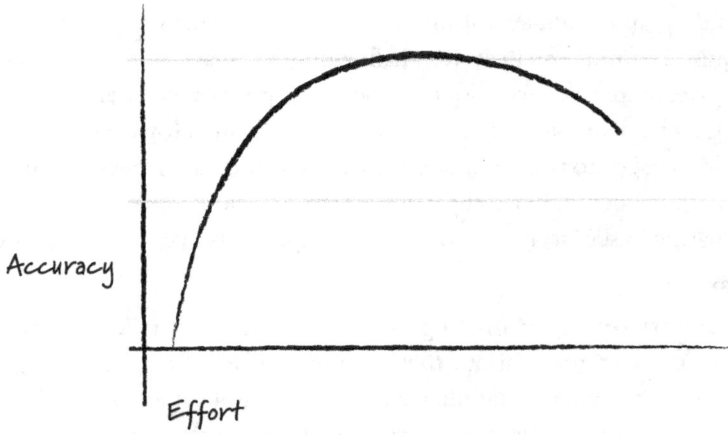

FIGURE 6.2 Accuracy vs. effort for estimating

Source: Cohn, M. 2006. *Agile Estimating and Planning.* Upper Saddle River, NJ: Prentice Hall. Reprinted by permission of Pearson Education, Inc.

a single story. Given this time, we would eventually create very detailed tasks. These define work creating classes and functions, creating art assets, and tuning variables. As it turns out, this level of detail is too speculative. By the time we start defining functions and variables, chances are we are defining things that won't be needed or will be changed during implementation.

The purpose of story estimation is meant to be efficient and to occupy the left side of the curve in Figure 6.2. It's a quick, low-effort estimating practice that provides accuracy valuable enough for forecasting but not enough for a team to commit to the work.

Where Are Story Sizes Estimated?

Chapter 5, "User Stories," described a story workshop where a hand-to-hand combat system was debated. The debate included not only my technical perspective and experience but also those of the animators and the lead designer. As a result, we had good cross-discipline agreement about the story before we estimated the work.

This is a benefit of story workshops. When teams estimate the size of stories, it drives the discussion of vision, design assumptions, and challenges of implementation. As a colleague once remarked, "It helps remove the fuzziness and hand-waving when you have to come up with a number."

These cross-discipline discussions refine a team's understanding of what they are trying to achieve. An estimate for a story needs to reflect this cross-discipline understanding and produce a value that everyone agrees with, regardless of the skills required to implement it. It's challenging to create a universal scale for all stories. For example, a story about a procedural physics effect and a story about animating a character are difficult to directly compare. However, over time, as a team builds a repository of estimated stories and the experience of implementing them, it becomes easier to find comparable stories.

Estimating user stories should be a quick process that involves the following:

- **Expert opinion:** Inviting domain experts to story workshops helps inform the group about the issues and effort of implementing something the expert is familiar with. For example, if a story includes an online component, a network programmer would provide value to the discussion about it.
- **Analogy:** Analogy is used to estimate story size. When stories are compared to each other, a far more accurate estimate can be achieved than estimating stories on their own. Using triangulation, a story is compared to one larger in complexity or size and one smaller to produce the best results. To provide the best results, a story that requires significant specialization, such as a weapon creation story, is best compared to other weapon creation stories.
- **Disaggregation:** Large user stories are more difficult to accurately estimate than smaller ones, so often these stories are disaggregated into smaller ones, which are more accurately estimated. However, stories shouldn't be broken down into a pile of tiny ones because a false sense of detail emerges, as described previously.

Story Points

User stories are typically estimated using story points, which are a relative measure of a feature's size or complexity. For example, modeling two vehicles is estimated at twice the points of modeling one vehicle and possibly the same as modeling a character. This relative measure of story points allows for a more accurate measure of size, as explained later in this chapter.

NOTE

Although points are not durations, it can be impossible to keep durations out of your mind when estimating points. For example, I mountain bike a lot, but I take downhill sections very slowly. Some of the people I ride with bomb down these rocky

> sections. I might estimate two different downhill sections to myself in time and say the first took 20 minutes and the second took 40 minutes. My friends would argue that the first was 10 minutes and the second was 20. We'd never agree on the times between us, but we'd agree that one was half the "size," or length, of the other. As long as we keep the time estimates to ourselves, they can work.

A story point estimate is not a commitment to when a story will be completed. There are two reasons for this. First, a story point estimate takes only a few minutes. A team's commitment to completing a story requires a more precise and time-consuming estimation process. This happens when they break a story down into individual tasks in sprint planning. Second, different teams have different velocities. For example, one team might implement a 10-point story twice as fast as another team based on their membership and experience.

NOTE

Story point estimation is a bit like estimating the price of a car to within $5,000 to $10,000. I don't need to know the exact price of a ***Porsche*** to know that I can't afford one, but if I know that the small truck that can carry my surfboard is around $20,000, I'll go to the lot to learn more.

Planning Poker

A favorite technique for estimating user stories is the Planning Poker game (Grenning 2002). Planning Poker combines expert opinion, disaggregation, and analogy in a fun and efficient practice. Planning Poker should be part of release planning meetings and story workshops. It should be used whenever new stories are introduced that need an estimate.

In Planning Poker, attendees discuss stories that have not yet been estimated. After a story is discussed, each person estimates the points they think should be assigned to the story by simultaneously raising a card with their estimate on it for all to see. The first vote often reveals a wide disparity of estimates. The group discusses the range, first by asking the outlying voters to describe the reasoning behind their estimate. This exposes the uncertainties and assumptions of the story. As a result, the vision, design, and implementation details are discussed and refined. These discussions often lead to adding conditions of satisfaction for a story or defining new stories that were not previously considered.

This practice is repeated until everyone produces the same estimate. If a couple of people have different but close estimates, they may concede to the group's estimated points and allow the meeting to move to the next story.

NOTE Don't average the votes. The different point estimates often hide what needs to be discussed! Assigning an average doesn't solve potential problems with the story.

Estimating an entire release plan can take four to eight hours. Often teams won't tackle all stories for a release in one sitting. They disaggregate and estimate the highest-priority stories and then meet once a sprint to estimate lower-priority or new stories for upcoming sprints.

Story Point Sizes and the Fibonacci Series

Story points provide a quick and relative estimate of size and complexity for a story. Alone they are not perfectly precise, but with a mass of stories, they average out well enough for planning.

Projects need to define a set of numbers that they use for story point estimates. The two rules of thumb for selecting a set of story points are that the entire scale be within two orders of magnitude. For example, a range of 1 to 100 or a range of 1,000 to 100,000 works. Second, the numbers used should be closely spaced out at the small end and widely spaced out at the high end of the scale. The reason is that our ability to judge the difference between stories with sizes of 20 and 21 points, for example, is not the same as our ability to tell the difference between two stories with sizes of 1 and 2 points.

A useful set of story points that follows these two rules is derived from the Fibonacci numbers. In a sequence of Fibonacci numbers, each number is the sum of the two preceding numbers. An example set of Fibonacci numbers useful for story point estimation follows:

0, 1, 2, 3, 5, 8, 13, 20, 40, 100

The numbers at the high and low ends of the set depart from the Fibonacci sequence. We use zero-point estimates for trivial stories that require very little effort, such as changing a user interface (UI) font color.[2] The upper range of these numbers departs from the Fibonacci series rule, but they exist to allow a couple of rounded-out values in the high range.

The team should constrain themselves to use only numbers within the set and not use values between them to create averages or compromises. This creates a false sense of precision with story point estimation and slows down a Planning Poker session!

---

2. Be careful not to accumulate too many zero-point stories...zeros add up with this math!

TIP If Planning Poker encounters a story whose estimate exceeds the highest point value, it's best to disaggregate that story into smaller stories before estimating each.

Ideal Days

The concept of story points is difficult to introduce. Teams accustomed to time estimates often find story points too abstract and instead use ideal days as a benchmark to begin estimating. An ideal day is the measure of work accomplished in a single day with no interruptions (phone calls, questions, broken builds, and so on). Because of this association with something real, the team more readily embraces ideal days.

Ideal days are still measures of size alone. A story estimated to be one ideal day in size doesn't mean it takes one day of actual work to complete. We want to avoid any translation of ideal days to actual days of effort. Ideal days, like story points, are valuable measures for quick relative forecasts of effort but not precise enough to use for making commitments.

Release Planning

Release planning is different from sprint planning. A release plan has more flexibility as features emerge from the sprints and team velocity is demonstrated.

NOTE Chapter 3, "Scrum," described releases as major goals that occur every several months, comparable to milestones or E3 or magazine.

Releases begin with a planning meeting that establishes major release goals, a release plan, potential sprint goals, and a completion date. A release makes progress through a series of sprints. As each sprint implements user stories, the burndown of story points measures the velocity of work. This is used to inspect progress and adapt the plan.

Release Planning Meetings

A release planning meeting uses the steps shown in Figure 6.3.

The product owner, stakeholders, team members, and domain experts attend the meeting. It begins with a review of the progress made in the last release and the product backlog. The group then deliberates on the major goals for the release. These goals, often referred to as **big hairy audacious goals** (BHAGs),[3] represent a challenge for the entire team and establish a vision to aid story prioritization. For example, a BHAG to "fight other players online" might raise the priority of spikes to demonstrate that the animation system works in an online setting.

TIP A release planning meeting can take most of a day. It's useful to find a location with minimum disruptions. A conference room at a local hotel is a good option.

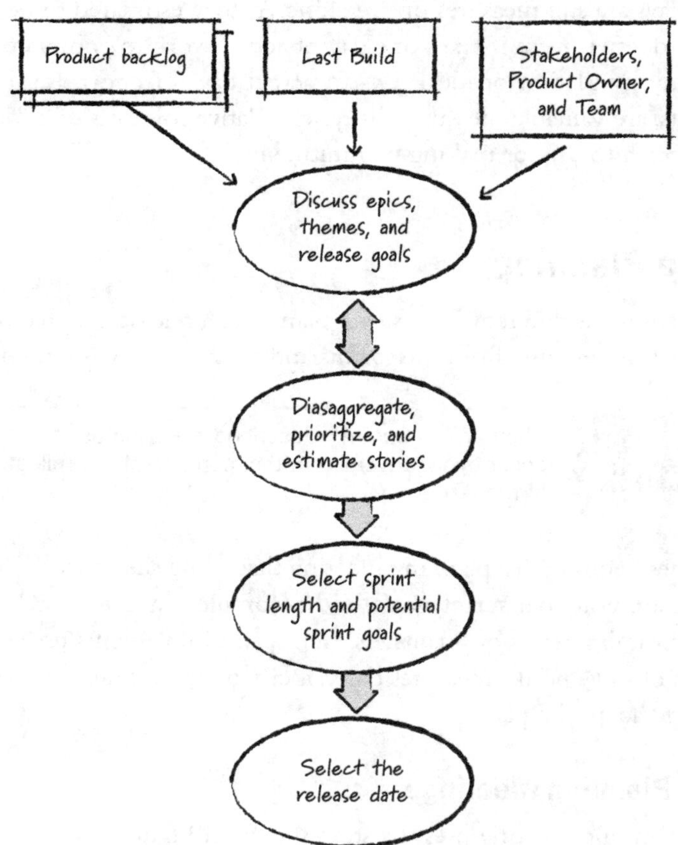

FIGURE 6.3 The flow of a release planning meeting

3. http://en.wikipedia.org/wiki/Big_Hairy_Audacious_Goal

After BHAGs for the release are agreed upon, user stories needed to implement them are identified, prioritized, and estimated using story points. The group uses the estimated story size and priorities to create a release plan, based on the velocity teams have demonstrated in past sprints, to lay out the sprint goals for the release. This is called the **release plan**.

The release plan identifies potential sprint goals for the release. Figure 6.4 shows a release plan based on a historical velocity of 15 story points per sprint.

Story	Points	Sprint
As a player...	5	
As a player...	5	Sprint 1
As a player...	5	
As a player...	10	Sprint 2
As a designer...	5	
As a player...	6	
As a player...	3	Sprint 3
As a player...	6	
As an animator...	7	
As a player...	5	
As a player...	8	
As a player...	4	Sprints 4–6
As a player...	9	
As a player...	5	
As a player...	6	

FIGURE 6.4 Splitting the release plan across future sprints

The goals for sprints 1 through 3 each contain stories that add up to 15 points. The stories for the more distant sprints in the release are lumped together. In this example, the product owner has called for six sprints in the release because the release plan and projected velocity tells them that this is how many sprints are needed (for example, 89 points at 15 points of velocity every sprint tells them they need six sprints).[4]

As sprints are finished, the goals and stories for the subsequent sprints are refined. For example, after sprint 1 is completed, the goal for sprint 4 is identified.

It's important to understand that the sprint goals identified in the meeting are a forecast of work that can potentially be accomplished by the team; they're not a commitment. They are useful benchmarks for measuring progress.

WHY NOT CREATE A RELEASE BACKLOG?

People often refer to a release backlog instead of a release plan. It's best not to create a different backlog for the release. The release plan is a subset of the product backlog that changes during the release. Having separate backlogs creates a lot of extra work and confusion over what backlog we are talking about.

Rolling Out the Plan

On larger projects, it's sometimes impractical to have the entire project staff attend the release planning meeting. In this case, only the product owner, domain experts, and discipline leads attend.

After release planning, the product owner presents, or **rolls out**, the release plan to the entire project staff. The owner describes the BHAGs and release plan and answers any questions raised. The project staff is then given the opportunity to organize themselves into Scrum teams that would best achieve the initial sprint goals in the plan.

Teams are usually organized around the BHAGS. For example, in a release that has single-player and online gameplay BHAGS, teams are organized around each. After the teams form, they can each hold a release planning meeting to further refine their area of the release plan.

Updating the Release Plan

Following each sprint review, the release plan is reexamined. Sometimes the sprint has identified new stories to be added. These are stories that were

4. We always round up.

either overlooked or not anticipated in release planning. Other times, stories are removed. These stories are considered unnecessary, or their priority was reduced enough to push them into a future release. As with the product backlog, the product owner makes the final decision on the addition, deletion, or reprioritization of any story in the release plan.

The release plan may also need refinement based on the team's actual velocity. Figure 6.5 shows an example of an original release plan on the left, which forecasted 16 user story points of velocity per sprint. However, the first sprint accomplished only 13. As a result, the product owner updated the new release plan—shown on the right—which dropped the last two (lowest-priority) stories.

The product owner also had the option of adding another sprint to the release if they didn't want to drop those stories.

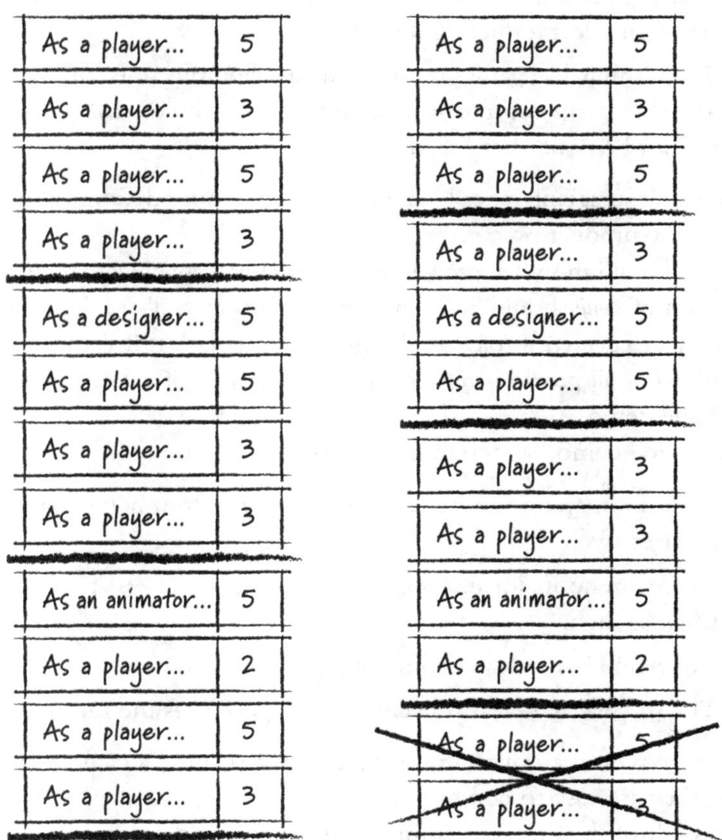

FIGURE 6.5 Updating the release plan based on velocity

> **NOTE**
> In practice, the release plan isn't dependent on the results of a single sprint. The velocity used to forecast the sprint goals for the release is usually based on the average velocity of the past several sprints.

Magazine Demos and Hardening Sprints

Scrum describes sprints as delivering a potentially shippable version of a product at the end of every sprint. This allows the product owner to decide to ship the product on short notice. This is a challenging goal for many large-scale game projects for three reasons:

- There is only one true release at the end of two or more years of development.
- Many features and assets require a number of sprints to implement (for example, production levels).
- To be shippable, games must often pass rigorous tests for hardware and first-party compliance. These tests can take weeks to conduct and cannot be done every sprint.

Nevertheless, sprints should achieve a minimum definition of *done* as defined by the product owner.

A release build should approach the potentially shippable goal more closely. Its definition of *done* should be higher than a sprint's. Still, a release build cannot always be expected to pass all shipping criteria unless it is the final release of the game. For all previous releases, a good example of a definition of *done* is the magazine demo.

A magazine demo has certain expectations:

- It has no major memory leaks preventing it from being played for an hour or two.
- There are no major missing assets. All stand-in assets are clearly identified as such.
- The game has a clean and usable user interface.
- The player has a clear objective and experiences the fun of the game.

These are typical requirements for a demo version of a game in any publication, so they are easy to communicate.

As a result of the different completion bars for releases and sprints, release builds require additional testing beyond what is tested for every sprint. If this testing identifies issues with the game that aren't found in sprint testing, the additional work created to address them creates the need for a special sprint at the end of the release called a **hardening sprint**.

Work for the hardening sprint is derived from the difference between the definition of *done* for sprint builds and release builds. If the definition of *done* is the same for both, there should be no reason for a hardening sprint.

NOTE

The need for a hardening sprint is often driven by testing practices considered too time-consuming to be done every sprint. For example, testing a magazine demo requires many hours of "burn-in" testing to ensure that there are no significant memory leaks.

Hardening sprints are often run using a list of bugs and polishing tasks that need to be worked on. They are not used to complete stories from the product backlog (see the sidebar "How to Run a Hardening Sprint").

HOW TO RUN A HARDENING SPRINT

At High Moon Studios, we created simple practices for planning and managing the work for a hardening sprint.

A hardening sprint was shorter than our typical three-week sprint; it was usually one week long. The sprint planning session started with a simple triage. The sprint backlog emerged from a play-through of the game during the meeting with the team, stakeholders, and product owner in attendance. During the play-through, anyone in the room could identify a potential fix for the sprint. If the product owner agreed with the value of the fix, it was written down on a whiteboard.

Following the review, the product owner roughly prioritized the bugs. This consisted of labeling each bug with an ***A***, ***B***, or ***C***. The A bugs were the most important to fix, the B bugs were medium priority, and the C bugs were not considered very important to fix. This prioritization raised much discussion; some A bugs were considered too challenging to fix in a single week and were demoted, while some C bugs were judged trivial to fix and were promoted.

The team then identified and estimated the tasks to fix all the A bugs and as many of the B bugs as they could within the coming week.

Unlike normal sprints, changes to the hardening sprint priorities were allowed. It was important for the product owner to be involved in evaluating the daily build during the hardening sprint. Sometimes new bugs caused the product owner to change the items or priorities of the bug list. As a result, teams weren't able to commit to a fixed set of tasks.

Not all fixes on the list were completed in the hardening sprint, but the prioritization helped the team accomplish work in the best order. For us, the hardening sprint was more like a series of one-day sprints to improve the game.

Summary

Agile planning is not an oxymoron. Agile teams plan in ways that allow iteration, transparency, and change. They adjust planning to match reality rather than trying to make reality match a plan.

Agile planning requires a product backlog that prioritizes the user stories that the stakeholders want in the game. The product backlog prioritization and team membership determine which stories might be completed every sprint. These stories, measured in size by story points, allow the measurement of work accomplished per sprint, which is the velocity. Velocity is used to examine the rate of development and predict future progress. Measuring velocity early and frequently allows the project to be steered when many options are available to it.

Release cycles allow major goals to be achieved over a longer time frame. Because of the longer time frame, releases have flexibility in planning that does not exist with sprints. Release plans can be altered in duration or in scope. Releases also demand a more refined definition of *done* (see Chapter 5) to bring an almost shippable level of polish, stability, and tuning to the game, rather than postponing it to near the end of the project.

For many projects, this is enough. The release cycle is sufficient to release versions of the product to consumers on a regular basis. Most video game projects don't have this luxury. They have pre-production and production phases that have a different focus and challenges. The next chapter describes these phases and how Scrum, agile planning, and lean practices can be combined for planning over the entire development life cycle.

Additional Reading

Cohn, Mike. 2006. *Agile Estimating and Planning*. Upper Saddle River, NJ: Prentice Hall.

PART III

Agile Game Development

Chapter 7

Video Game Project Planning

In Chapter 2, "Agile Development," a major challenge identified with adopting agile for game development was matching phase-less agile practices with the needs of game development stages, such as pre-production and production.

A typical Scrum project is always kept in a near-shippable state. The reason for this is that the work traditionally separated across multiple phases (design, coding, testing, optimization) is part of every sprint. By doing this, agile projects keep the debt of late project work, such as fixing bugs, to a minimum.

Agile game development follows the same model of combining all phases into each sprint. However, game project stages create a different form of debt, or necessary work that must be accomplished, such as production assets, which requires some new practices to be introduced over the course of the project.

This chapter addresses the needs for stages and the challenges they create. It focuses on production—the most expensive stage that derails many Scrum teams. By introducing lean ideas, Scrum teams manage complex asset production pipelines while maintaining the benefits over traditional preplanned methods.

Midnight Club Story

Of the score of games that I have worked on, only a few have shipped on time and within budget. Of these, Midnight Club was the most successful. Midnight Club was a PlayStation 2 (PS2) launch title where players illegally race in the large open cities of London and New York. The project was a grueling 18-month struggle with a new platform and new publisher.

The game was originally designed to include six cities. We considered two major risks to delivering a good game in time for the launch of the console. First was the uncertainty of developing for the PS2. Early on, its capabilities were compared to those of supercomputers, but over time we learned that it was a challenging platform that had some significant performance bottlenecks. Second, we were uncertain about the effort to produce six large cities in the time we had before launch.

We focused pre-production on creating one city that would run well on the PS2. This effort took four times longer than we anticipated. Armed with this knowledge, we were forced to scale our plans down to three cities. Our publisher, *Rockstar Games*, took these cuts in stride. They knew how hard we were working.

During production, we slowly realized that we had a crucial decision to make. The time to create the necessary polish for shippable cities was taking even longer than we had planned. We had to choose between shipping three low-quality cities or two polished ones. After much teeth gnashing, *Rockstar* Games decided to ship with two cities.

In the end, it was the best decision and contributed to the game shipping as a PS2 launch title that sold millions of copies. A major reason for maintaining the schedule was the constant attention to the production costs of creating and polishing the cities. For many game projects—especially those with fixed ship dates—the production costs and schedule pressures create the greatest risks.

Minimum Required Feature Sets

Many projects outside the game industry are challenged with an obligation of delivering on certain expectations from the start. For example, a word processor would have to have undo, printing, font management, and so on. This minimum feature set might require a year or more of effort before a product can be released.

Similarly, video games are challenged with a minimum set of requirements, including the following:

- About eight to twelve hours of single-player gameplay content
- Fixed ship dates such as the Christmas season or movie corelease dates
- Minimum required feature sets—such as online multiplayer for a first-person shooter—that must be shipped with the game

These requirements require budget and staff planning for the long term, beyond releases. For example, production costs are refined over the course of pre-production releases to identify the number of content creators and the time needed to produce eight to twelve hours of gameplay.

Minimum required features sets necessitate similar long-term plans. For the first-person shooter example, the following is a minimum required feature set:

- Single-player gameplay
- AI
- Weapons
- Online multiplayer gameplay

These features create a debt of work, much like the production debt, that takes multiple releases to deliver. Often, stakeholders demand that resource management plans be developed to support a predicted ship date for these features.

How does resource management planning work with agile planning? A proven approach is to identify a range of resource needs to implement epic-level stories and continually refine both through sprints and releases.

This is a balancing act of cost and value. Imagine you are buying yourself a new PC, but you have only $2,000 to spend, not a cent more. You'd start with a breakdown of the parts of the PC and the cost of each:

Component	Cost
CPU, motherboard, and memory	$800
Graphics card	$500
Monitor	$400
Case, mouse, and keyboard	$200
Hard drive	$100

You might decide later to buy the latest graphics card that costs $100 more. This money has to come from another part of the computer. This is how long-term planning works with epics. Large epics are defined and thought about to produce a cost of time and resources. If any budget item is wrong, the time has to come from another bucket. That needs to be a deliberate and visible decision and needs to be publicly proclaimed.

For each item, the first estimate might be largely based on experience with previous games, which is not very accurate. For the first-person shooter example, a product owner identifies the large online multiplayer epics that a team of eight might complete in six to eight months. Some of these epics are not disaggregated until more is known. For example, cooperative online gameplay with AI may or may not be valuable or even possible within this resource plan until more is known, so the epic that might contain that feature is not disaggregated until more is known and a team is available to work on it.

This provides the flexibility necessary as more is discovered about the challenges, velocity, and opportunities for online as the game emerges. It does not ensure that every minimum required feature will be completed within budget and schedule—no planning process does that—but it enables decisions to be made earlier that help steer the project in the right direction.

The Need for Stages

For many games developed using agile, there is still a need to separate some of the development activities. There are three major reasons for this:

- **Publishers require concepts:** To gain publisher approval (which includes marketing and often franchise or license owner approval), developers need to create a detailed concept treatment at the start of a project. They are unable to stray too far from this vision throughout the project.
- **Games need to deliver eight-plus hours of gameplay:** Games typically deliver eight to twelve hours of single-player gameplay. Games tell stories that need a great deal of production content to be created using mechanics discovered during pre-production.
- **One ship date:** For large-scale games, there is only one ship date at the end of a 24+ month development cycle. Intensive hardware compliance testing is often delayed until the end.

REAL RELEASES

Massively multiplayer online games (MMOs), such as World of Warcraft or Eve Online, which regularly deliver expansion packs to existing customers, balance the pressures of schedule and scope to determine ship dates on a release-by-release basis. Other games, such as iPhone or casual online games, have similar release cycles. This model is emerging more and more through expansion packs and episodic content as gaming platforms become more connected and embed more storage space.

The Development Stages

Agile game projects spread activities such as concept, design, coding, asset creation, optimizing, and debugging more evenly throughout their life. This doesn't mean that the project is a homogenous string of sprints.

Most game development projects have stages regardless of whether they are agile or not. These stages change how teams develop the game:

- **Concept:** This stage occurs before pre-production. Concept development is almost purely iterative. Ideas are generated, possibly prototyped, and thrown away on a regular basis. This stage is usually timeboxed to deliver one or more concept development plans to a green-light approval process required by the publisher or a license holder.
- **Pre-production:** Teams explore what is fun and how they are going to build assets to support it during production. They also create levels and other assets that represent production quality. This stage is fully iterative and incremental. Teams iteratively discover what is fun and incrementally adapt development planning with this knowledge.
- **Production:** The team focuses on creating an eight- to twelve-hour experience using the core mechanics and processes discovered during pre-production. This stage focuses on efficiency and incremental improvements. Teams iterate less on core mechanics discovered during pre-production because they are building a great deal of assets based on them. Changing those mechanics during production is usually very wasteful and expensive. For example, consider a team in production on a platformer genre game. Platformer games challenge the player to develop skills to navigate treacherous environments (such as Nintendo's Mario series). The production team creates hundreds of assets that depend on character movement metrics such as "how high the character can jump" or "the minimum height that the player can crawl under." If these metrics are changed in the midst of production, it wreaks havoc. For example, if a designer changes the jump height of the character, hundreds of ledges or barriers would have to be retrofitted. This creates a great deal of wasted effort during the most expensive phase of development. It's critical to discover and lock down such metrics during pre-production.
- **Post-production:** With the content brought to shippable quality, the team focuses on polishing the whole eight- to twelve-hour game experience. This stage improves the game incrementally. Following this, the game is submitted to hardware testing. Although much of this testing is spread throughout the entire project, some of it cannot be. For example, Microsoft and Sony hardware testing is expensive and only occurs in the months prior to shipping the game.

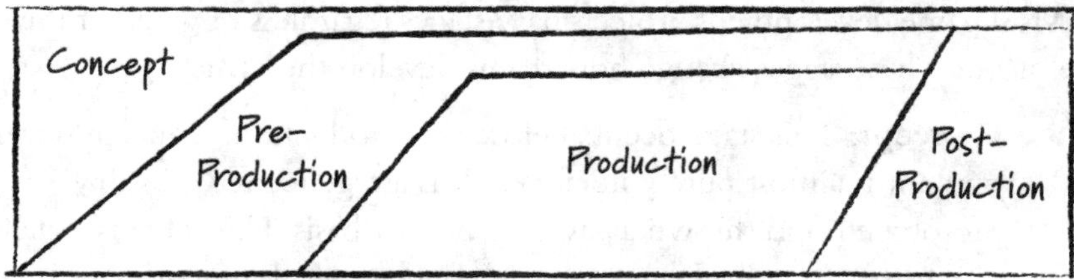

FIGURE 7.1 Overlapping stages

Mixing the Stages

Stages aren't isolated to distinct periods of time. For example, although a great deal of concept work is done up front, concept development needs to be refined as the game emerges over the entire project.

Figure 7.1 shows a typical distribution of efforts on an agile game project. Note that although more design and concept is done up front and more tuning, debugging, and optimization is done at the end, many overlap with one another. For example, rather than an official "production start date," teams see a gradual buildup of production activities and a drop-off of pre-production work in the middle of the project.

Managing Stages with Releases

Releases are a series of sprints linked together to deliver major features and assets. Similarly, a game project is a series of releases that deliver a finished game to the consumer. Figure 7.2 shows a typical series of two- to three-month releases that make up a two-year project.

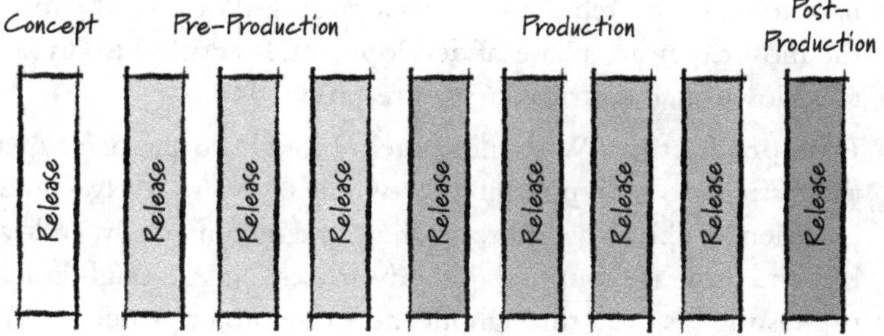

FIGURE 7.2 Releases in a multiyear project

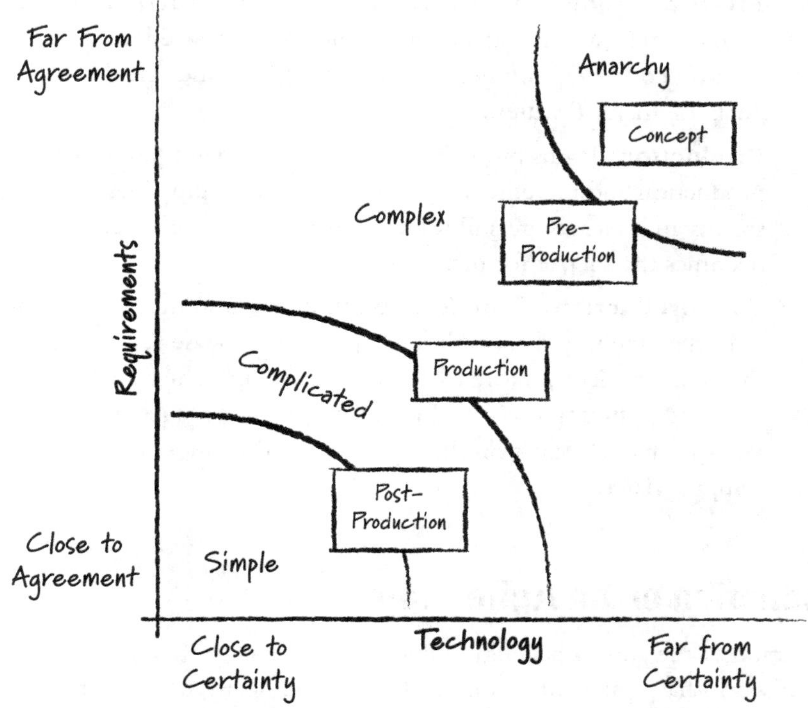

FIGURE 7.3 Stages of decreasing uncertainty

Source: Schwaber, K., and M. Beedle. 2002. *Agile Software Development with Scrum.* Upper Saddle River, NJ: Prentice Hall. Reprinted by permission of Pearson Education, Inc.

Each of these stages requires a different emphasis on the practices used. The transition between stages such as pre-production and production can be gradual, with various asset types transitioning at different times.

The reasons for the change in practices are illustrated by an enhanced version of the Stacey diagram shown in Figure 7.3. As the game progresses from concept to post-production, the level of technical and requirements uncertainty drops. As the Stacey diagram indicates, the practices should reflect these levels of uncertainty.

The framework used is still Scrum, but teams adjust the practices for the current stage:

- **Concept:** Sprints are shorter, and most of the stories in the very small backlog are spikes. The main goal of the conceptual stage is to create knowledge for the team and stakeholders, not value for the consumers. Release goals are concept treatments and perhaps a prototype to demonstrate to stakeholders.

- **Pre-production:** Scrum is used to discover the fun of the game and incrementally and iteratively build value and knowledge about production costs. Development is paced by sprints and releases. Release goals are major features.
- **Production:** Teams produce assets that were identified in pre-production and incrementally improve the asset pipelines. Although sprints and releases are still used, the pace of asset production becomes the metric for measuring velocity.
- **Post-production:** Teams focus on tuning, polishing, and bug fixing tasks they identify daily. Although sprint and release reviews are held, the goals are driven more by the daily backlog (which includes bug fixes and polishing tasks) and upcoming key dates such as submission. Post-production starts on the alpha date and includes the beta and shipping dates.

Production on an Agile Project

Production is the most challenging and expensive stage. It represents a large debt of work that is dependent on pre-production decisions and timing.

For Scrum teams, the complex pipelines of asset creation don't fit perfectly with the iterative flow of work in a sprint. Because of this, many teams entering production abandon Scrum in favor of waterfall practices. The problem in doing this is that they abandon many of the agile benefits.

This section addresses the issues with production for an agile team. It introduces some lean concepts that allow teams to continually improve their production rate and the quality of the assets they produce.

Production Debt

Have you ever seen a schedule for a game project that picks a day for production to begin? A date is chosen, a year or so in advance, that predicts when the team is to begin creating production assets (usually levels).

Where does this date come from? How do we know how much time is needed for pre-production and production? How do we know whether the time given is enough? How many times have you entered a nine-month production stage with twelve months of work? Many games enter production too early because the schedule says they need to do so. The problem is that the core mechanics and budgets that production depends on are still being iterated. This creates wasted work, because large numbers of assets must be reworked as this information emerges.

The work that needs to be done in production to create the eight to twelve hours of content many games need is called **production debt**.

Measuring Production Debt in Pre-Production

One of the goals of pre-production releases should be to measure and refine knowledge about the size of the production debt. During the first few releases, that debt is uncertain. For example, a project early in development might estimate its production debt to be 1,000 people-months of work, plus or minus 20%. Changes to the feature set may impact those ranges as well. Toward the end of pre-production, it should be more accurate, such as 1,050 people-months, plus or minus 5%. Figure 7.4 shows how this range of estimates will change over time. Although this estimate will never be perfect, it is always better than the first guess made at the start of the project.

These estimates are refined with sprint and release goals that call for assets with increasingly higher quality. By developing these assets, the team learns more about the actual cost required to create them. These estimates aren't frozen in production either. During production, the team should be finding ways to improve how assets are created to further reduce costs.

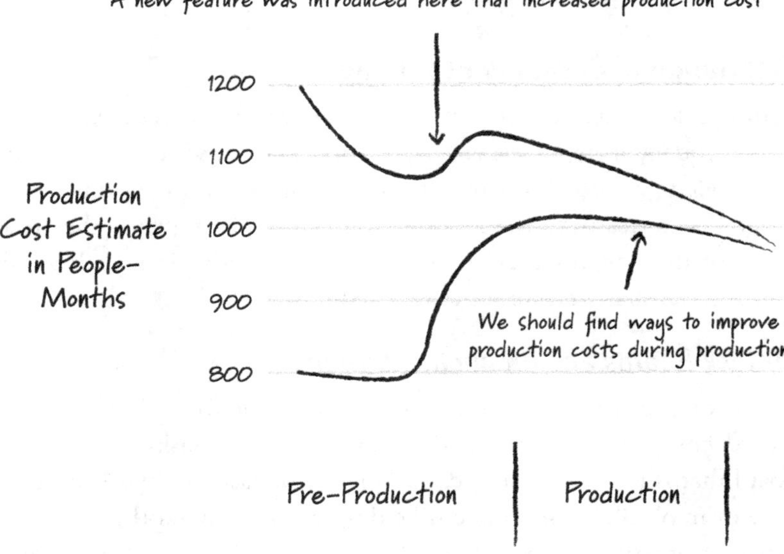

FIGURE 7.4 Production cost estimates over time

Why Measure Production Debt?

Measuring the cost of production during pre-production is important to help make decisions about the features that impact that cost. If the product owner does not know the cost impact of such features, they are inclined to accept them on face value.

Imagine you are working on a first-person shooter game that has twelve months of production scheduled to build ten levels. During development, the team implements technology that enables every part of the world to be destroyed or have holes blown in it. This is a great new addition, but it doubles the amount of work required to build a level.

If the product owner knows this, they can make an early decision. The following are some choices:

- Drop the feature because the project can't afford it.
- Drop half the levels.
- Start production earlier.
- Extend production and the ship date.
- Scale up the production resources.

Some of these choices are better than others, but they are all better than the one taken if production debt isn't measured: trying to stuff 24 months of production effort into 12 months of schedule.

The Challenge of Scrum in Production

Production is dominated by an assembly-line approach to asset creation characterized by sequential steps of specialized work. These asset production streams are easily stalled or starved of work at various points within by impediments.

When Scrum teams fit asset production streams into sprints, they discover that some of the benefits they've enjoyed in pre-production, such as ad hoc iteration and transparency, are somewhat reduced.

Scrum Task Boards and Production Streams

At the start of a sprint, a team commits to completing the tasks they estimated they could complete by the end of the sprint. Those tasks are placed on a task board that is reviewed every day. Many of the tasks are worked on out of sequence or in parallel. If someone is held up waiting for another task to complete, then they work on something else. This organic flow of task execution fosters communication among the team and prevents impediments from stopping them cold. Scrum task boards are great for supporting this.

However, for a long series of asset production steps that must be completed in order, the team loses much of this benefit. Tasks must flow in an ordered and steady pace to ensure that the specialists on a production team are not waiting for work. Scrum task boards don't clearly show this flow.

For example, consider the asset production stream for a single character to be produced in a sprint in Figure 7.5. The team estimates they will complete this work before the end of the sprint. As this stream shows, each task has to occur in order before it is handed off to the next one.

When this stream of work is placed on a task board, it looks like Figure 7.6.

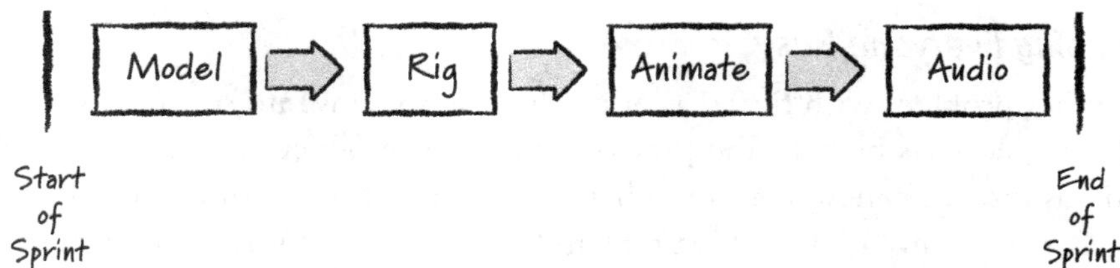

FIGURE 7.5 A production stream in a sprint

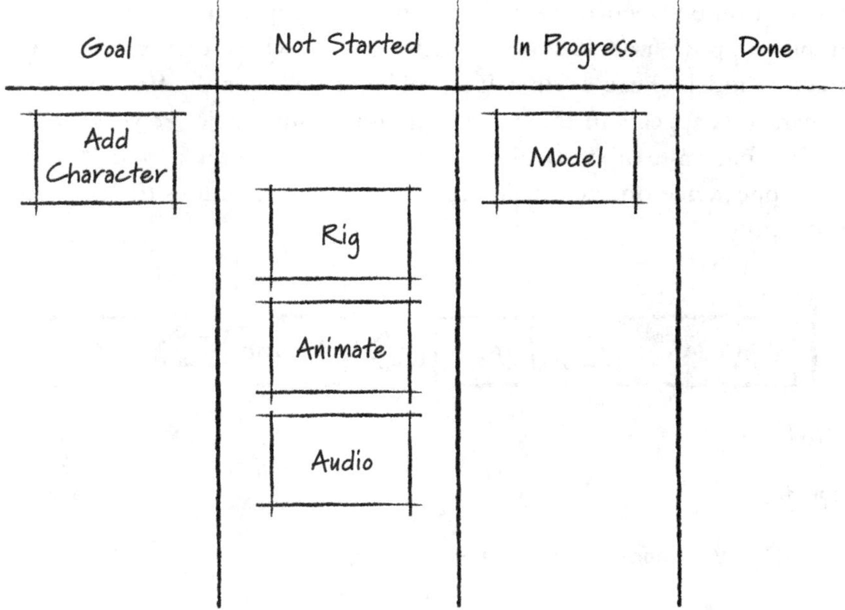

FIGURE 7.6 A character production stream visualized on a task board

This task board shows that the character model is being created first. One problem with displaying streams on a task board is that the flow rate of the stream is not sufficiently visualized. This lack of visualization fails to alert a team to problems.

For example, what happens if modeling takes longer than estimated? Figure 7.7 shows the likely result. The modeler, rigger, and animator are able to finish their work, but the last person in the chain, the audio designer, does not have enough time to do their work before the end of the sprint.

The team needs to see the impact of delays within the stream while they are occurring at any time.

Keeping Everyone Busy

Another problem with fitting asset production streams into sprints is keeping all the specialists busy. In the previous character production stream example, what is the audio designer doing before the animation is completed?

Scrum teams address this problem in a number of ways. One way is to share the composer with another team that needs audio. The other is to pool the audio designers into a team that has its own backlog. Another is to batch up the audio work for a number of characters until the audio designer joins the team for a sprint. None of these solutions is ideal because each increases the separation between an asset's creation and its appearance in the game. For example, suppose modelers are pooled together where they create a dozen character models ahead of time. If a problem is revealed the first time one of the characters appears in the game, it might require major rework of all 12, which is a big waste of effort. Shortening the time between a model's creation and its appearance on the screen creates more opportunities to "do it right" the first time.

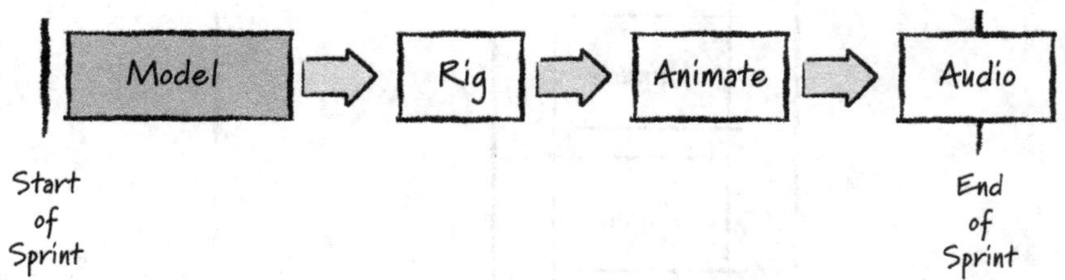

FIGURE 7.7 What happens if modeling is delayed

Less Use of Iteration

Asset production pipelines are similar to assembly lines. In this sense, a Scrum team completely empties the assembly line by the end of every sprint, which doesn't make sense for assembly lines. They have to be continuously filled because each step in the line only works on what was passed from the previous step. An assembly-line run like a sprint creates many gaps in the line that leave team members waiting.

This is the reason that many Scrum teams abandon agile when they enter production. However, production is never 100% efficient. The team cannot foresee every potential problem. They need to seek improvements in pipelines right up until the game is shipped. For this reason, the agile values should be maintained in production. If production is driven by fixed schedules and deadlines, the best the team can hope for is to meet those deadlines, but unplanned problems will continue to appear and threaten them. Practices that are still agile are needed—practices that anticipate change, that encourage continuous efficient flow, and that focus attention on continually improving how assets are produced.

This is where "lean" thinking can help. **Lean** is a set of principles applied to production environments that have more certainty about what is being created but still want to introduce improvements continually. The remainder of this chapter will describe what lean is and how it and practices like kanban can help a team remain agile during production.

Lean Production

Discovering what lean means is challenging. It seems that every month someone is branding their own version of lean. Still, some common threads run through most of these lean brands, which I refer to as **lean thinking**.

The origins of lean thinking precede World War II. Large-scale manufacturing industries were beginning to understand that the greatest untapped resource was the brains of the assembly-line worker. Encouraging them to take more ownership for improving workflow and quality paid dividends.

Since then, lean thinking has found its way into every industry. It helps teams focus on continual improvement, deliver fast, and improve the entire flow of product creation.

Lean thinking lends itself to the challenges of production (refer to Figure 7.3). Its practices, like XP programming practices, are a good complement to Scrum. They help teams create transparency within asset production streams and wring out the highest amount of quality and efficiency.

It's outside the scope of this book to explain every lean principle (see the "Additional Reading" section at the end of the chapter). Instead, the chapter introduces some lean thinking concepts and practices through a level production example.

A LEAN THINKING METAPHOR

"Lean thinking is a proven system that applies to product development and production, as evidenced by Toyota and others. And although most often applied to products, it is also used in service areas—both within Toyota and in domains such as health care. The image and metaphor we like to convey a key thinking mistake—and opportunity—is the sport of relay racing.

"Consider the relay racers standing around waiting for the baton from their running colleague. The accountant in the finance department, looking aghast at this terrible underutilization 'waste' indicated in some report, would probably mandate a policy goal of "95% utilization of resources" to ensure all the racers are busy and 'productive.' Maybe—he suggests—the runners could run three races at the same time to increase 'resource utilization' or run up a mountain while waiting. Funny...but this kind of thinking lies behind much of traditional management and processes in development and other domains. Of course, in contrast, here is a central idea in lean thinking:

"'Watch the baton, not the runners'"[1]

Visualizing Flow with Kanban

A kanban board is a bit similar to a Scrum task board.[2] In Japanese the word *kan* means "card," and *ban* means "signal," so **kanban** refers to "signal cards." Kanban represents a "pull system" for work. A kanban card is a signal meant to trigger action, such as "work on this next" or "I need an animation."

A team employs a kanban board to visualize an asset production stream and provide the transparency that a Scrum task board cannot.

We'll use an example level production stream to demonstrate how kanban and lean thinking are applied to production. Figure 7.8 shows a simplified level production stream, from concept to tuning.

1. Larman, C., and B. Vodde. 2009. *Scaling Lean and Agile Development: Thinking and Organizational Tools for Large-Scale Scrum*. Boston: Addison-Wesley. Reproduced by permission of Pearson Education, Inc.
2. Some call this board the **Heijunka board**.

FIGURE 7.8 A simplified production stream for levels

The first step is to represent the stream on a kanban board, which uses columns to represent individual workflow steps and capacity. Figure 7.9 shows a simplified kanban for the level production stream.

There are six columns, which representing the steps of this production stream, including the product backlog. The cards within the columns represent individual levels in production. As the work for each step of a level is completed, a card for the next level to work on is pulled from the column immediately to its left, if that level is ready.

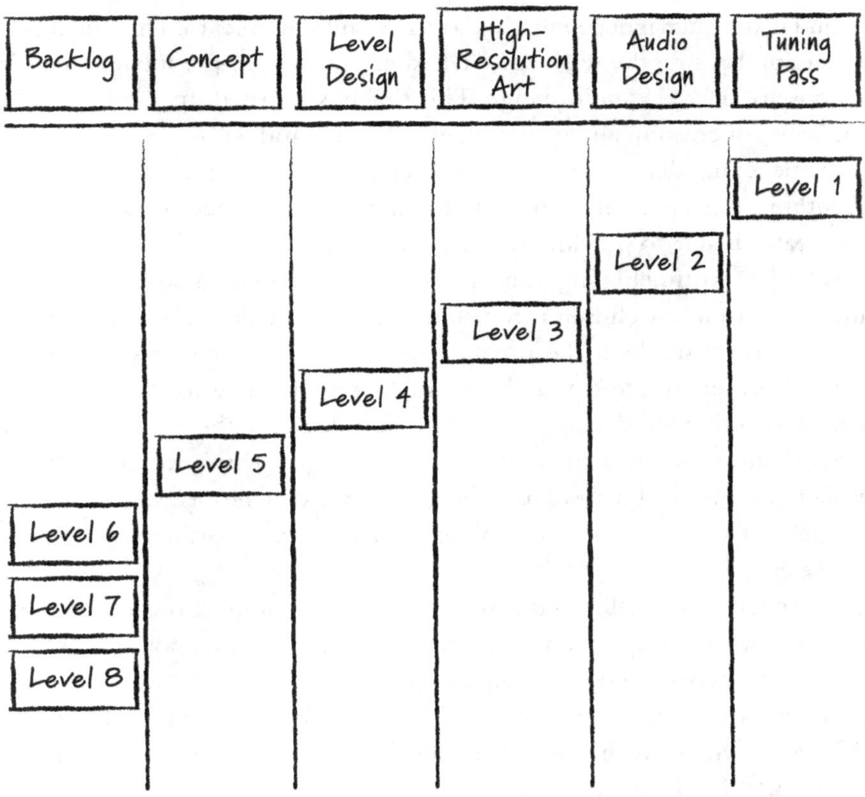

FIGURE 7.9 A simple kanban board

Leveling Production Flow

Now that the team has a kanban board representing the level production stream, the team members can start applying lean tools to smooth out the fluctuations of production. This allows them to create production assets at a more constant and predictable rate.

There are two basic tools for leveling production flow. The first is establishing timeboxes for each step of the production stream. Following this, the flow is leveled by balancing the resources supporting every step.

Timeboxing Every developer who uses Scrum recognizes that a sprint is a two- to four-week timebox. Teams don't change that timebox. The benefit is to create a measurable cadence of value being added to the game.

In lean production, this is taken a step further. Each step of a production stream is timeboxed. For example, audio design for a level might be timeboxed to ten days. This is different from a similar Scrum task in pre-production that the audio designer independently estimates and commits to. This changes for production because the team has established, during pre-production, the ideal timebox for a level's audio design. This timebox is based on the trade-off of time (cost) of creation and quality desired by the product owner.

Timeboxing does not mean content creators are forced to meet a set quality within a fixed amount of time. The quality is determined by what the content creator is able to provide within the time limit.

The key to timeboxing assets is balancing quality and cost, measured in time. If the timebox chosen is too short, then the quality of the asset will be too low. For example, if the timebox for a section of high-resolution level geometry is set to one day, an artist might only be able to create a section filled with untextured cubes! On the other hand, if the timebox selected were two months, the artist might deliver a section with too much detailed geometry. It would be absolutely beautiful, but that beauty would come at too great of a cost to the stakeholder compared to the value it provides to the player.

Balancing asset quality and cost is the job of the product owner. They have to judge what the player values. Figure 7.10 demonstrates a notional curve of the trade-off between cost and value to the player.

It's not a straight line, because of diminishing returns; a player driving past a 10,000-polygon fire hydrant does not experience 50 times the value of a 200-polygon fire hydrant.

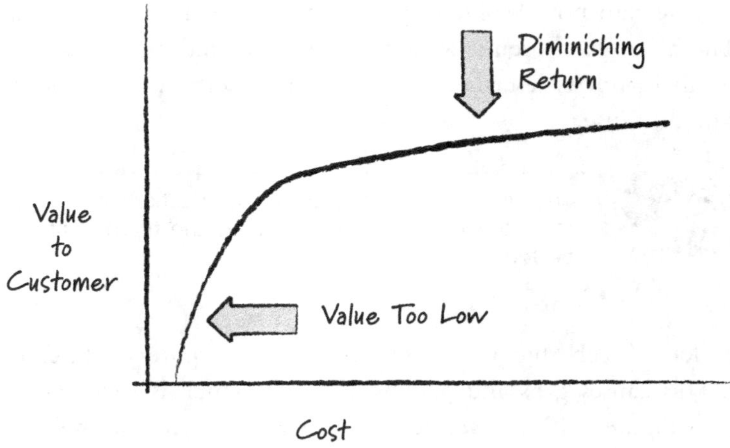

FIGURE 7.10 The cost/trade-off curve of assets

> **NOTE** As the product owner of a driving game, I asked the artists to create "95-mile-per-hour art." This quality bar depends on what the player cares about when they play the game; the player doesn't care about a high-resolution fire hydrant they pass at 95 miles per hour!

Figure 7.11 shows the area of the trade-off curve where the timebox selection is made. Pre-production refines the shape of this curve and the best range for a production timebox.

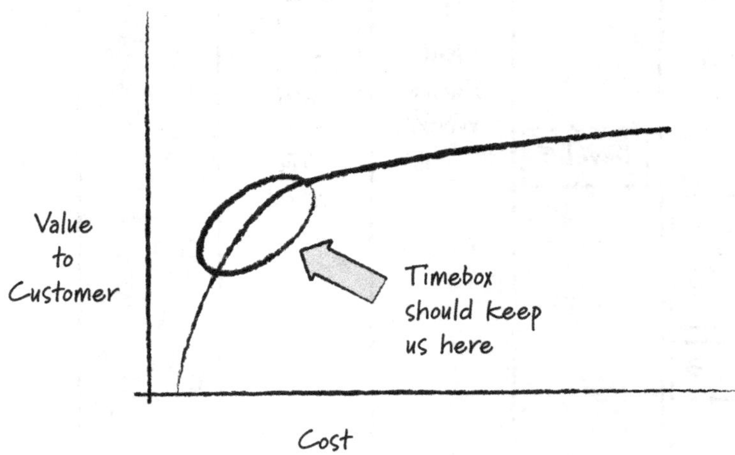

FIGURE 7.11 Selecting a timebox for an asset

Timeboxes are not absolutely precise. Some levels take more time than others. The timebox chosen is an average of best- and worst-case times. The team uses small buffers, described next, to avoid underflow or overflow of work that this might cause.

NOTE The timebox changes during production; it shrinks as it is refined and moves to the left as the team improves how it performs.

Leveling Flow Each step in the stream usually requires a different-length timebox. This causes gaps and pileups of work, which is to be avoided. For example, in Figure 7.12, if level design takes a week but the high-resolution geometry takes two, then the design work piles up. Conversely, if conceptualization requires two weeks for each level, the level designer eventually runs out of work and has to wait.

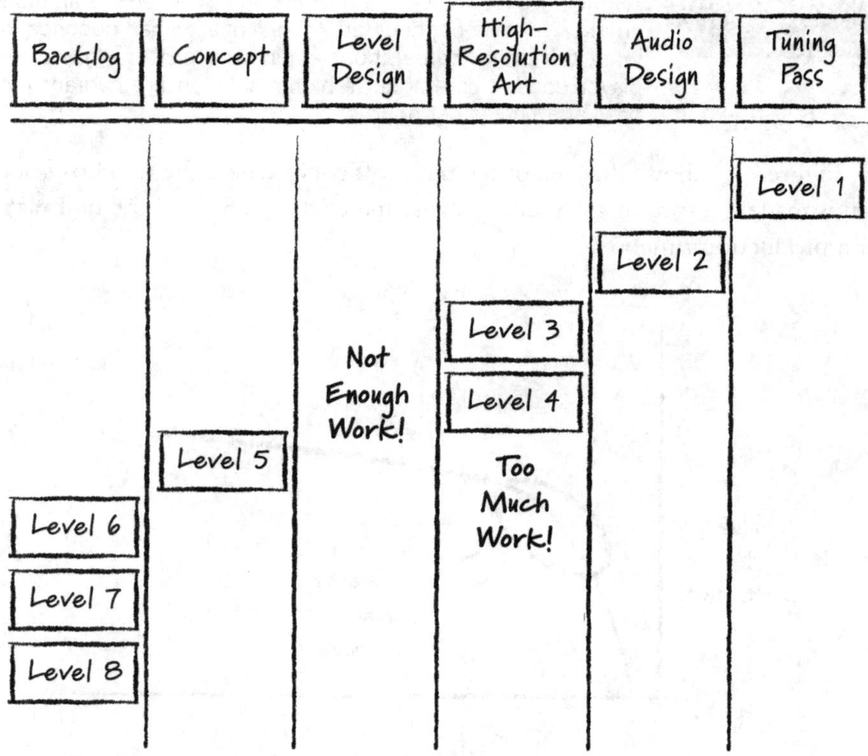

FIGURE 7.12 A kanban board showing starvation and overflow

Workflow needs to be balanced so that everyone always has work to do and that large amounts of work in progress don't pile up at any step. One way of doing this is to balance the amount of time each step takes, called its **cycle time**.

For example, if the team wants a ten-day cycle time for each step, they start by examining the timeboxes for each person working on the stream (see Table 7.1).

Concept art and audio design already have a cycle time of ten days. However, the other steps have different cycle times. For example, tuning takes less than ten days per level. This means the designer who tunes levels runs out of work from time to time and has to find other things to do. This could mean helping out another team, level design, or QA.

For steps that require more than ten days per level, the team needs to add people or find improvements to the process. For example, since the high-resolution artists require thirty days per level, the team could dedicate three high-resolution artists to balance the flow. Artists can work together in a number of ways, but each has challenges:

- Have all high-resolution artists work on the same level. This may not be an option if the editing tools do not support simultaneous editing on the same level.
- Break up the high-resolution step into a specialized flow (for example, texture artist, prop artist, static geometry artist). It may be hard to balance these specialties.
- Have the high-resolution artists working on multiple levels in parallel. This solution might pose challenges with creating consistent quality and pace.

TABLE 7.1 The Starting Cycle Times for an Unbalanced Stream

Step	Timebox per Person
Concept	10 days
Level design	20 days
High-resolution art*	30 days
Audio design	10 days
Tuning pass	7 days

* **High-resolution art** is the creation of detailed geometry, textures, and lighting.

Each member of the team adds capacity, represented by a kanban limit for each column as shown in Figure 7.13. This number defines how many cards (levels) should reside in each column. When the number of cards in a column does not match its limit, it signals to the team that there is a potential problem.

Our kanban board now looks like Figure 7.13.

The team has now balanced the level production stream and established the rate at which levels are completed, called the **takt time** (see the sidebar "Takt Time and Cycle Time"), which is also ten days. They apply lean tools to maintain and even reduce takt time so to continually improve the cost and quality of the levels.

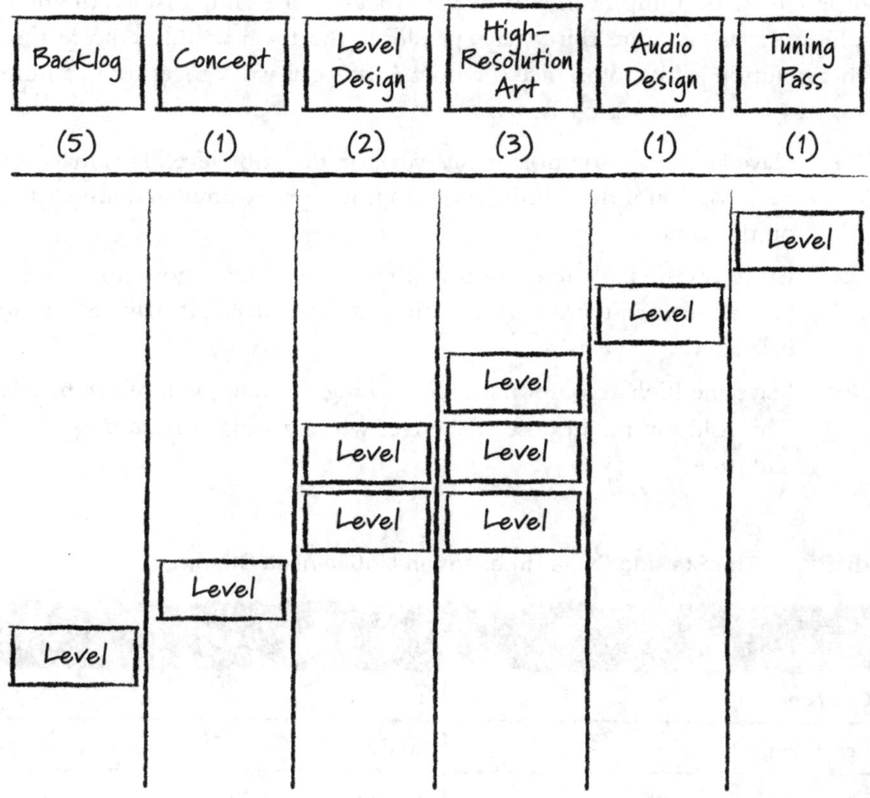

FIGURE 7.13 A kanban board showing balanced flow

TAKT TIME AND CYCLE TIME

Lean uses two measures of time for asset production streams. One is takt time, which is the rate of external demand for completed assets to be delivered. For video game production, this is determined by a schedule established in pre-production. One goal of lean practices is to continually put pressure on reducing takt time—increasing the rate at which finished assets are delivered—by finding improvements in the pipeline.

Cycle time is used to measure the interval of time between the start and finish of a step or an entire stream.

Ideally, the cycle time of each step is less than or equal to the takt time. This is the goal of leveling flow. In the level creation example stream, the high-resolution art step required a 15-day cycle time. This could not be reduced to the takt time goal of five days by simply improving the pipeline. The solution was to create three high-resolution art stations working in parallel to meet the demand for one level of high-resolution art to be completed every five days.

Continual Improvement

One of the main advantages of using lean production is that teams maintain the drive to continually improve what they are making and how they are making it. This is a benefit over fixed production schedules, where teams concentrate on keeping pace with deadlines.

In production, teams apply the same agile planning paradigm of using velocity measurements to forecast the pace toward achieving a goal. This allows fixes and improvements to be quickly appraised.

This section uses the level production example to describe some of the ways lean thinking enables teams to continually improve how they work together to increase the quality and production pace of assets.

Improving Cycle Time The pace of iteration has a direct impact on quality. For example, if the iteration time on changing a texture and seeing it in the game is reduced from ten minutes to ten seconds, an artist iterates on textures more, and the game looks better.

The same principle applies to asset production streams. We want to shorten a stream's iteration time to allow improvements to be introduced as quickly as possible. These include pipeline, tool, workflow, and teamwork improvements. Shortening the iteration time of such changes enables more of them to be implemented and seen.

In lean production, we focus on improving the iteration time, or cycle time, for the entire stream rather than the individual steps. The following factors influence a stream's cycle time:

- **Asset size:** Large assets, such as full levels, have large cycle times. If a team completes portions of a large asset, they reduce its cycle time.
- **Batch size:** This is the number of assets processed at one time at any individual step. The larger the batch size, the longer the cycle time. An example of this is completing a dozen character models before handing them all off to the rigger.
- **Waste:** This is the effort spent on things that don't add value to the final asset. For example, the time spent waiting for an approval is non-value-added time, or waste.
- **Knowledge, skill, and empowerment:** The greatest factor in determining cycle time is the knowledge and skill of everyone who adds value along the stream and their ability to influence change. For example, knowing when and where to reuse an asset rather than building one from scratch has a large impact on cycle time.

Smaller Assets By breaking large assets into smaller ones, teams receive faster feedback. There are three types of feedback:

- **Gameplay feedback:** Very large assets, such as levels, can have monthlong cycle times and, despite how detailed their design, deliver uncertain gameplay. This long cycle time provides little opportunity for feedback to influence the asset. As a result, levels are shipped based on their initial design assumptions. By breaking levels into smaller areas, teams are given valuable feedback about the gameplay emerging and use this knowledge to influence subsequent portions of the level.
- **Production feedback:** Improvements to the production flow are applied more quickly and cheaply. For example, if the team discovers that a particular piece of static geometry interferes with character motion in the first section of the level, they fix that section and change their standards of work to apply the improvement on every subsequent section. This is a big time-saver.

- **Velocity feedback:** It's very difficult to gauge the effectiveness of individual practice changes or tool improvements when the cycle time is measured in months. If the cycle time is reduced to weeks, then changes to the pace of work from improvements are more apparent.

One level production team I was working with did this by breaking up their levels into seven smaller "zones." Zones were the sections of levels that were streamed in and out of memory as the player moved.

Once they began building zones, their cycle times became one seventh of what they were before. Zones were completed every few weeks, and each one added improvements in quality and production that fed into subsequent zones. This team eventually reduced their cycle time by more than 50%.

Smaller Batches Traditional production pipelines focus on the efficient utilization of resources, rather than the flow of asset production streams. The imbalance of disciplines often causes project managers to level resources so that nobody runs out of work to do. Since "resource leveling" predictions are never too precise, large inventories of works in progress are built in, between the steps.

For example, if a project has dozens of levels to ship, it may start producing batches of concept art or level props well before the end of pre-production. To a certain degree, this is necessary, but it often goes too far. For example, a half dozen levels of concept art created before gameplay is fully understood leads to waste if the concepts have to be redone or, worse, levels are produced using these obsolete concepts.

With lean thinking, teams try to reduce or eliminate batches of work. Because of the uncertainties within the timeboxes for each step, they often need to create small buffers of works in progress between the steps of an asset production stream. They choose the smallest possible buffer size, because buffers increase the cycle time. The buffers should prevent waiting but not excessive pileups of work between each stage of work.

Figure 7.14 shows how buffers are represented on a kanban board. Buffers have limits, like every other step, that signal when the buffer is overflowing or underflowing.

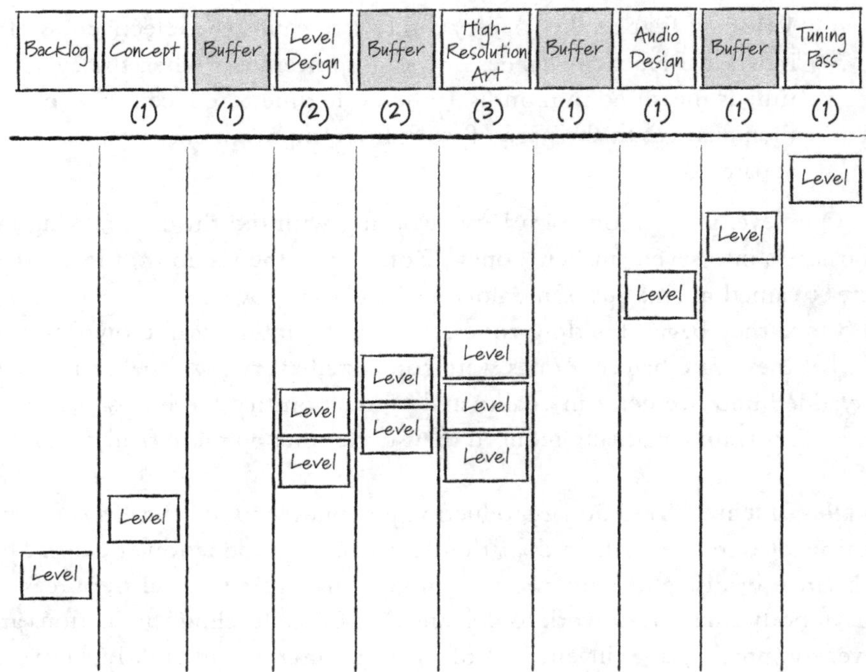

FIGURE 7.14 A kanban board with buffers

Reducing Waste A good portion of the time spent in production is wasted on work or activities that don't add value to the final product. Examples of this are the time waiting for exports, waiting for asset approvals, or syncing with the latest assets. Reducing these wastes greatly benefits productivity and cycle times.

Many of these wastes are identified and corrected by the team itself. The subtle pressures of takt time and timeboxing largely drive this. Timeboxes exert a pressure on the content creators to use their time wisely. As a result, it encourages them to seek ways to be more effective in how they work and point out the problems that were not so impactful when they had more time (see the sidebar "Lean Thinking and Boats").

LIMITING CREATIVITY?

One concern about lean is that it limits the creativity of artists in production. I have found that the opposite is the case. A quote from TS Eliot seems to apply: "When forced to work within a strict framework, the imagination is taxed to its utmost and will produce richest ideas. Given total freedom the work is likely to sprawl."

One production team I was working with had a ten-day takt time for level sections. This pace was challenging and exposed many problems with the flow of work. The biggest problem was with the concept art step. The team had only one concept artist available who was sitting with the other concept artists in another part of the studio. It often took more than ten days to create a dozen drawings for each section. The team recognized this as a bottleneck.

In team discussions, it turned out that the level designers and high-resolution artists didn't really need all the drawings created. Because the concept artist was separate from the team, much of the concept art was based on poor assumptions about the level and gameplay. For example, gameplay was linear, but much of the concept art represented open areas. The concept artist was surprised to hear that much of his work was useless. The solution the team created was to move the concept artist next to the level designer and high-resolution artists. This enabled them to discuss the layout of levels as concept art was created. As a result, far fewer drawings needed to be created, and the quality of the levels improved.

This is an example of reducing the waste of handoffs. By applying this practice to other handoffs, the team was able to create similar improvements across the entire production stream.

This is one example of dozens of changes the team made. By the end of production, they had improved takt time by more than 50% while significantly improving quality.

LEAN THINKING AND BOATS

A useful metaphor for how lean thinking encourages continual improvement is that of a boat traveling down a river. The river is filled with boulders of various sizes, which impede the flow of water. When the water level of the river is high, the crew piloting the boat doesn't encounter the boulders and isn't concerned about how they are slowing them down.

However, when the water level in the river drops, the boulders begin to appear. They are then recognized not only as impediments to the flow of the river but also as real danger! Now the crew reacts to the boulders and steers around them.

In this metaphor, the boat is the project, and the flow of water represents the flow of money or time being spent on it. The boulders stand for the things that slow development down like unreliable build systems or asset pipelines that take hours to create a build.

Lean thinking not only causes the water level to be lowered but gives teams the equivalent of a cannon, through transparency and practices, to start blowing the boulders away. This makes it possible for the boat to go faster and straighter with less water.

Knowledge, Skill, and Empowerment Like Scrum practices, lean practices create transparency in the production pipeline, which makes quality, velocity, and waste visible. One of the first things revealed is the variation of quality and velocity between separate teams. This visibility enables leads to know where to focus mentoring. In many cases, all that is required is to help a struggling content creator use a tool correctly or understand how they reuse assets to improve their effectiveness.

Lean thinking focuses skills on the final product, rather than on individual steps. Part IV, "Agile Disciplines," discusses this in greater detail.

Many of the lean tools described require the team to be empowered to make decisions and take ownership of their practices. In the previous example, the team decided to move the concept artist with the rest of the team. In many studios, teams are not allowed to make such decisions. It comes back to the lack of transparency. With transparency, teams are entrusted to make greater and greater decisions because of the performance metrics that ensure their decisions demonstrate higher productivity and quality. The difference in the number, quality, and frequency of beneficial changes increases as ownership of them is spread. Leaders might be skilled and insightful, but they can't be everywhere. They need to rely on empowered teams to recognize and solve issues daily.

Outsourcing

Outsourcing has established its benefits for asset production. However, many studios have found that outsourcing limits the amount of iteration that takes place in the creation of large assets such as key characters or levels. This limited iteration impacts quality or introduces expensive rework that limits outsourcing's cost benefits.

Lean production outside the game industry evolved to work with external suppliers. Suppliers to lean companies need to become lean themselves. Lean suppliers deliver smaller batches of parts to the main production line. This is done to allow quality improvements to be introduced more frequently and at lower cost.

How does this translate to game asset production? With our example, we don't want to outsource the entire level production stream. The key is to outsource parts of the production stream that don't require larger iterative cycles that should remain in the studio. For level production, studio teams retain large layout tasks and outsource the component assets used in these layouts. An example of this is environment sets, or collections of assets, common throughout a level. If

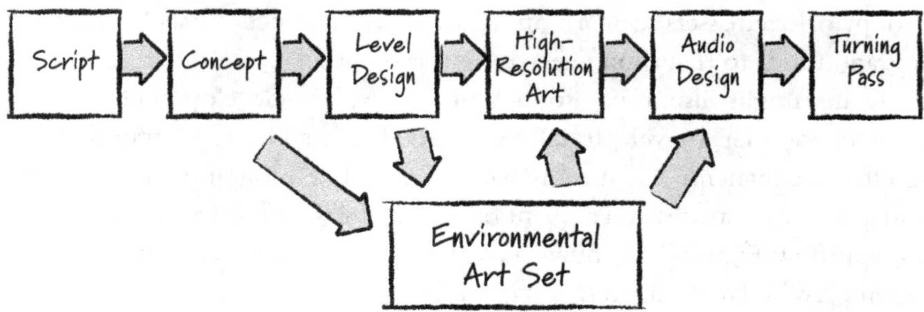

FIGURE 7.15 Outsourcing a portion of the stream

a project needs a large city level, they outsource all the props such as light posts, mailboxes, vehicles, building components, ambient sounds, and so on. These environmental sets are brought into the layout steps (high-resolution art and audio layout). This enables continued iteration of the layouts at the studio.

Figure 7.15 shows a production stream with the environmental art outsourced.

The outsourced assets are identified in level concept and design to give sufficient lead time. These assets are delivered as they are developed, rather than in a single batch.

> **NOTE**
>
> Many layout tools support late introduction of outsourced components. An example is the Unreal Engine 3 editor. The packaging system allows for levels to be laid out with proxy assets that are automatically replaced as the high-quality outsourced assets are delivered. For example, the studio artists could use blue rectangles in place of doors, and when the outsourced doors are delivered, a single instance change replaces them all.

Working with Scrum

When the project enters production, asset production teams may not use practices such as sprint planning and tracking. However, these practices are still used by other teams to continue innovating new features.

Sprints are still valuable in production. Asset production teams demonstrate the assets that have been completed since the last sprint review. Production teams don't plan sprints. Instead, they periodically fill a backlog buffer with a set of prioritized assets to work on next. The team selects a backlog buffer size limit and fills it to that limit every time it is emptied.

Teams might also mix production and feature development work. For example, consider a level production team that has a few programmers adding effects, enhancing AI, and improving tools. The programmers plan typical sprints with user stories and a sprint backlog, while the level creators use a kanban workflow. Figure 7.16 shows how the two task boards are combined using a Scrum "swim lane" added to a kanban board.

Retrospectives and daily scrums are still essential practices for production teams to address impediments and to improve how the team performs together.

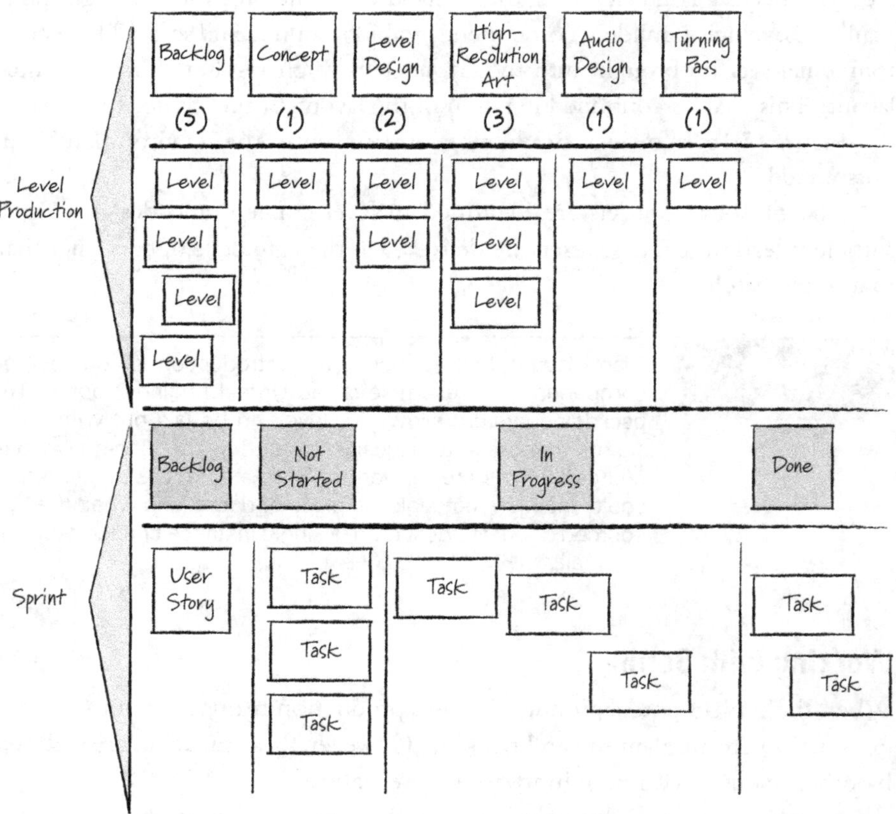

FIGURE 7.16 A kanban board with a sprint swim lane

Transitioning Scrum Teams

Scrum teams exploring gameplay in pre-production don't instantly reorganize their workflow into asset streams overnight. They gradually build up to them by iterating on assets that approach production quality and refining each stage or workflow. Each team approaches this transition differently, but the common set of steps is as follows:

1. Explore what is correct (fun and cost).
2. Refine the timeboxes.
3. Understand how much content is needed and who is needed to create it, and refine the production budget.
4. Establish the asset streams.
5. Start adding columns to task boards with kanban limits.
6. Level the flow. Adjust the teams.

As the teams level the flow of an asset stream, their size might far exceed ten members. Some teams might break the team into two, but more often they maintain themselves as a single team. This allows them to "see the whole" asset stream as one continuous flow. The downside is that it makes team meetings, such as daily scrums and retrospectives, less productive because of the communication overhead.

Summary

The additional challenge of stages with game projects doesn't diminish the value of agile or require complex plans or project management structures. It requires product owners to be aware of impacts that features have on production costs and for teams to adapt their practices as they enter production.

Additional Reading

Poppendieck, M., and T. Poppendieck. 2006. *Implementing Lean Software Development: From Concept to Cash*. Boston: Addison-Wesley.

Ladas, C. 2009. *Scrumban: Essays on Kanban Systems for Lean Software Development*. Seattle: Modus Cooperandi Press.

Chapter 8

Teams

I've worked on creating various products, from the F-22 fighters to games, for more than 20 years. The highlights of my career are clearly marked in my mind by the project teams I was working with. These teams were more consequential to enjoyment and productivity than the company or project we were working for at the time.

Working with the project team on the first Midtown Madness game was a highlight. The team was largely composed of developers who had never worked on a game before. Microsoft, our publisher, and the studio we worked at, Angel Studios, left us largely alone to develop the game. As a result, many of the smaller details of the game were left to us to discover. We were never far away from being canceled either…in some cases hours away. We had to prove ourselves.

What emerged was a team with a shared vision, a sense of ownership, and pride. We worked hard on the game. For example, we started a LAN party with the game every day at 6 p.m., and at 8 p.m. we met in a conference room to talk about improving the experience. I'd often have an idea pop into my head during the night, and I'd rush back in during the early hours of the day to try it, often finding teammates who had arrived earlier or had even spent the night working on their own idea. Although we spent long hours on the game, it seemed more like a hobby we were passionate about than a job, but it never felt like a "crunch."

The game we shipped was a success, but the real reward was the experience of working with that team. Much of the chemistry of that team is a mystery to me. There doesn't seem to be a formula for how such teams can be created, but I've found that it's quite easy to prevent such teams from forming. Scrum's focus is on allowing such teams to form, if possible, and nurturing them to grow. This chapter will explore some of the basic Scrum principles and practices that support such teams and how large projects of more than 100 people can use these practices and allow individuals on teams to still have a shared vision, sense of ownership, and pride. It will also explore various team structures that have been formed on large game projects.

This chapter describes the central role of teams in Scrum, the role of leadership, and how small Scrum teams scale for large projects.

Great Teams

Great teams are one of the most influential factors for creating a successful game. Great teams are also the most difficult teams to foster. They cannot be created through the application of rules or practices alone. Studio and project leadership are required to facilitate them.

Great teams share the following characteristics:

- **Follow a shared vision and purpose:** Everyone on the team understands the goal of what they are working on.
- **Complement other team members' skills:** Team members depend on each other to achieve their goals by applying their unique skills to a shared goal.
- **Exhibit open and safe communication:** Team members feel safe to communicate anything to one another.
- **Share decision making, responsibility, and accountability:** The team succeeds or fails together, not as individuals. Everyone earns their spot on the team daily. There is no room for titles or egos.
- **Have fun together:** They spend time together and enjoy each other's company. They care for one another.
- **Deliver value:** Great teams take pride in their work and deliver high value consistently.
- **Demonstrate shared commitment:** Great teams have a unified cause. When one member has a problem, the entire team will pitch in to help them out. As a result, great teams deliver value because they focus on the whole rather on their own parts. Great teams are committed to their goals. They'll go the "extra mile" to achieve a goal that they believe in.

Scrum creates a framework, through its practices and roles, to support these teams. They require facilitation and support of leadership and management to evolve. Great teams are uncommon. They create experiences—like the one I mentioned in the chapter introduction—that people strive to be a part of over their entire career.

When baking a cake, a few ingredients are needed before you start. If you are missing any of these, such as eggs, flour, and so on, you can't make a cake. However, just how these ingredients are prepared together and baked into the cake is the main difference between a memorable wedding cake and something that might taste like it that came from an Easy-Bake oven.

Leadership and talent are the required ingredients for a great game, but like the cake, how these ingredients are brought together, such as in a team, is the main determinant of the quality of the game. Scrum doesn't provide the ingredients for great teams but helps them "mix and bake" what's there to achieve that goal.

A Scrum Approach to Teams

Scrum creates conditions that enable such teams to achieve greatness through its practices and principles:

- **Cross-discipline teams:** Enables teams to deliver features and mechanics that have clear value to customers and stakeholders
- **Self-management:** Enables teams to select the amount of work they can commit to every sprint and complete that work through whatever means they find appropriate
- **Self-organization:** Enables teams to have a degree of authority and responsibility to select their membership
- **True leadership:** Provides leadership focused on mentoring and facilitation to free the best performance possible from the team

The rest of this section will examine the principles and practices in greater detail.

EXPERIENCE

"At the heart of scrum is the interaction of the team. A daily meeting around the task board is interactive, vibrant, collaborative, visual, and tactile. It is a visual way of showing the goal the team is striving toward and the progress they are making. They, each and every member of the team, are peers.

"They own the goal. It's a team effort. They gather around the board to align themselves with each other, to honor others' contribution to the effort, and to course-correct when they are missing the mark. They argue, discuss, share, learn, continually improve, celebrate, boost each other up, and create solutions.

"There is another thing that Scrum does for the team: It creates transparency. Since Scrum depends on collaboration and continual forward progress, problems are addressed by the team as they crop up instead of dealing with them later or covering the problem under a layer of 'spin.'

"A structured, militant environment will never create a team. A team works together toward a shared goal. A group works together toward a goal given to them. Scrum is messy and noisy. It lives, it breathes, it stretches, it morphs, and it expands. Interaction is the heart of the team. The heart of Scrum is the team."

—Shelly Warmuth, freelance writer and game designer

Cross-Discipline Teams

When the various documents are written and schedules are created, the priorities of each discipline's schedules don't often mesh. Programmers often read the design document and architect a number of systems based on the goals established in the document. Complexity and risk prioritize this work, not feature value.

For example, if the design identifies characters that walk on walls, then they architect that requirement into the character system. This requires a great deal of work to alter the physics system and the camera system. The programmers consider these changes as high priority, since they affect core systems at a fundamental level. As a result, they begin working on these changes from the start. The problem is that the "walking on walls" feature may not be very important to the designers. The feature may even be dropped when it is seen.

This lack of synchronized prioritization between disciplines leads to delays in building knowledge about the game: knowledge that comes only from using each mechanic in a working game.

Scrum requires a synchronization of the disciplines every sprint. This forces change in how each developer works daily regardless of their discipline. A cross-discipline team uses value to explore a solution, which addresses the needs for technology, design, and animation. This drives changes in the way each discipline works to avoid one discipline getting too far ahead of the others, such as creating speculative architectures. Programmers on a Scrum team may eventually adopt test-driven development practices, discussed in Chapter 10, "Agile Technology," to enable value-prioritized development without the cost of late changes that up-front architectures attempt to avoid.

Cross-discipline Scrum teams minimize the delays and costs that are incurred by large discipline-focused hierarchies. Team members share the same goal and therefore the same priorities, which encourage collaboration. Practices such as the daily scrum reinforce a team's commitment to the sprint goal and to solving the problems that ordinarily would "fall between the cracks" between the disciplines on a daily basis.

Self-Management

Scrum addresses the problems of communication on large teams not by adding management layers but by dividing the project staff into small teams. Scrum teams are usually composed of five to nine cross-disciplined developers who take on major game features and create vertical slices of those features every sprint. Teams take on an increasing level of self-management by doing the following:

- Choosing the amount of work to accomplish for the coming sprint and committing to its completion
- Deciding the best way to work together
- Estimating their own work and monitoring progress toward their committed goal daily
- Demonstrating sprint goals achieved to the stakeholders every sprint
- Taking responsibility for their performance and finding ways to improve it

Team self-management doesn't happen overnight. It requires mentoring and practice to achieve. It requires trust to be built between management and the teams and the clear definition of the dividing line of responsibilities.

Self-Organization

Team self-organization is the most challenging practice for teams trying to achieve self-management. Self-organizing teams select their own members whom they believe can help them achieve the best results.

The benefits of self-organization are an essential part of a self-managing team. When teams "own" their membership, then they treat team commitments with a great deal more ownership. When people are assigned to a team built by management, it's something that they have no control over, and, as we've seen, a lack of control prevents full commitment.

Teams are allowed to change their membership between sprints, but most often they only make changes before the first sprint of a new release. Shortly after a release plan is discussed with the project staff, they negotiate among themselves to exchange members. The teams take the following into account when self-organizing:

- **What are the release goals and initial release plan?** Sometimes release goals require a complete reorganization of the teams. For example, a game that has focused on single-player mechanics might work on online gameplay during the next release. This might require a new distribution of skills.
- **What disciplines and skills are required to implement the release goals?** For example, if a team that has been implementing a shooting mechanic is now being called upon to create AI characters that shoot back, they need to bring an AI programmer on board. If some simple changes need to be made to the codebase, perhaps a junior programmer is the best fit.
- **What are the priorities of the release goals?** If teams compete for people, the higher-priority release goal determines where people go. For example, if both a shooting and driving team need AI and there is only one experienced AI programmer, the higher-priority goal determines that the AI programmer first goes to the shooting mechanic team.
- **Do the team members have chemistry?** Although it is often ignored, the chemistry of people working together on a team has as much impact as any of the practices. For example, teams often benefit from having one outspoken member but suffer from having two. Both might be equally talented, but together they just don't work well. Teams recognize this and should be able to control their membership to avoid it.

Like many other Scrum practices, a team isn't expected to master self-organization from the start. Most studios starting Scrum avoid this practice at first and slowly over time allow the team a greater degree of influence over who is added and removed from the team. Eventually the team will make the decisions on their own, with leadership influencing their decisions and providing help with conflicts and problems that exceed the team's authority. The rewards are profound. Self-organizing teams deliver unequalled levels of performance and enjoy their work far more than conventionally managed teams (Takeuchi and Nonaka 1986).

When people first hear about self-organization, they are skeptical. It reminds them of painful childhood memories of not being chosen for a sports team. Inexperienced teams treat this practice as a popularity contest. They will need the assistance of management to help them make the best choices (see Chapter 16, "Launching Scrum"). Experienced agile teams, which understand team commitment, end up making better choices that benefit their velocity.

Occasionally, teams "self-organize people off" between sprints. The team removes poor performers or poor team players (see the sidebar "When Someone Is Kicked Off a Team"). This is necessary to allow teams to truly take ownership and commit to their work.

WHEN SOMEONE IS KICKED OFF A TEAM

It's pretty rare for a team to unanimously eject someone from their team. Usually the person ejected has ignored months of team and leadership feedback about their poor performance or teamwork. However, being ejected from a team cannot be ignored. It is a strong statement from a group of your peers.

After this occurs, another team willing to take this person has to be found. They have to be made aware of the issues that led to their ejection from the last team. Teams cannot be forced to accept people they don't want.

If it's the first time this person has been ejected and several other teams are around, the person will be able to join another team easily. Most of time this person corrects the issues and becomes a valuable member of another team, or the person simply finds a team where the chemistry is better.

On rare occasions, they don't work well on the next team either. After a few ejections, it's common to find that no other team will accept this person. It then becomes management's duty to release this person from the company. Sometimes the person gets the message and leaves before this happens.

I've only seen this happen a few times. It's unfortunate, but it makes a statement to the teams: They control their destiny. They are responsible and have the necessary authority to make changes to improve their performance. When this authority doesn't exist, it doesn't allow a team to achieve its potential. Teams that can't self-organize will feel that they are stuck with the members on their team and there is nothing they can do about it. They feel helpless to make the change they need and don't make the same level of commitment they possibly could.

When you see the performance of teams that achieves their potential, you stop questioning the value of these practices. It does take a leap of faith to allow them into your studios. Unfortunately, some don't reach this point and don't see the potential of great teams realized.

Team Size

Scrum literature recommends teams have sizes of seven to nine members (Schwaber 2004). This is based on studies (Steiner 1972) and firsthand experience that shows that team productivity peaks at these sizes.

A challenge for agile game development is to build cross-discipline teams that don't exceed this range. For some teams, the number of disciplines desired to achieve a goal can be large. For example, a level prototyping team may need the following:

- Two level artists
- One prop artist
- One texture artist
- One animator
- One sound designer
- One concept artist
- One level designer
- One gameplay designer
- One graphics programmer
- One gameplay programmer
- One AI programmer

This is a 12-member team that begins to exhibit some of the problems seen on larger teams. For example, some members are more likely than others to not speak up and be heard. This inhibits the team from raising their performance through commitment and shared accountability.

Another problem with larger teams is that subteams or cliques tend to form. I was on a team such as the previous one. The designers and artists formed separate cabals that raised communication barriers. Whenever I visited one of these cliques, they would criticize the other. These criticisms weren't shared between the two factions, so problems lingered. This had a major impact on the quality of the prototype levels and the speed at which they were created. ScrumMaster intervention eventually resolved this, but a smaller team would have self-corrected this problem sooner.

A team like this might consider separating into two teams with smaller goals that "stage" the development of prototype levels, but that introduces dependency and accountability issues. I encourage teams to try different arrangements for a few sprints, and if that doesn't address the problems, they can reform into a larger team again.

NOTE Some studios have used teams of three to five people in size and report that it worked very well.

DRAWING THE LINE

At High Moon Studios, we established some "laws" that were meant to describe the practices and rules that projects and their teams had the authority over and others that they did not. We referred to these laws as the "state laws" that defined project and team authority and "federal laws" that defined decisions that were made for them.

For international readers, in the United States federal laws govern the entire country, while state laws govern those within a state. If the two conflict, federal laws take precedence.

One example of a federal law was the use of a studiowide engine and pipeline technology. Studio management didn't want the teams creating significantly different engine and pipelines for their own games. We wanted the benefits that came from individuals understanding a shared technology as they moved from one project to another. An example of a state law was how the project organized themselves into individual teams and implemented items from the product backlog.

Leadership

When I was a child, my father decided to teach me to swim, as his father had taught him, by tossing me into a lake where the water was over my head. After watching the bubbles come up for half a minute, he dove in and pulled me out. I didn't learn to swim that day. In fact, I learned to avoid even trying for the rest of the summer. With my children, we have adopted a more gradual approach of coaching them to take on greater swimming challenges from a few seconds of dog paddling through the point where they can swim back and forth across an Olympic-sized swimming pool.

Leadership in an agile organization has a similar challenge. Agile organizations need to grow leadership at every level but find the approach between micromanaging teams and throwing them in over their head that will bring about success. Both of those extremes will lead to failure.

Project Leadership

The responsibilities of project leaders (lead programmers, lead artists, lead designers, and so on) may change as teams adopt agile:

- **Design and planning:** Leads still define the design (gameplay, technical, concept, and so on) for their discipline in concert with the other disciplines and oversee how the design is implemented.
- **Resource allocation:** Leads will estimate how many people in their discipline are needed on the project, what areas they will work on, and approximately when they will work on them, but these will only be estimates. The teams will slowly take over the responsibility of identifying areas of need on a per-sprint and even release basis.
- **Task creation and management:** Leads no longer break down work into tasks that they estimate, assign, and track. Teams manage this themselves. Leads still participate in sprint planning and helping members of their discipline improve their task identification and estimating skills.
- **Review and promotion:** Although leads may continue to review every member of their discipline on a regular, usually annual, basis, the performance of the team becomes a more important part of their the information for the review (see the "Reviews" section).
- **Mentoring:** Leads work with less experienced developers to improve their productivity. The lead role shifts from managing primarily through project management tools to one where they "go and see" what is occurring with each developer as frequently as possible (see the "Mentoring" section).

Team self-management challenges the lead role definition. It's difficult for many leads to give up making detailed decisions for teams on a daily basis and allow them to risk failure, even for smaller challenges. However, the benefits of growing self-management behaviors become apparent as some of the more mundane management duties of a lead, such as task creation, estimation, and tracking, are taken over by the team. For example, a project staff of 80 developers generates and tracks approximately 1,600 tasks during a four-week sprint.[1] This is an overwhelming volume of detail for any lead

1. 10 teams × 8 people × one task per day × 20 days per sprint

group to manage and draws their time away from the more valuable leadership duties of their role.

Mentoring

The most important role of the lead is to mentor developers to improve how they work. An example is when lead programmers pair with associate programmers to teach them how to improve their coding and design practices.

> **NOTE**
>
> Junior programmers often implement simulation solutions that are far too expensive in the CPU resources they consume. I recall one new programmer who was tasked with implementing a wind effect. They started implementing a complex fluid dynamic engine that used 90% of the CPU time to simulate thousands of air particles. A lead programmer intervened and showed them a few tricks to introduce a good effect in a few hours that required hardly any CPU time.

Scrum creates opportunities for leads to continue working on games and lead by way of example instead of through a spreadsheet. Rather than spending half their day with a tool creating and tracking tasks, they interact with people working one on one.

Reviews

Another critical role of leadership is to provide career support for the developers in their discipline. In companies that employ a matrix management structure, this takes the form of a yearly management and salary review. This reinforces discipline-centric performance over team-centric performance.

For example, if an artist is evaluated on how productive they were creating assets over the past year, then they focus on faster asset creation to improve this metric. As a result, when a teammate interrupts the artist about a game problem, it reduces the number of assets they create; the artist then tries to isolate him or herself to reduce these interruptions for the benefit of a better review. This is not a good cycle.

Leads in agile environments have introduced frequent team-based peer reviews to supplement, if not replace, the yearly review process. This allows feedback about teamwork and cross-discipline collaboration to be introduced. Individual lead roles for each discipline will be described in greater detail in coming chapters.

DIRECTOR ROLES

The game industry is filled with director roles, such as art directors, technical directors, and so on. Usually these roles are given to members of a discipline who show the greatest level of craftsmanship but who also have authority over the work, rather than a group of people. Often these roles exist to oversee and approve or disapprove of the work being done in their area. Scrum teams need to adjust their practices to meet the needs of these roles, such as described in Chapter 11, "Agile Art and Audio."

Game Teams and Collaboration

Game development requires a high level of collaboration between diverse disciplines. For example, a character in a game has animation, physics, textures, models, sounds, and behaviors that need to work seamlessly together to produce the whole. A single discipline cannot accomplish all of these functions alone. They need to work closely with other disciplines to create features.

Unfortunately, as team sizes grow, disciplines tend to pool together. This delays integration of their work and leads to many problems. Scrum focuses development on frequently integrated features that drive close cross-discipline collaboration. Daily cross-discipline collaboration leads developers to think of themselves as game developers first and as programmers, designers, arts, QA, producers, and so on, second.

In this section, we'll examine various team structures that are used by agile game teams to promote collaboration across the project and across disciplines.

COLLABORATION, INTERRUPTED

There is no shortage of ways in which companies try to build morale with large cross-discipline teams. I've been involved in a few of these potentially dangerous exercises myself in the past.

I still recall the day that a team-building exercise nearly maimed me. It was on a paintball field located in high chaparral land east of San Diego. I was lying flat on my back, nearly out of ammunition, while nearly 30 electrical engineers were trying to shoot me.

I was a young software engineer working for a military avionics company. During my career in the defense industry, I witnessed the animosity between electrical engineers and software engineers. To the electrical engineers, we lacked true engineering discipline and were overpaid. They often considered our code as a "necessary evil." We saw the electrical engineers as elitist in attitude and outdated in their technical philosophy.

Personally I believed the electrical engineers hated us because we were often the heroes of a project. The software we wrote often worked around the flaws in their hardware that threatened a project in its final hours.

It started with a division into two teams. Naturally, one team consisted of the electrical engineers, and the other consisted of us software engineers.

I won't lie and say we were better fighters that day. We weren't. I won't make excuses and accuse them of cheating, although they brought some suspicious-looking tools with them. The plain fact was that the software team lost most games, and we lost them badly.

I faced the greatest challenge during the last game of the day. We were playing an elimination match in a small plywood "village." The goal of the game was for one team to eliminate every player on the opposing team to win.

It was another bloodbath for the software team. We were quickly decimated. I survived by hiding, with several other programmers, on the roof of a plywood hut. The partial cover of three walls protected us, and the only way to enter the roof was through a hole in the floor from the room below.

One by one, my roof mates were killed off in heroic displays of gallantry and ignorance of the value of cover. I was content to hunch low and survive.

Suddenly the referees blew their whistles signaling the end of the game. They believed that all the software engineers were dead! I jumped up, roaring in defiance at what I hoped was one or two remaining enemies. My roar was quickly choked when I saw that nearly the entire enemy team of 30 electrical engineers was still alive. Endless seconds seemed to pass as we considered each other. Then one of the referees announced, "Game on!" and blew his whistle. I will never forget the sight of all those electrical engineers, shouting with gleeful nerd rage, running toward me as I ducked back into cover.

I held out for a while. I even managed to kill a few of the enemy engineers. I would love to say that I was a hero that day, but it was not to be. Someone eventually shot me. The electrical engineers completed their victory over us, and we went back to work with renewed feelings of antagonism.

Feature Teams

Features teams are cross-discipline teams that develop core game features. For example, the small cross-disciplined team shown in Figure 8.1 could take full responsibility for a driving mechanic.

A major benefit of feature teams is the sense of ownership they experience. Participating in the full development of a few mechanics is far more satisfying to most developers than participating part-time on many. For many developers, this gives a greater sense of accomplishment.

DISCIPLINE	ROLE
Designer	Tune driving controls and layout test levels
Designer	
Artist	Create vehicles and props and test level geometry
Artist	
Programmer	Program vehicle drive-train, physics, and artificial intelligence for opponent vehicles
Programmer	
Programmer	
Audio Designer	Sound support for vehicales, level, and gameplay

FIGURE 8.1 An example driving mechanics team

A feature team should have everyone they need to build the mechanics. In practice, this is difficult to accomplish. Sometimes teams need to share disciplines in short supply. An example of this is an effects (FX) artist who is utilized 25% of the time by any single team. Often this person is shared among multiple teams.

Functional Teams

Functional teams are composed of developers who are mostly of the same discipline yet still work on a key feature. Although less common than feature teams, functional teams have their benefits. One example is a platform team comprised of mostly programmers. These programmers are experts in optimizing performance for a particular platform such as the PlayStation 3 (PS3) or Xbox 360. Concentrating these individuals on a single team focuses effort on challenging problems that are wasteful for feature teams to solve on their own. For example, if the PS3 programmers are spread across multiple teams, then their efforts creating a working PS3 build are diluted.

Functional teams are typically used only for foundational or infrastructure work. Using functional teams for higher-level, cross-discipline work often leads to solutions that are more suitable for the discipline than the game.

An example of a poorly conceived functional team was one formed to create the character AI for a game. This team consisted of AI programmers who wanted to create the best-architected AI possible. Unfortunately, their efforts led to AI functionality that was handed off to other teams that neither understood how the AI worked nor benefitted from many of the features designed into it. Ultimately this team broke up, and the AI programmers were scattered around the project to implement AI needed by various teams.

Production Teams

Production teams are cross-discipline teams that are used for game development projects that have a production phase. These teams have a more defined pipeline of work for creating content and applying some of the lean and kanban practices described in Chapter 7, "Video Game Project Planning."

Production teams may exchange members as needed with other production teams to maintain a steady flow of asset creation. Production teams often form from feature teams as a mechanic transitions from pre-production to production. For example, most of the programmers might leave the level pre-production team as it enters production, to be replaced with more modelers, texture artists, and audio designers.

Shared Infrastructure Teams

Shared infrastructure teams provide shared support services such as engine development and cinematic and audio services that multiple games rely on. These teams are dominated by one discipline, such as composers on the audio team, but also have other disciplines on the team, such as programmers, to support their pipelines and tools.

A frequently asked question is how shared infrastructure (SI) teams should organize themselves in an agile project environment. Since they support multiple teams, they receive requests for features that cannot be as easily prioritized as they are for a single team. This can create confusion and conflict between the SI team and their "customers," the games that depend upon them.

There are a number of valuable practices for these teams:

- SI teams require their own backlog and product owner. Having more than one backlog and one product owner is a recipe for disaster. The team should have every benefit that other agile teams have in an understandable backlog and single vision.
- Customer teams should identify priorities during release planning and include the SI team (or at least their lead and product owner) in their release planning. SI teams usually need a longer planning horizon than a single sprint.

- SI teams should factor support into their velocity whether it is identified for tasks or not. Setting aside a certain percentage of your bandwidth for unexpected maintenance is critical.
- Loaning SI team members out to another team for a sprint is OK, but it should be identified in release planning. It's very valuable to have SI team members see how their "product" is being used.
- The SI product owner should ideally be at the executive level (or in frequent contact with them) to arbitrate conflicting product priorities. Deciding to support one game over the other is a company-level (strategic) decision and should have the input from the people who run the studio. For example, the CTO should be the product owner for the SI team.
- With their own product owner and backlog, an SI team can feel like a real team and take ownership of their work.
- SI teams are also the model for "live support teams" that support one or more games that have been shipped. An example of this is a team that supports MMOGs and their large player communities.

Tool Teams

A tool team consists of a number of tool creators (programmers, technical artists, QA) whose customers are users of a common tool set and pipeline.

Like a shared infrastructure team, a tool team often supports multiple projects and has their own product backlog.

Tool teams have the added benefit of releasing tools to customers who are in the same building, not just stakeholders who represent them. Having tool users who can participate in backlog definition, prioritization, planning, and reviews is a major benefit to the tool developers. Tool development can be even more exploratory than game development and benefits greatly from using an agile approach.

Pool Teams

A pool team is a collection of developers from a single discipline. Unlike other teams, they don't have their own sprint goals. They exist to support teams that do. Examples of this are a pool of animators that could support a feature team that needs a large number of animations in a single sprint.

Another benefit of a pool team is to provide a service center for art production. This is also referred to as **in sourcing**. Environment artists and animators are in greater demand during production, and pool teams help level the resource requirements in a larger development studio.

Pool teams require more planning and management during a release to ensure that they are fully utilized. Pool teams are more commonly used in late pre-production or production.

Integration Teams

It's challenging to share a common vision with larger projects with more than 40 developers. The vision among separate teams can drift, even with a hierarchy of product owners. As a result, some projects have "integration teams" that integrate mechanics, developed initially by feature teams, into a unified experience.

These teams are similar in structure to feature teams. The difference is that they are responsible for the overall theme of the game. For example, in an action-racing game, eventually the core team takes over the driving mechanics from the team that developed it once it is mature enough. From this point forward, they modify and maintain both mechanics to seamlessly work together.

OBJECTION: POOL TEAMS AND CORE TEAMS—THESE DON'T SOUND VERY "SCRUM" AT ALL

Ideally, every team should be a functional team, but the sheer number of specialties required for game development leads to pool and core teams. Scrum is more about teams finding ways to perform best rather than "following the rules out of the book."

Scaling and Distributing Scrum

Although the ideal Scrum teams size is five to nine people, modern game development projects typically require more developers. Sometimes the developers are separated across multiple locations. Scrum has practices that allow it to scale and distribute multiple Scrum teams.

This section will examine the practices commonly used to scale up Scrum: holding the Scrum of Scrums meeting, creating a hierarchy of product owners, aligning sprint dates, creating communities of practice, and avoiding dependencies. It will conclude with discussing the challenges and solutions of distributed development.

The Problem with Large Teams

Project staff sizes for many console and PC games have grown steadily from the "good old days" of the lone developer who designed, coded, illustrated, scored, and tested the game on their own to project team sizes that now often exceed 100 people. Unfortunately, the effectiveness of a 100-person project is usually not 100 times that of a one-person project. This loss of effectiveness has many sources, the main one being the overhead of communication.

Consider the combinations of any two people who may need to communicate on a project. These "lines of communication" grow much faster than the number of people on the project (see Figure 8.2). For example, a project with 100 people has 4,950 possible lines of communication between members.[2] This is far too many for everyone on the team to grasp in order to know who to talk to when a question or issue arises. As a result, hierarchies of management were created to oversee this complexity.

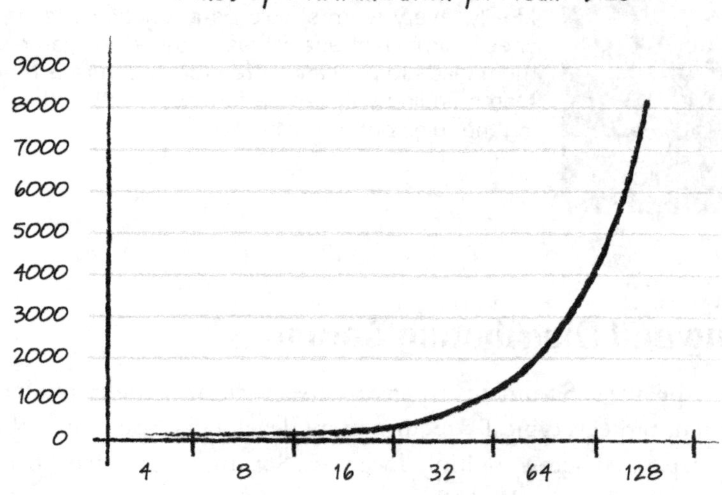

FIGURE 8.2 Team size and lines of communication

2. The formula for lines of communication is $n*(n-1)/2$, where n is the number of people on the project.

Such hierarchies create barriers between any two people who need to solve problems quickly. For example, if an animator needs a fix in the animation code, they have to send a request for their change to their lead. That lead, in turn, passes the request to a project manager. The project manager sends the request to the lead programmer who then communicates the change to a programmer to make the change. This entire process depends highly on every link in the communication chain working quickly and on the information being passed accurately. Unfortunately, this doesn't usually happen.

The Scrum of Scrums

The central practice for scaling Scrum is the Scrum of Scrums meeting. Figure 8.3 shows how a larger project could divide into subteams and how each team sends a member of their team to the Scrum of Scrums.

This meeting enables one or more representatives from every team to gather to inform other teams about their progress and impediments. Who attends the meeting often depends on what needs to be reported. It's very effective for identifying shared or potential problems that one team can solve for all the others.

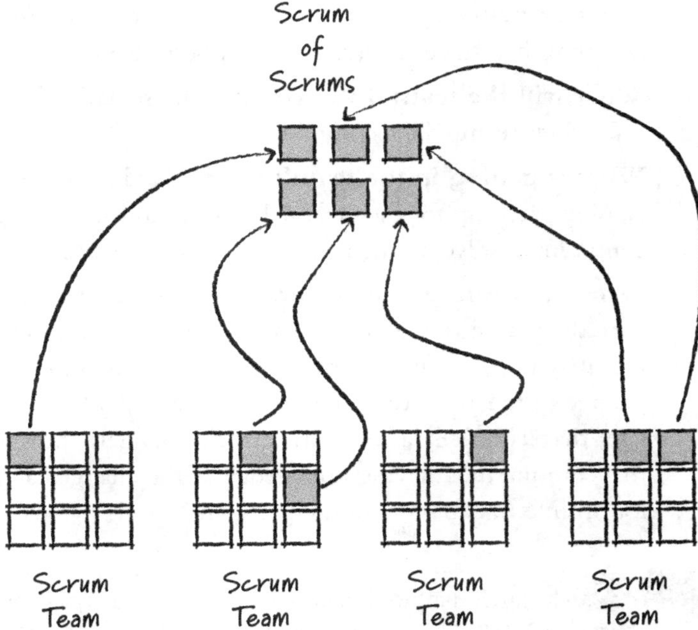

FIGURE 8.3 The Scrum of Scrums meeting

For example, an engine technology team often works with multiple teams to improve the engine technology. Changes to this technology often create impediments for teams when rolled out because of unforeseen bugs. Imminent changes to the shared technology are described at the Scrum of Scrums so any resulting problems are quickly identified and resolved. In this case, a technical lead from the shared technology team attends the meeting to report the pending changes.

The Scrum of Scrums is different from a team's daily scrum meetings:

- **It doesn't have to be daily:** It can be weekly or semiweekly. The group that meets should decide on the best frequency for it.
- **It is for problem solving:** The meeting is not timeboxed to 15 minutes. Potential solutions are addressed in the meeting. This meeting may be the only time when these individuals meet during the week, and the problems they discuss have larger impact on the project.
- **The questions are different:** The meeting starts with everyone answering slightly different questions:
  - **What did the team do since we last met?** Each team's representative describes, in general terms, what their team has accomplished since the last Scrum of Scrums meetings.
  - **What will the team do next?** The representatives discuss what their team will accomplish next.
  - **What is getting in the team's way?** What impediments are causing problems for each team? These are usually issues that the team cannot solve on their own or communicate to other teams.
  - **What is a team about to throw in the other team's way?** Like the previous engine example, teams often commit changes that may impact other teams. Perhaps a team is committing a change to the animation engine, which every other team uses, later that day. If characters start moving strangely shortly after this commit, then having knowledge of the change can save a lot of time tracking down the problem.

DON'T NAME INDIVIDUALS

It's important to discuss a whole team's progress and not the progress of each individual on each team when answering the first two questions at the Scrum of Scrums. Otherwise, the meeting takes far longer!

The Scrum of Scrums doesn't have a product backlog, but it creates a short backlog of shared impediments that are addressed at every meeting. An example of a shared impediment is when the one FX artist for the studio is out sick and it impacts multiple teams. Many impediments that are identified take days to resolve, so tracking them is beneficial.

A ScrumMaster for the Scrum of Scrums isn't necessary, but teams often assign one of their members to the role to help keep the meeting on track.

A Hierarchy of Product Owners

The demand for a product owner's time on game teams can be greater than the demand for product owners in other industries. The reason is that teams are challenged with knowing if the "fun" they are creating is the "fun" the product owner wanted. Questions such as how "bouncy" a physics response should be or how "snappy" an animation transition needs to be are subjective and may need daily feedback from the person who owns the vision for the game: the product owner.

For large projects, with a dozen or more teams, this creates a problem. The product owner's time becomes spread too thin, and they cannot effectively maintain a shared vision for the game across all teams. Without a shared vision, each mechanic will drift from the original vision as it evolves, and the game becomes less consistent and appealing.

An effective practice is for the product owner for a large project to delegate some ownership. One way of doing this is to establish a hierarchy of product owners. A lead product owner guides the project, and each core mechanic has a product owner. Figure 8.4 shows an example of such a product owner hierarchy.

The lead product owner oversees the two product owners who work with one or two Scrum teams. The lead product owner continues to work with teams directly, such as the user interface team, but they delegate "product owner as pig" responsibility to the teams that have their own product owner.

Each product owner works with their teams during the sprint, helping them plan the sprint and working with them daily to ensure that they achieve the sprint goal. For example, as a product owner on a team implementing a driving mechanic, my role included educating the team about the shared vision for the mechanic. This often required conversations about the balance between a "sim" vs. "arcade" feel for the controls, vehicle physics, and the environment.

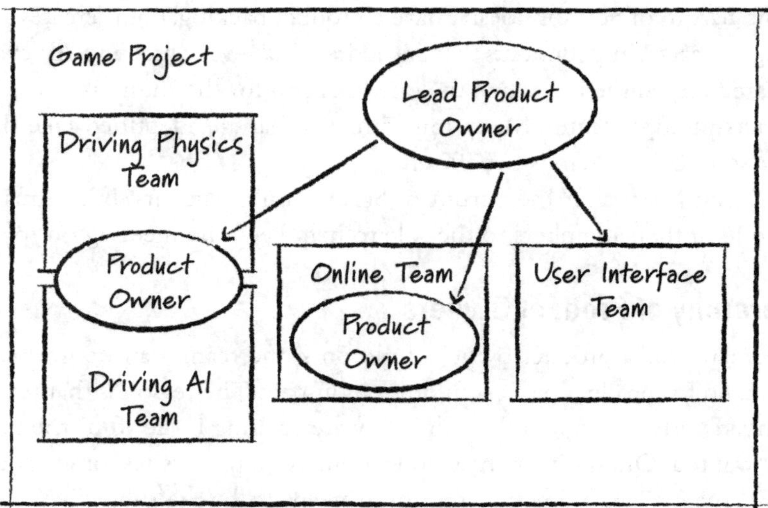

FIGURE 8.4 An example product owner hierarchy

The product owners need to ensure that there is a shared vision for the entire project. This includes frequent meetings among them all, including the Scrum of Scrums meetings, to address any questions about the game's vision.

Product owners take direction from the lead product owner between sprints and release planning. There is often a difference of opinion on the best path to achieve release goals between the product owners. The insight of a team's product owner is invaluable in finding the best path, but the lead product owner is responsible for safeguarding a consistent vision for the game across all mechanics and features.

A product owner team creates a shared vision on a large project and ensures consistency of vision everywhere.

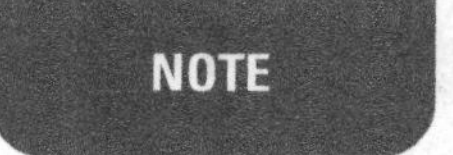

Integration teams are a type of team that helps ensure a shared vision on a large project is maintained as the features and mechanics are integrated.

Aligning Sprint Dates

Separate Scrum teams working on a project may align their sprint planning and review dates or have independent schedules. Figure 8.5 shows the difference between the two dispositions.

For teams with independent schedules, there are some benefits. The biggest one is that each team doesn't have to vie for time with the product owner. For multiple teams with aligned dates, it can be challenging to schedule the product owner's time, especially for planning the next sprint.

Nonetheless, it's usually best to align the sprints (Cohn 2009). The benefits to the game are as follows:

- **Teams can exchange members:** Following the sprint review, nobody has a commitment to any sprint goal, so it is easy for teams to trade members for the next sprint.
- **An integrated view of the game is encouraged:** Teams with the same sprint review date can integrate all work into a single build so that the entire game is reviewed. This encourages more cross-team collaboration and an integrated view of the game.

A hierarchy of product owners on larger teams eliminates the problem of the lead product owner being spread too thin when teams using synchronized sprints need to plan the next sprint.

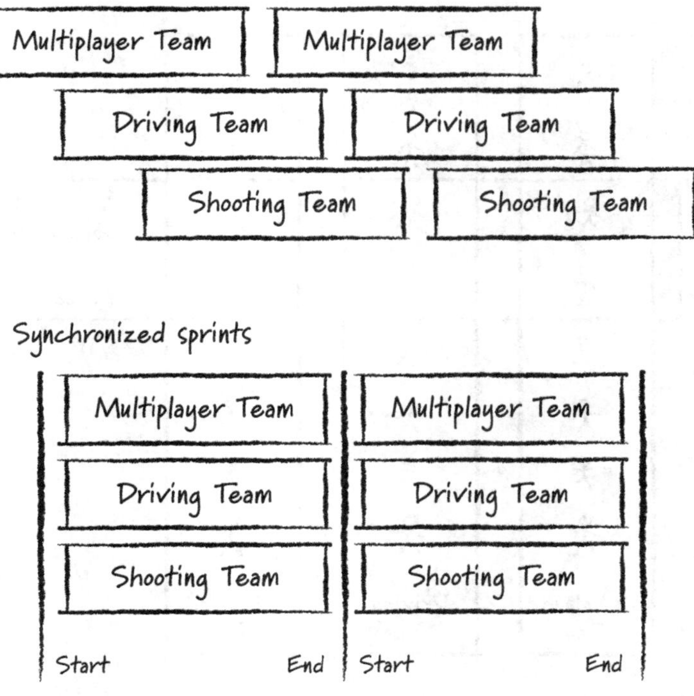

FIGURE 8.5 Independent and synchronized sprints

Communities of Practice

Another challenge created by large Scrum projects is the potential loss of communication caused by the separation of discipline, or functional expertise, across multiple cross-discipline teams. For example, if all the graphics programmers are spread across multiple teams, what is to prevent them from solving the same graphics problems in different ways?

NOTE

We had this problem when all the AI programmers were split up across three feature teams. Each team implemented a unique AI state machine. One team implemented a script-based system, another implemented a C++-based system, and the third team developed one that was manipulated with a graphical interface.

The solution is to establish **communities of practice** that can share knowledge and eliminate the duplication of effort. Figure 8.6 shows how the AI programmers from across multiple Scrum teams can form an AI community of practice.

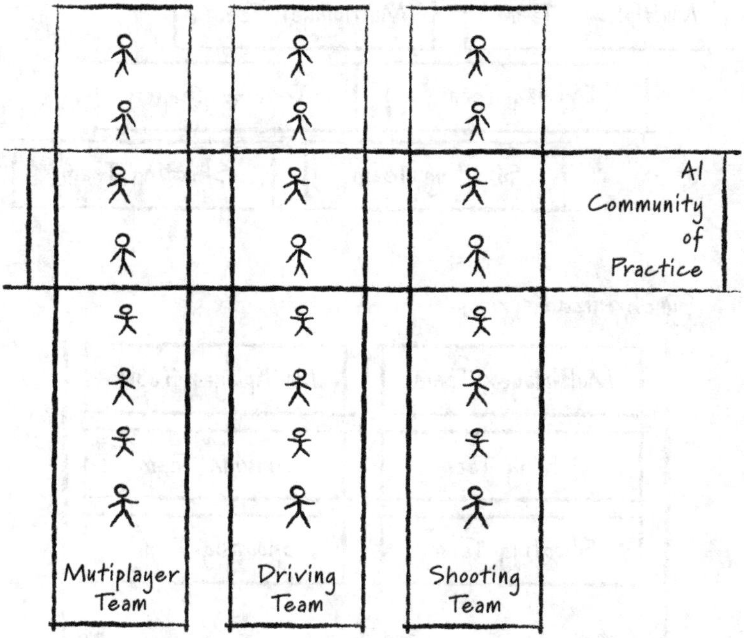

FIGURE 8.6 An AI community of practice

Each community can decide how frequently they need to meet and address the issues they are facing. The AI community might discuss common solutions they could each implement. The ScrumMasters can form a community to share improvements to their team's practices. The designers could form a community to complain about everyone else.[3]

Communities of practice do not have their own sprint goals or assign work outside their own teams. Their only purpose is to share information.

Avoiding Dependencies

Interteam dependencies inside a sprint can prevent teams from achieving their goals. Consider a team whose sprint goal is to implement a wall-climbing mechanic but has to rely on another team to provide the animation. Because of the separation of teams and goals, it's likely that the mechanic team will hand off their work to the animation team near the end of the sprint rather than collaborating daily. At best, this limits the number of iterations that can occur with the mechanic. At worst, the goals that the animation team has for their own sprint might prevent them from handing back the wall-climbing animation in time.

When projects begin using Scrum, these dependencies are quite common, and they are the source of many impediments and sprint failures. Over time, teams change their membership to reduce dependencies and establish other practices to prevent their impact.

Changing membership to create more self-contained, cross-discipline teams is the easiest solution. If the team implementing mechanics needs full-time animation work throughout the sprint, having an animator join them is best.

In many cases, there isn't enough work to justify a specialist joining one team full-time. In these situations, teams can share specialists within a sprint or trade them between sprints. Doing this requires a bit more planning and foresight to avoid overlapping demands for a specialist's time. There are two places where this is done: at release planning meetings and at lookahead meetings.

Release Planning

In release planning, teams identify potential sprint goals for the next several sprints. Using these goals, they identify sprints where part-time specialists or a concentration of disciplines (such as a bunch of texture artists) might be

3. One design group I knew actually did this...they were able to keep it mostly constructive!

needed. Often these will uncover conflicting needs among teams. The best way to resolve these is to raise or lower the priorities of stories creating the conflicts. For example, if two teams require the same FX artist full-time during the same sprint, then the product owner changes the priority of one of the stories requiring FX work enough to shift the sprint for one team to remove the overlap.

Lookahead Planning

Release planning does not identify specific goals for more than several sprints because change is more likely. As a result, regular lookahead planning meetings are held during the release to update the goals for approaching sprints.

Lookahead planning takes an hour or two during each sprint. It can be combined with prioritization meetings. It identifies changes to team membership that may be necessary and any pending conflicts that the product owner and teams need to navigate around.

BORROWING AN AUDIO ENGINEER

Our team was working on a driving mechanic. We were able to implement much of the simple audio ourselves. However, the sprint goal of adding complex audio behavior for the drivetrain was approaching. This required engine sounds that would be realistic throughout the entire RPM range and blend between gears. This was a difficult problem to solve, especially since our vehicle was licensed, and the drivetrain physics (revolutions per minute [RPM] and torque curve) didn't match those of the actual vehicle. We asked the audio pool team if we could borrow one of their audio engineers for the sprint. We moved our goals around a bit with the product owner to accommodate a sprint where that team could free him up. This worked out well for both teams.

Problems occur with little warning on a day-to-day basis that require a specialist on another team to help out. For example, one of our projects had one UI scripter that could implement UI changes rapidly. Almost every day he was requested to help another team for an hour or so. Because of the demand for his time, his team would allow him to commit to only half the available hours during a sprint.

Requests like these can be handled in the Scrum of Scrums meeting described earlier. Whether or not a specialist can help another team within a sprint lies with the current team to which the specialist belongs.

> **NOTE**
>
> Scrum doesn't solve the problem of specialists who become bottlenecks, but it makes such problems transparent and therefore easier to solve. In the case of the UI scripter, the solution might be to hire more people who can script or cross-train others to be able to write UI scripts. The ideal solution depends on the project and the studio's needs.

Distributed Teams

To reduce costs and help balance staffing demands, studios frequently distribute the development of games. With this model, teams distributed across two or more locations develop core mechanics and features of a game in parallel. This is different from outsourcing, which typically focuses on distributing certain types of production work, such as asset creation or technical support.

The challenges of distributed development are mainly those of communication, which are much more likely to impact distributed teams.

This section examines the challenges that face distributed teams and some of the agile tools available to overcome them.

Challenges

Three common challenges affect distributed teams:

- **They lack a shared vision:** It's more common for distributed teams to experience their visions "drifting apart" because of physical separation. This divergence leads to conflicting or incompatible efforts from the teams.
- **They have a less collaboration:** Physically separated teams cannot collaborate as closely as colocated teams. If the differences in time zones is great enough, a single question can take a day to answer.
- **Iteration and dependencies can destroy the benefits:** The potential savings in cost for distributed teams is easily lost when time and effort is wasted through iteration delays and dependencies between teams.

Agile Tools

Many of the agile practices discussed help distributed teams overcome these challenges. They give teams the opportunity to maintain a shared vision, increase collaboration, and avoid going down separate paths.

Scrum Teams Align with Location Usually each distributed team is a separate Scrum team. There are occasions when it's beneficial to have members of a Scrum team distributed to share knowledge and create bonds between locations (Cohn 2009), but for the most part having each Scrum team colocated is best.

When each Scrum team is colocated, they can more effectively collaborate on a shared sprint goal. Such teams need a local product owner but should find ways to hold sprint review and planning meetings with other teams and the lead product owner either in person or through a video-conferencing system.

Shared Scrum of Scrums A video- or phone-conferenced Scrum of Scrums meeting is essential for distributed teams. These don't have to occur every day, but they should be held at least once a week. If teams are spread across many time zones, the time of the conference call should not be fixed so as to impose a constant burden on one team more than the others. The meeting time is changed on a regular basis so that attendees from different locations have to come in early or stay late.

Shared Release Planning It's critical for a release plan to be developed and shared to the greatest degree possible among the teams. Often this will include flying one or more members from each location to a central place where the meeting is held. It's often a necessary cost that cannot be avoided with distributed teams. You either spend money on airfares and hotels or spend much more on the costs incurred by divergent goals.

There are many ways to organize depending on the how the teams are distributed. The sidebar "A Global Game Development Story" tells the story of how one company organizes their releases across three continents and sixteen time zones.

Improved Sharing of Builds, Assets, and Code A problem with large projects is how to share the large number of changes that occur. Frequent small changes can perpetually break the build, and bulk changes committed weeks apart can bring teams to a halt for days at a time. With colocated teams, this problem is bad enough. With distributed teams, defects passed across in shared builds, assets, and code can be disastrous. When a single question can take a day for an answer, tracking down a problem and the necessary expertise to solve it consumes days rather than hours or minutes. Extra care must be taken to protect distributed teams from external defects. This requires a focus on improved commit practices and testing described in Chapter 9, "Faster Iterations."

Processes and Tools Agile methods value "individuals and interactions over processes and tools." A wider team distribution can impede interactions and place more weight on processes and tools. Distributed teams often use more tools to track and display sprint progress and product backlogs and share knowledge. Wikis and other documentation tools are beneficial and are used more with colocated teams.

A GLOBAL GAME DEVELOPMENT STORY

CCP games, the developer and publisher of EVE Online, was founded in 1997 with development split between studios in Reykjavik, Iceland; Atlanta, United States; and Shanghai, China. It has grown to have more than 400 employees and to host more than 300,000 active subscribers in a single online world.

In the fall of 2008, CCP undertook the development of its tenth expansion pack called Apocrypha. Apocrypha was the most ambitious expansion of the EVE universe. It added major technical features and significantly extended the size of the EVE world. The goal of the company was to release the expansion pack within six months following a four-month development cycle (see Figure 8.7).

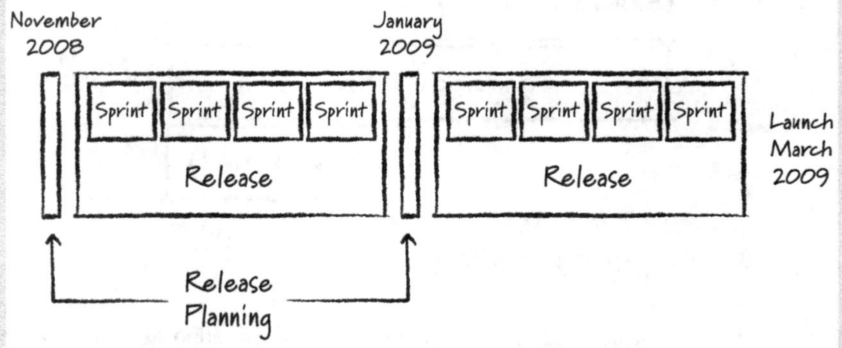

FIGURE 8.7 The Apocrypha timeline

This ambitious goal required CCP's worldwide development studios to work in parallel. Features and content developed simultaneously across three continents had to seamlessly come together to achieve their goal. Normally this would be the introduction to a disaster story, but CCP pulled it off. CCP is a longtime adopter of agile methods, specifically Scrum.

In the case of Apocrypha, with more than 120 developers in 13 Scrum teams spread across three continents, 9 product owners were required. These product owners took their direction for the game from a project management group in Iceland.

Release Planning

The stakeholders identified two release cycles of development to release the expansion pack in March 2009. Ideally, release planning should gather every developer, but it was nearly impossible to collect 120 people from around the world in one location, so CCP had to create some innovative practices to perform release planning.

Apocrypha release planning meetings took place over a single 12-hour period. A high-definition video conferencing network facilitated this meeting and allowed every developer to take part.

Since most of the development staff, including the project management group, was in Reykjavík, the meeting was focused there. It started at 9 a.m. Because of the time difference, it was far too early for the developers in Atlanta to attend. It was the end of the day for the developers in Shanghai, so they and the Reykjavík group met first. Hours later the Shanghai team would leave, and the Atlanta team would join to discuss the release (see Figure 8.8).

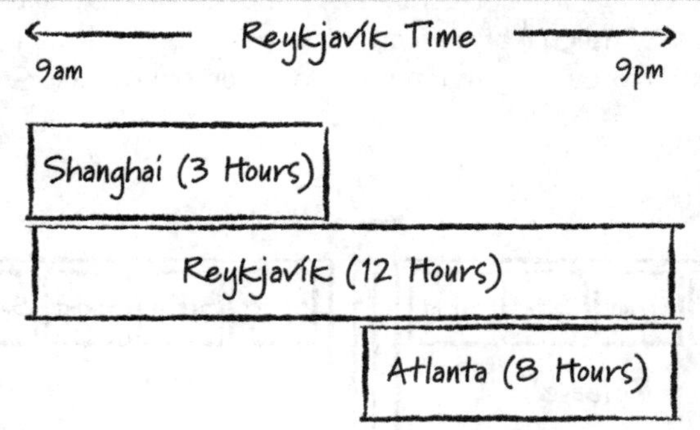

FIGURE 8.8 Overlapping meeting times

You can see a time-lapse video of this amazing meeting in Reykjavik on YouTube at www.youtube.com/watch?v=gMtv1zDUxvo.

It's important to note that the time zone limitations and the limitations of video conferencing allowed only two teams to meet at one time. In this case, Atlanta and Shanghai could not attend together. To avoid potential problems, two developers from Shanghai flew to Reykjavík to participate at the core meeting and to represent the Shanghai teams.

Each pair of locations would discuss the release goals and begin breaking them down into smaller goals that were reasonably sized to fit into a sprint. The conferencing network enabled multiple simultaneous meetings to occur. This was necessary since many questions raised during this process required a great deal of live conversation among the entire staff or individual teams.

The goal of the release planning meeting was to generate a set of potential sprint goals for each of the 13 teams that would fulfill the release BHAGS. This wouldn't be the last time that the teams would communicate. Daily issues were communicated, and a build of the game was demonstrated every sprint, which were two weeks long. Changes to the release plan were made every sprint to adjust for the realities of development.

After two releases, Apocrypha was ready to do final testing and polishing, and on March 10, 2009, it shipped on schedule.

Solving the Problems

A globally distributed development team can be successful in creating a high-quality product within budget and within the schedule limits. The raw ingredients for this success can be summarized in several points:

- **Local vision and ownership:** Scrum enables individual cross-disciplined teams to take ownership of their sprint goal and achieve it independently. Having a product owner on-site who is responsible for the vision of what the team is creating is essential.
- **Iterative development methodology:** Creating an integrated, potentially shippable version of the game every two weeks from work done around the world forces problems to the surface and demonstrates real progress. Without this, critical problems can remain submerged until late in the project, when it is too late to avoid delays and cost overruns.
- **High-bandwidth communication:** Communication on large colocated teams is difficult enough. On large distributed teams, it can be the main challenge. Teams must have the tools to communicate effectively, such as a networked conferencing system, that are reliable and ubiquitous, as well as a methodology that creates transparency, such as Scrum.

Distributed teams will never be as effective as colocated teams, however. What is lost from daily face-to-face communication cannot be made up through conference calls. But it can come close enough to ensure that the teams are productive.

Summary

There is no single formula for creating the best teams on a game project. The teams and practices described here result from adapting the existing Scrum roles and team to improve how people work together and how a vision is unified and shared. Exploring roles and team structures is an ongoing process. Teams must use the retrospective practice to find ways to improve how they work together and with the stakeholders of the game. By allowing teams to take ownership and authority over some of the daily aspects of their life, they are more likely to take responsibility for their work. This doesn't happen overnight. It takes years in many cases and will create head-on collisions with studio leadership culture. The results are worth the effort.

Scrum scales up to projects of any size but drives changes in team structure, the project owner role, and practices such as the Scrum of Scrums.

Scrum also drives changes across disciplines, focusing the team on changing how they work day to day to improve communication and the pace of iteration. It also drives changes in how each discipline works. The remainder of this part of the book will address these changes.

The goal is to create teams that can take more ownership of development and have greater purpose in what they do.

Additional Reading

DeMarco, T., and T. Lister. 1999. *Peopleware: Productive Projects and Teams, Second Edition*. New York: Dorset House Publishing.

Katzenbach, J. R., and D. K. Smith. 2003. *The Wisdom of Teams: Creating the High-Performance Organization*. Cambridge, MA: Harvard Business School Press.

Larman, C., and B. Vodde. 2009. *Scaling Lean and Agile Development: Thinking and Organizational Tools for Large-Scale Scrum*. Boston: Addison-Wesley.

Leffingwell, D. 2007. *Scaling Software Agility: Best Practices for Large Enterprises*. Boston: Addison-Wesley.

Schwaber, K. 2007. *The Enterprise and Scrum*. Redmond, WA: Microsoft Press.

Chapter 9

Faster Iterations

In agile circles, iteration means one thing: It's the timebox in which product increments are made. For Scrum, the iteration is a sprint. For game developers, the term *iteration* means something more. It refers to the practice of creating an initial version of something (artwork, code, or a design), examining it, and then revising it until it's sufficiently improved.

Unfortunately, iterating isn't free. It takes time to revisit a past bit of art, code, design, audio, or other game element. The challenge facing all teams is to find ways to reduce the cost of iteration. A team that reduces the cost of iteration benefits in two ways: They iterate over gameplay elements more often, and they do so more frequently. These benefits result in an increase in their velocity.

Scrum focuses game developers on improving iteration time everywhere. The benefits of doing this are reinforced daily among cross-discipline teams and over the course of sprints through the measurement of velocity. As described in Chapter 6, "Agile Planning," velocity is measured as the number of story points accomplished every sprint. Stories not only require coding and asset creation but also debugging, tuning, and a degree of polishing to be considered done. These additional requirements drive the need for more iterations, and the longer the iteration time, the slower the velocity. Faster iteration improves velocity.

This chapter examines where the overhead of iterating code, assets, and tuning comes from and ways that a team and a project can reduce it and greatly increase their velocity.

A SEA STORY

One of the best things about developing games is that mistakes don't kill people or cost tens of thousands of dollars. The pace of development can be slowed under these conditions.

My last job before I joined the game development industry was developing autonomous underwater vehicles. These vehicles were meant to perform dangerous operations such as searching for underwater mines. Once launched, these multimillion-dollar vehicles were counted on to conduct their mission and return to us.

No matter how much we tested the software and hardware before a mission, some problems always surfaced at sea (no pun intended). Often these problems resulted in the vehicle not returning at the appointed time or location. When this happens, you realize how big the ocean really is.

As a result, changes to the vehicle were very carefully tested over the course of weeks. Even the smallest mishap would "scrub" a day at sea. This long iteration cycle slowed development progress to a crawl.

Where Does Iteration Overhead Come From?

Iteration overhead comes from many places:

- **Compile and link times:** How long does it take to make a code change and see the change in the game?
- **Tuning changes:** How long does it take to change a tuning parameter, such as bullet damage?
- **Asset changes:** How many steps does it take to change an animation and see it in the game?
- **Approvals:** What are the delays in receiving art direction approval for a texture change?
- **Integrating change from other teams:** How long do changes (new features and bug fixes) from other teams take to reach your team?
- **Defects:** How much time is lost to crashes or just trying to create a stable build?

These time delays between iterations last seconds to weeks in duration. Generally, the longer the time between the iterations, the more time is wasted either waiting or having to find lower-priority work to do before another iteration is attempted.

Measuring and Displaying Iteration Time

The complexity of a game, asset database, build environment, and pipeline grows over time. While this happens, iteration times tend to grow—there is more code to execute, and more assets in the database to sort through. Iterations are rapid at the start of a project but grow unacceptable over time. Before you know it, half your day is spent waiting for compiles, exports, baking,[1] or game loads.

The key to reducing iteration overhead is to measure, display, and address ways of reducing iterations continually.

Measuring Iteration Times

Iteration times should be measured frequently. To ensure that such measurements are performed frequently, the measurement process should be automated. A simple automated tool[2] should do this on a build server with a test asset, for example. A nice feature to add to this tool is to have it alert someone when this time spikes.

> **NOTE**
>
> One time a bug nearly doubled the bake time for a game, yet no one reported it during any of the daily scrums for a week. It seemed that people became immune to long iterations, which was more worrying than the bug itself.

Displaying Iteration Times

An iteration time trend chart displays the amount of time that an individual iteration time, such as build time, is taking and shows its trend over time. Like the sprint burndown, this chart displays a metric and its recent trend. Figure 9.1 shows an example iteration trend chart.

Showing a longer-term trend of iteration time is important since it is often hidden in daily noise. How frequently the chart is updated depends on how often a particular iteration time is measured and the need for updating it. Significant iteration metrics (based on how many people execute the iteration and how often) should be calculated daily, and the charts should be updated weekly.

---

1. **Baking** refers to the process of translating exported assets into a particular platform's native format.
2. If not automated, it is easily skipped or forgotten.

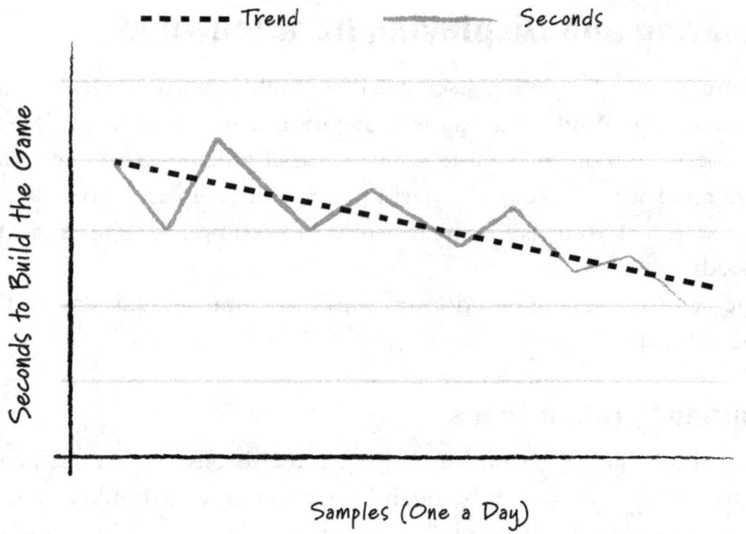

FIGURE 9.1 Recent iteration times and trend line

> **NOTE** A tool that automatically measures iteration time should also alert someone immediately when that time spikes.

EXPERIENCE: PS3 ASSET BAKING

When iterating on art assets, the largest amount of the time it takes to iterate on changes typically comes from baking or exporting an asset to a target platform's native format. On a PS3 project I worked on, every asset change required a 30-minute bake. Since the actual game executable was used to perform the baking, this time continued to creep up as features were added. It reached the point where everyone working with the PS3 spent half the day waiting for this process!

The team began by plotting asset iteration time on a daily basis. Over time, they dedicated a portion of their sprint backlog toward optimizing the baking tools and process. During a release, the team saw the trend of bake times slowly declining (33% in three months).

Without this regular measurement and display, it would have been easy for the team to lose track of the overall trend. Without keeping an eye on the metric, the bake times would have crept up gradually. Equally important was the value of introducing a large number of very small optimizations and seeing the effect over time. Often the "one big fix" simply doesn't exist, and nothing else is done because a significant benefit isn't immediately visible. The burndown demonstrates the value of "a lot of small fixes."

Personal and Build Iteration

It's useful to consider two types of iteration: personal iterations for each developer iterating at their own development station and the build iterations when code and asset changes are shared across the entire project. Both require constant monitoring and improvement.

Improving personal iteration is mainly a matter of improving tools and skills. Build iteration requires not only tool improvements but attention to the practices shared across teams to reduce the overhead inherent in sharing changes with many developers.

Personal Iteration

Personal iteration time includes the time it takes to do the following:

- Exporting and baking assets for a target platform a developer is iterating on
- Changing a design parameter (for example, bullet damage level) and trying it in the game
- Changing a line of code and testing it in the game

These are the smallest iteration times, but since they happen most frequently, they represent the greatest iteration overhead. Removing even five minutes from an export process used a dozen times a day improves velocity by more than 20%![3]

Some common improvements can speed up personal iteration times:

- **Upgrade development machines:** More memory, faster CPUs, and more cores increase the speed of tools. This is usually a short-term solution since it hides the real causes of delay.
- **Distributed build tools:** Distributed code-building packages reduce code iteration time by recompiling large amounts of code across many PCs. Tools also exist for distributed asset baking.
- **Parameter editing built into the game:** Many developers build a simple developer user interface into the game for altering parameters that need to be iterated.
- **Asset hot-loading:** Changed assets are loaded directly into a running game without requiring a restart or level reload.

---

3. This is based on four to five hours of useful work done per day.

NOTE The ideal iteration is instantaneous! It's far more difficult to achieve this ideal after a game engine has been created. For a new engine in development, I consider zero iteration time and hot loading to be necessary parts of the engine that must be maintained from the start of development.

Build Iteration

Build iteration is the process that spreads changes from one developer to all the other developers on the team. Sometimes this cycle is weeks long, but since members of the team do other things while waiting for a new build, it is not given as much attention as personal iteration times. However, the larger the team, the more impact the build iteration has on the team's effectiveness. It often results in a near disaster when there is a rush to get a working build out for a sprint or release. Bottlenecks and conflicts inevitably occur when everyone is trying to commit changes at the same time. The solution is to reduce this overhead so builds are safely iterated more frequently.

Figure 9.2 shows the build iteration cycle discussed.

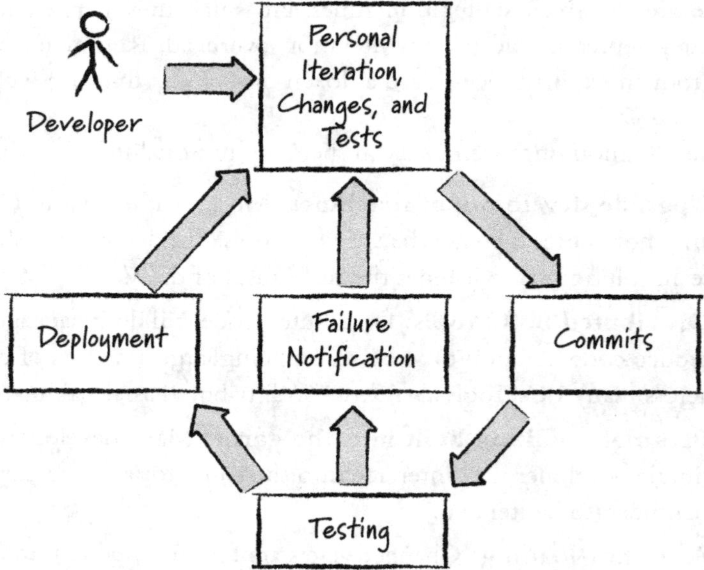

FIGURE 9.2 A build iteration cycle

Following personal iteration, a developer commits changes to a repository or revision control system. This is followed by a battery of tests. If these tests find a problem, the developer is notified and asked to fix the problem. Otherwise, if the tests pass, the build is deployed to the team.[4]

Commits

Commits are changes made to a project repository for the rest of the team to access. For example, an animator commits a new set of animations for a character to the repository, and subsequent builds show characters using those new animations.

There are two main concerns regarding commits:

- The commits should be safe and not break the build.
- The build is in a working condition so that any failure is more likely to be tied to the last commit and quickly fixed.

The developer must first synchronize with the latest build and test their changes with it. This is done to avoid any conflicts that arise with other recent commits. If the latest build is broken, it must be fixed before any commit is made.

When builds are chronically broken, they slow the frequency of commits, which means that larger commits are made. Since larger commits are more likely to break the build, they create a vicious cycle that dramatically impacts a team's velocity.

NOTE

Chapter 10, "Agile Technology," discusses continuous integration strategies to minimize the size of code changes commits.

Testing

Once changes are committed, there should be a flurry of more extensive tests made to ensure that those commits haven't broken anything in the build. There are two competing factors to consider. First, we want to ensure that the build is solidly tested before it is released to the team. Second, a full suite of tests often takes the better portion of a day to run, which is too long. We need to balance testing needs with the need to iterate quickly on build changes.

---

4. If your project is not doing this, stop reading and implement it now!

Test Strategies A multifaceted approach to testing is best. A combination of automated and QA-run testing catches a broad range of defects.

Figure 9.3 shows a pyramid of tests run in order from bottom to top. The tests at the bottom of the pyramid run quickly and catch the more common defects. As each test passes, the next higher test is run until we get to the top where QA approves the build by playing it.

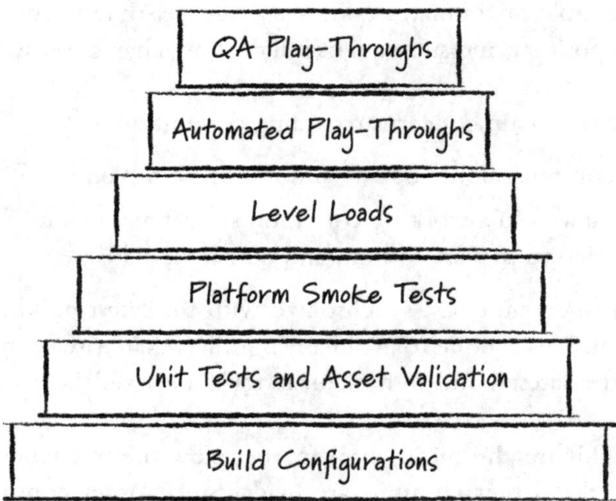

FIGURE 9.3 A testing pyramid

The tests are as follows:

- **Build configurations:** This testing simply creates a build (executable and assets) for each platform. This discovers whether the code compiles on all your target platforms with multiple build configurations (for example, debug, beta, and final). This could cover dozens of platforms for a mobile game.
- **Unit tests and asset validation:** This includes some of the unit tests (if they exist) and any asset validation tests. Asset validation tests individual assets before they are baked and/or loaded in the game. These are examples of asset validation tools:
  - Naming convention checks
  - Construction checks, such as testing for degenerate triangles
  - Platform resource budget checks (for example, polygon count or memory size)

NOTE Unit tests are described in more detail in Chapter 10.

The list of validation tests should be built up as problems are discovered.

- **Platform smoke tests:** These tests ensure that the build loads and starts running on all the platforms without any crashes.
- **Level loads:** One or more of the levels are loaded to ensure that they run on all the platforms and stay within their resource budgets. Usually only the levels affected by change are loaded, but all of them are tested overnight.
- **Automated play-throughs:** A game that "plays itself" through scripting or a replay mechanism benefits testing. In fact, implementing this type of feature into the game from the start is worth the investment. If conditions at the end of the play-through do not meet expectations (such as all the AI cars in a racing game crossing the finish line in a preset range of time), an error is flagged.
- **QA play-throughs:** If the build passes all previous tests, then QA plays through portions of the game. QA is not only looking for problems that were missed in the previous tests but also looking for problems that tests could not catch such as unlit portions of the geometry or AI characters that are behaving strangely.

Test Frequency As development progresses, the time required for running all of these tests grows to the point where it is impossible to keep up with every commit. At this point, the scope of build approval needs to be tiered. The following list shows three tiers of build tests that apply increasing levels of testing:

- **Continuous build tests:** These builds have passed the unit and asset tests for the committed modules or assets. These tests take minutes.
- **Hourly build tests:** These builds have passed every test up to the level load test.
- **Semidaily build tests:** Two or three times a day, QA selects the latest hourly build and plays through them for 30 minutes.
- **Daily build tests:** These are builds that have been completely rebuilt (code and asset cooking) and for which every possible automated test has been run. These take hours to run and are usually done overnight.

As each build is approved, it is flagged (or renamed, and so on) to reflect the testing tier it passed. This lets the team know how extensively the build was tested and to what degree they should trust it.

> **NOTE**
> Sprint review builds should pass all the daily build tests!

Failure Notification

When a commit is made that breaks the build, two things must happen:

- The person(s) who made the last commit must be notified immediately in a way they can't ignore. This can take the form of a dialog box that pops up on top of all other windows.
- The rest of the team should be notified that the build is broken and that they shouldn't "get the latest" code and assets until the problem is fixed. This notification requires less intrusive means to communicate. An example of a notification is an icon in the system tray that turns red.

> **NOTE**
> At High Moon, whenever the build was broken, every development machine warned their user by playing a sound bite. One time I broke the build and 100 PCs started playing the Swedish Chef's theme song from the ***Muppet Show***.

THE LOAF OF QUESTIONABLE FRESHNESS

Most of the time when a commit is broken, it is because of someone ignoring the established testing practices. Teams often devise "motivational tools" to help ensure that teammates remember to perform these practices. An example of this took place on the Midtown Madness team in the late nineties at Angel Studios. We didn't have extensive build testing automation then. We had a dedicated PC, the "build monkey," where any change committed had to be tested separately following every commit. Verifying the build on the build monkey could be a tedious task. Some people occasionally found excuses to skip it, sometimes to the detriment of the team.

After a while, I thought of a cure. I purchased a loaf of Wonder bread, and we instituted a new practice: If you broke the build monkey, you had to host the loaf of bread on top of your monitor (everyone had CRT monitors back then, with plenty of warm space on top) until someone else broke the monkey and took ownership of the loaf.

At first things didn't change. At first, no one seemed to mind a loaf of bread on their monitor. However, as time passed, this changed; the bread became stale and then moldy. Someone on the team started calling it "the loaf of questionable freshness." Eventually, we all desperately wanted to avoid being the owner of the loaf. As a result, build discipline improved, the monkey stayed unbroken, and eventually the loaf of questionable freshness was given a proper burial.

Technology has changed these practices a bit (in other words, we can't fit a loaf of bread on top of an LCD monitor). These days automated test tools play embarrassing music, or the team holds impromptu ceremonies for team members who break the build (have you ever come back to your workspace to find it completely wrapped in Saran wrap?). It's all done with a sense of fun, but it works.

Deployment

The last step in build iteration is to deploy a working build back to the developers. There are two main considerations here: communicating stability and reducing transfer time.

Communicate Stability Communicate the level of testing performed on working builds to reflect the testing tier each one passed.

In the past, we've used a simple homegrown tool that shows all the builds available on the server, their build date, and the test status. The developer selects a build to download based on their needs. Usually, the developer downloads the latest build that was fully tested (usually the daily build). When a developer wants very recent changes, they select the hourly build.

NOTE It's useful to keep a few weeks' history of builds around in case a subtle bug needs to be regressed to discover which commit introduced it.

Reduce Transfer Time Reduce the amount of time to transfer the build from the servers to personal development machines.

Games require many gigabytes of space, and when 100 developers transfer builds daily, it challenges the company network. It's common for a new build to take 30+ minutes to transfer from a server to a personal machine. Reducing this time is crucial. There are a number of ways to attack this problem:

- **Server/client compression/decompression:** There are a number of tools to improve the transfer speed of large amounts of data over a network.

- **Partial transfer:** Does everyone need to transfer every asset? Do some developers need just a new executable? Make it possible to do selective transfers.
- **Overnight transfer:** Set up a tool for pushing daily builds (if working!) to all the developer stations overnight.
- **Upgrade your network:** Move to higher-bandwidth switches and mirrored servers. This is costly, but a simple return-on-investment calculation usually shows that the improved deployment time pays for itself in productivity gains.

Focusing a Team on Build Iteration

When I was a child, I desperately avoided cleaning my room. As I became older, my mother told me that "she was not put on Earth to clean up after me." Imagine my surprise! However, when I had to clean up after myself, I quickly learned that it was better to avoid making the mess in the first place. At the very least, I learned to clean up a mess before it dried on the carpet!

Improving build iteration and debugging is the responsibility of every team. Making it the responsibility of one group of people removes some of that sense of responsibility. However, creating a better build system to catch problems and deploy builds requires specialists and expertise beyond the capabilities of any one team. It isn't efficient for every team to create their own system. They are better off adopting a studio-maintained system and focusing on their game.

The role of creating and maintaining the build system is often the responsibility of an engine or tools team. These teams have a sprint goal but also set aside a certain percentage of time to handle problems that occur on a day-to-day basis. Members of this team see patterns of failure and work to plug any holes that enable problems to slip through. Additional build server tests are the easiest remedy, but often teams need to improve their practices to avoid commit failures. An example of this is to show individuals how to write better unit tests or improve their unit test coverage or to work with an artist to avoid using nonstandard texture sizes or formats.

The team that supports the build servers and tools also needs a metric that shows their progress. A useful metric used for measuring build stability and availability is to record the percentage of time a working build is available to everyone on the team. The ideal is 100%. A perfect level of stability will not be maintained forever, but it is a powerful goal.

NOTE

On one team, the "working build availability percentage" started at 25%. They recorded this metric daily and plotted it on a burn-up chart. After a year, it averaged 95%. Some weeks after a major middleware integration, the availability rate dropped back to near zero, but the burn-up chart enabled the teams to see the long-term picture and slowly improve the trend.

A WORD ABOUT REVISION CONTROL

A detailed discussion of revision control is outside the scope of this book; for a detailed discussion, see Lakos (1996). However, an agile approach to development influences what system you use and how you use it.

Summary

The source of iteration overhead comes from many factors. These sources must be relentlessly tracked down and reduced. Left unattended, they will grow to consume more time and bring velocity to a crawl.

Faster iteration time is a big win. It improves velocity and quality by enabling more iterations of features and assets. Faster iterations improve the life of a developer and the quality of the game. When a designer has to wait 10 minutes to test the effects of a wheel friction tweak on a vehicle, they'll likely find a value that is "good enough" and move on. When the iteration time is instantaneous, they'll tweak the value until it's "just right."

Additional Reading

Crispen, L., and J. Gregory. 2009. *Agile Testing: A Practical Guide for Testers and Agile Teams*. Boston: Addison-Wesley.

Lakos, J. 1996. *Large-Scale C++ Software Design,* Reading, MA: Addison-Wesley.

PART IV

Agile Disciplines

Chapter 10

Agile Technology

Software developers have been battling the challenge of creating complex software projects since the first program was written.[1] Even in the infancy of computers, the challenge of programming with primitive tools pushed the limits of what people could accomplish. Seminal books on project management such as *Mythical Man Month*, written in the sixties, address challenges that are seen to this day.

COMPLEXITY IS NOT NEW

The complex Apollo program was almost undone by unanticipated glitches in the Lunar Module's navigation and guidance computer in the final seconds before the historic landing. That computer had only 4,000 words of memory[2] (one-millionth of the memory in a typical desktop computer).

This chapter will begin with a description of some of the major problems encountered when creating technology for games. The remainder of the part discusses some of the agile practices—including the XP methodology—used to address these problems.

I've avoided low-level technical discussion and code examples in this chapter on purpose. The goal is to communicate the issues and solutions that people in every discipline can understand.

The Problems

Technology creation is the greatest area of risk for many video game projects. Video games compete on the basis of technical prowess as much as gameplay and visual quality. Consumers want to experience the latest graphics, physics, audio effects, artificial intelligence, and so on. Even if a game isn't using the

1. http://en.wikipedia.org/wiki/Bernoulli_number
2. http://en.wikipedia.org/wiki/Apollo_Guidance_Computer

next-generation hardware, it's usually pushing the current generation to new limits.

This section addresses the typical technical problems that often impact development. These problems impact all disciplines and lead projects down dead-end paths.

Uncertainty

In 2002 I joined Sammy Studios as the lead tools programmer. What intrigued me about Sammy was the vision for the studio's technology. It was to give the artists and designers the best possible control over the game through customized tools, while engine technology was to be largely middleware-based. This was in stark contrast to my previous job where engine technology was the main focus and tools meant to help artists and designers were considered far less important.

The first tool I was tasked with developing was meant to tune character movement and animation. This tool was meant to integrate animation and physics behavior and allow animators to directly construct and tune character motion. The tool effort was launched with an extensive 80-page requirements document authored by the animators. This document had mock-ups of the user interface and detailed descriptions of every control necessary for them to fully manipulate the system. I had never seen this level of detail in a tool design before, least of all one created by an artist. At my last company, the programmers developed what they thought the artists and designers needed. This resulted in tools that didn't produce the best results.

Another programmer and I worked on this tool for several months and delivered what was defined in the design document the animators wrote. I looked forward to seeing the amazing character motion that resulted from this tool.

Unfortunately, the effort was a failure. The tool did what it was supposed to, but apparently the animators really couldn't foresee what they needed, and none of us truly understood what the underlying technology would eventually do. This was shocking.

We reflected on what else could have been done to create a better tool. What we decided was that we should have evolved the tool. We should have started by releasing a version with a single control—perhaps a slider that blended two animations (such as walking and running). Had this tool evolved with the animators' understanding of their needs and the capabilities of the emerging animation and physics technology, we would have created a far better tool.

We had developed the wrong tool on schedule. This suggested to us that a more incremental and iterative approach was necessary to develop even technology that had minimum technical and schedule risk.

EXPERIENCE: A MOVING TARGET

Years ago we signed a game project with a Japanese publisher. They didn't want any design documentation at all. They wanted us to explore gameplay for an idea they had. The idea was to create a SWAT game with squad-based AI. The team developed technology and gameplay for six months. Then the publisher changed their mind and wanted it to be a first-person sci-fi shooter that didn't have squad behavior. The team pursued this for several more months. Other changes came and went. The team eventually shipped as a third-person cowboy-based shooter.

During development, progress slowed to a crawl. One of the main reasons for the lack of progress was that the codebase had become so convoluted from all the changes in direction. It was only through the heroics of a few programmers refactoring major portions of the code that any progress was made.

Change Causes Problems

At the core of any game's requirements is the need to "find the fun." Fun cannot be found solely on the basis of what we predict in a game design document. Likewise, technical design and architecture driven by a game design document are unlikely to reflect what we may ultimately need in the game. If we want flexibility in the design of the game, then the technology we create needs to exhibit equal flexibility, but often it does not.

Cost of Late Change

The curve in Figure 10.1 shows how the cost of changing something in a project grows over time (Boehm 1981). Changes made late in a project can result in costs that are a magnitude or more greater than if those changes had been made early. Many reasons for this exist:

- Design details are forgotten by the programmer who wrote the code. It takes time to recall the details and be as effective as when the code was written.
- The original author of the code may not be around to make the change. Someone else has to learn the design and architecture.

- Changing assets that were created based on the original code's behavior can take a lot of time and effort.
- A lot of code may have been built on top of the original design and code. Not only does the original code have to be changed, but all the other code built upon the expected behavior of the original code has to be changed as well.

So, it's important to identify and make changes as early as possible.

Both uncertainty and the cost of change point to the benefits of short iterations of development. Short iterations test features quickly, which reduces uncertainty for those features. Uncertainty implies the potential for change. Since the cost of change increases as time passes, carrying uncertainty forward also carries the potential for increased cost. For example, some projects implement online functionality late in development and discover that much of their core technology (such as animation and physics) does not work across a network. Had they discovered this earlier in the project, the cost of fixing the problem could have been far less.

> **NOTE** This potential cost of change being carried forward is also referred to as **technical debt**. The concept of debt is used for many elements of game development in this book.

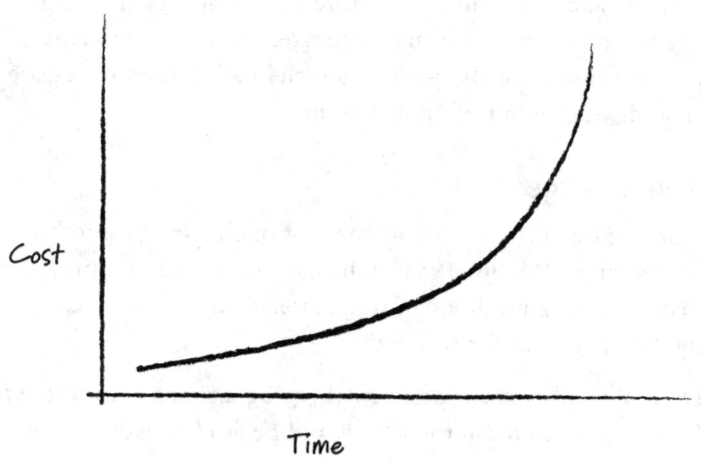

FIGURE 10.1 The cost of change

Too Much Architecture Up Front

One approach to the problem of creating technology for changing requirements is to "overarchitect" a solution. This means implementing a solution that encompasses all the potential solutions. An example is a camera system for a game initially designed to be a first-person shooter. A programmer might architect a camera system that includes general-purpose tools and camera management that handles a variety of other potential cameras, including third-person cameras and others. The goal is that if and when the designers change their minds about the game (such as going from a first-person view to a third-person view), then the changes to the camera can be accommodated through the architected system.

There are two problems with this approach:

- **It slows the introduction of new features up front:** At the start of the game, the designer wants a simple first-person camera to begin prototyping gameplay. They have to wait for the baseline architecture to be created (or brought in from an existing codebase) before the camera is introduced.
- **Architectures designed up front often need to be changed:** The assumptions built into the architecture are often proven wrong during development and need to be changed anyway. Changing larger systems takes more time than smaller systems.

EXPERIENCE: BUILD WHAT YOU NEED, NOT WHAT YOU THINK YOU MIGHT NEED

"Too many developers spend months working on the technology for their next game before starting the game itself. Sometimes, they never make it to developing the game! The most pragmatic solution to this is using preexisting technology. However, if custom technology is required, then only create what is needed as you go.

"A trap many developers fall into is thinking 'We'll be using this feature in the next five games, so it's worth putting a lot of time into it now.' If this is done for all features, the first game will never be finished, let alone the next five. My rule of thumb is that until I've solved a problem at least a couple of times, I don't have enough information to make a generalized solution.

"A great way of achieving these goals is adopting an agile development practice. We are using Scrum for our current game, keeping us focused on creating just enough infrastructure to reach our current sprint/milestone."

—Alistair Doulin, blogger[3]

3. www.doolwind.com/blog

An Agile Approach

This section describes agile solutions to these problems. These solutions focus on an iterative and incremental approach to delivering value and knowledge early.

Extreme Programming

Scrum, by design, has no engineering practices. Many teams using Scrum soon find that their original engineering practices can't keep up with the changing requirements. These teams often turn to the practices of Extreme Programming for help.

XP was a methodology developed after Scrum that adopted many of the Scrum practices. XP iterations and customer reviews, though slightly different, aren't hard to integrate into Scrum teams used to these concepts. XP introduced new practices for programmers. Among them are the practices of test-driven development (TDD) and pair programming.

It's outside the scope of this book to cover the concepts and practices of XP in great detail. There are great books that already do that (see the "Additional Reading" section at the end of this chapter). Numerous studies have shown that XP increases the velocity of code creation and its quality (Jeffries and Melnik 2007).

Programmers pair up to work on tasks. They apply the TDD practices, described next, to implement technology in small, functional increments. This enables functionality to emerge incrementally that remains stable in the face of change. The goal is to create higher-quality code that can be changed with minimum cost.

Test-Driven Development

TDD practices include writing a number of unit tests for every function introduced. Each unit test will exercise the function to be written a single way by passing in data and testing what the function returns or changes. An example of this is a function that sets the health of the player in a game. If your game design defines 100 as full health and 0 as being dead, your unit tests would each set and test valid and min/max parameters and check to make sure those values were assigned by the function. Other unit tests would try to assign invalid numbers (greater than 100 or less than 0) and test to make sure the function handled those bad values correctly.

If you follow the strict TDD practices, the tests are written before you write the logic of the function that will allow those tests to pass, so the tests actually fail at first.

Unit tests and their associated code are built in parallel. When all the tests pass, the code is checked in. This happens quite frequently when the team is using TDD, sometimes every hour or two. This requires a server that acquires all changes as they are checked in and runs all the unit tests to ensure that none of them has broken the code. This server is called a **continuous integration server** (CIS). By running all the unit tests, it catches a majority of the problems usually caused by commits. When a build passes all the unit tests, then the CIS informs all the developers that it is safe to synchronize with the changes. When a submission breaks a unit test, the CIS lets everyone know that it is broken. It then becomes the team's job to fix that problem. Since the culprit who checked in the error is easily identified, they are usually the one who gets to fix the problem.

This provides big benefits to the team and project. As a project grows, the number of unit tests expands, often into the thousands. These tests continue to catch a great deal of errors automatically that would otherwise have to be caught by QA much later. These tests also create a safety net for refactoring and for other large changes that an emerging design will require.

One of the philosophical foundations of XP is that the programmers create the absolute minimal amount of functionality to satisfy customer requests every iteration. For example, suppose a customer wants to see one AI character walking around the environment. Many programmers want to architect an AI management system that handles dozens of AI characters because they "know that the game will need it sometime in the future." With XP, you don't do this. You write the code as if the user story needs only one AI character. When a story asks for more than one AI character in a future sprint, you then introduce a simple AI manager and refactor the original code. This leads to an AI manager that is a better fit for the emerging requirements.

A major benefit of TDD is that it requires "constant refactoring" of the codebase to support this behavior. There are a number of reasons for this, but here are two of them:

- Systems created from refactoring, coupled with implementing the absolute minimum needed, often match final requirements more closely and quickly.
- Refactored code has much higher quality. Each refactoring pass creates the opportunity to improve it.

The barriers to TDD are as follows:

- There is an immediate slowing of new features introduced into the game. Writing tests take time, and it can be hard to argue that the time gained back in reduced debugging time is greater.
- Programmers take their practices very personally. Rolling out a practice like TDD has to be done slowly and in a way that clearly demonstrates its value (see Chapter 16, "Launching Scrum").

NOTE

Personally I don't fully agree with the purist approach that XP programmers should always do the absolute minimum. I believe that knowledge and experience factor into how much architecture should be preplanned. It's very easy to plan too much ahead and "overarchitect," but I believe there is a sweet spot found between the two extremes.

TDD is very useful and is not a difficult practice for programmers to adopt. In my experience, if a programmer tries TDD for a while, the practice of writing unit tests becomes second-nature. The practice of refactoring takes longer to adjust to. Programmers resist refactoring unless it is necessary. This practice reinforces the mind-set of writing code "the right way, the first time," which leads to a more brittle codebase that cannot support iteration as easily. Lead programmers should ensure that refactoring is a constant part of their work.

EXPERIENCE: WHEN XP GOES TOO FAR

"There is a danger that implementing the simplest solution and evolving the design may produce an architecture that makes extensions difficult. Experience enables a programmer to avoid choosing an implementation that will make later extensions difficult.

"Using XP I once implemented what seemed a perfectly valid and simple system. But when the problem being tackled became too complex, I realized that a different architecture would have been more appropriate. I felt that doing the refactoring was too much work, however, so I decided to limp along with the current architecture."

—Stephane Etienne, CTO, High Moon Studios

Pair Programming

Pair programming is a simple practice in principle. Two programmers sit at a workstation. One types in code while the other watches and provides input on the problem they are both tasked with solving.

This practice often creates a great deal of concern:

- "Our programmers will get half the work done."
- "I do my best work when I am focused and not interrupted."
- "Code ownership will be destroyed, which is bad."

Changing personal workspaces and habits can generate a lot of fear, uncertainty, and doubt. This section will examine how the benefits of pair programming outweigh or invalidate these concerns.

Benefits of Pair Programming Let's look at the benefits of pair programming:

- **Spreads knowledge:** Pair programming isn't about one person typing and the other watching. It's an ongoing conversation about the problem the pair is trying to solve and the best way to solve it.

  Two separate programmers solve problems differently. If you were to compare these results, you'd find that each solution had strengths and weaknesses. This is because the knowledge of each programmer does not entirely overlap with that of the other. The dialogue that occurs with pair programming helps to share knowledge and experience widely and quickly. It results in solutions that contain the "best of both worlds."

  Although this is good for experienced programmers, it is an outstanding benefit for bringing new programmers up to speed and mentoring entry-level programmers. Pairing brings a new programmer up to speed much more quickly and therefore rapidly improves their coding practices.
- **Assures that you'll get the best out of TDD:** TDD requires that comprehensive tests be written for every function. The discipline required for this is made easier by pairing. First, it's in our nature to occasionally slack off on writing the tests. From time to time, the partner reminds you to write the proper test or takes over the keyboard if you are not fully motivated. Second, it's common to have one programmer write the tests and the other write the function that causes the tests to pass. Although this doesn't need to become a competition between the two, it usually ensures better test coverage. When the same programmer writes both the test and function, they may overlook the same problem in the function and tests. The saying "two heads are better than one" definitely applies to pair programming!

- **Eliminates many bottlenecks caused by code ownership:** How many times have you been concerned about a key programmer leaving the company in midproject or getting hit by the proverbial bus that drives around hunting down good programmers? Pairing solves some of this by having two programmers on every problem. Even if you are lucky enough not to lose key programmers, they are often too busy on other tasks to quickly solve a critical problem that arrives. Shared knowledge that comes from pair programming solves these problems.
- **Creates good standards and practices automatically:** Have you ever been faced with the problem, late in a project, that one of your programmers has written thousands of lines of poor-quality code that you depend on and it is causing major problems? Management often tries to solve this problem by defining "coding standards" and conducting peer reviews.

  The problem with coding standards is that they are often hard to enforce and are usually ignored over time. Peer reviews of code are a great practice, but they usually suffer from not being applied consistently and often occur too late to head off the problem.

  Pair programming can be thought of as a *continuous peer review*. It catches many bad coding practices early. As pairs mix, a company coding standard emerges and is improved daily. It doesn't need to be written down because it is documented in the code and embedded in the heads of every programmer.
- **Focuses programmers on programming:** When programmers start pairing, it takes several days to adjust to the unrelenting pace. The reason is that they do nothing but focus on the problem the entire day. Mail isn't read at the pair station. The Web isn't surfed. Shared e-mail stations can be set up for when a programmer wants to take a break and catch up on mail. E-mail clients and web browsers are a major distraction from the focus that needs to occur for programming.

EXPERIENCE

At High Moon Studios, we didn't enforce pair programming 100% of the time. For example, programmers didn't always pair up to solve simple bugs. However, it was done long enough to become second-nature. Had we abandoned pair programming, I would have wanted to make sure that we retained the same benefits with whatever practices replaced it.

Problems with Pairing There are some problems to watch out for with pair programming:

- **Poor pair chemistry:** Some pair combinations should be avoided, namely, when the chemistry does not work and cannot be forced. If pairings are self-selected, it works out better. In rare cases, some programmers cannot be paired with anyone. Any large team switching to pair programming will have some programmers who refuse to pair. It's OK to make exceptions for these people to program outside of pairs, but they still need a peer review of their work before they commit. As time passes, they will often do some pairing and may even switch to it. You just need to give them time and not force it.
- **Pairing very junior people with very senior people:** Pairing between the most experienced programmers and junior programmers is not ideal. The senior programmer ends up doing all the work at a pace the junior programmer cannot learn from. Matching junior-level programmers with mid-level programmers is better.
- **Hiring issues:** Make sure that every programming candidate for hire knows they are interviewing for a job that includes XP practices and what that entails. Consider a one-hour pair programming exercise with each candidate in the later stages of a hiring process. This does two things: First, it's a great tool for evaluating how well the candidate does in a pair situation where communication is critical. Second, it gives the candidate exposure to what they are in for if they accept an offer. A small percentage of candidates admit that pairing is not for them and opt out of consideration for the job. This is best for them and for you.

Are XP Practices Better Than Non-XP Practices?

It's difficult to measure the benefit of XP practices when the team first starts using them because the pace of new features immediately slows down. This corresponds to studies (Jeffries and Melnik 2007) that show that a pair of programmers using TDD is about 1.5 times as fast as one separate programmer introducing new features. The additional benefits we've seen with XP/TDD more than offset the initial loss of productivity:

- **Very high stability in builds at all times:** It adds to the productivity of designers and artists as well as programmers when the build is not constantly crashing or behaving incorrectly.

- **Post-production debugging demands vastly reduced:** More time is spent tuning and improving gameplay rather than fixing bugs that have been postponed.
- **Better practices required in Scrum:** Iterative practices in Scrum have a higher level of change. TDD helps retain stability through this change.
- **Less wasted effort:** A project wastes less time reworking large systems by avoiding large architectures written before the requirements are fully known.

BRANCHING VS. CONTINUOUS INTEGRATION

Branch and merge commit strategies often result in weekly commits that bundle hundreds of lines of changes together in a big lump that causes problems that can require days to fix.

This is the reasoning behind continuous integration; it enables frequent commits that—coupled with unit testing—work well to ensure that the changes are testable, small, and safe. They also make the commit process quick and usually painless.

Debugging

One of the biggest differences between an agile game development project and a traditional game development project has to do with how bugs are addressed. In many projects, finding and fixing bugs does not happen until the end when QA focuses on the game. The resulting rush to fix defects usually leads to crunch.

One of the ideals of agile game development is to eliminate the "post-alpha bug-fixing crunch." By adding QA early in the project and addressing bugs as we find them, we significantly reduce the amount of time and risk during the alpha and beta portions of a project.

Debugging in Agile

An agile project approaches bugs differently. Fixing bugs is part of the work that needs to happen before a feature is completed each sprint. In an agile project, we are trying to minimize debt, especially the debt of defects, since the cost of fixing those bugs increases over time. Although QA is part of an agile team, this doesn't relieve the other developers from the responsibility of testing their own work.

When a bug is identified, we either add a task to fix it in the sprint backlog or a story to fix it in the product backlog.

Adding a Task to Fix a Bug to the Sprint Backlog When a bug is found that relates to a sprint goal and it's small enough to fix, a task to do so is added to the sprint backlog. Fixing bugs is part of development velocity. Adopting better practices to avoid defects increases velocity.

In some cases, if enough bugs arise during a sprint, then the team may miss achieving all the user stories.

Adding a Bug to the Product Backlog Sometimes a problem is uncovered that does not impact a sprint goal, cannot be solved by the team, or is too large to fix in the remaining time of the sprint. For example, if a level production team that contains no programmers uncovers a flaw with AI pathfinding on a new level, a user story to fix this is created, added to the product backlog, and prioritized by the product owner. Often such bugs are addressed in a hardening sprint if the product owner decides to call for one (see Chapter 6, "Agile Planning").

If the team is uncertain about which backlog the bug belongs on, they should discuss it with the product owner.

A Word About Bug Databases

One rule I strongly encourage on every agile team is to avoid bug-tracking tools and databases before the "feature complete" goals (often called **alpha**). It's not that the tools are bad, but tools encourage the attitude that identifying a bug and entering it in a database is "good enough for now." It's not. In many cases it's a root of the evil that creates crunch at the end of a project.

When a team enters alpha and the publisher ramps up their off-site QA staff, then a bug database may become necessary.

Optimization

Like debugging, optimization is often left for the end of a project. Agile game development projects spread optimization across the project as much as possible. Unfortunately for projects that have large production phases and single true releases, much of the optimization must be left to the end of the project when the entire game is playable.

Knowledge is the key element that helps decide between what is optimized early in the project and what is optimized in post-production. Projects optimize early to gain knowledge about the following:

- **Is the game (feature, mechanic, and so on) fun?** It's difficult to know what is fun when the game is playing at 10 fps. There must be an ongoing effort to avoid a debt of badly written code or bloated test assets that need to be redone in post-production.
- **What are the technical and asset budgets for production?** Projects shouldn't enter production unless the team is certain about the limitations of the engine and tool sets. Knowing these limitations will vastly decrease rework waste. The following are examples:
  - **How many AI characters can be in the scene at any one time?** Often this variable depends on other parameters. For example, a game may afford more AI characters in a simpler scene that frees up some of the rendering budget for AI.
  - **What is the static geometry budget?** This should be established early, and it should be very conservative. As the game experience is polished with special effects and improved textures, the budget often shrinks. In post-production, it's easier to add static geometry detail than to remove it from scenes.
  - **What work will be necessary to get the game working on the weakest platform?** Sometimes the weakest platform is the most difficult to iterate on. It's better to know as early as possible if separate assets need to be created for another platform!
  - **Does the graphics-partitioning technology work?** Don't count on some "future technical miracle" to occur that enables levels to fit in memory or render at an acceptable frame rate. How much work needs to be done to make a culling system work? Make sure the level artists and designers know how a culling system works before they lay out the levels.

So, what optimizations are left until post-production? These include lower-risk optimizations such as those made to the assets created in production to reduce their resource footprint. Such optimizations are best made after the entire game is fully playable. Here are some examples of post-production optimization:

- **Disc-streaming optimization:** Organize the data on the hard drive and disc to stream in effectively. This is always prototyped to some degree in pre-production.
- **AI spawn optimization:** Spread out the loading and density of AI characters to balance their use of resources.
- **Audio mixing:** Simplify the audio streams, and premix multiple streams when possible.

A project can't discount the benefits from engine improvements made during production. At the same time, they can't be counted on. It's a judgment call about where to draw the line. As a technical customer, I set the goal of a project to achieve a measurable bar of performance throughout development as a definition of *done* for releases. An example of a release definition of *done* is as follows:

- 30 frames per second (or better) for 50% of the frames
- 15 to 30 frames per second for 48% of the frames
- Less than 15 frames per second for 2% of the frames
- Loading time on the development station of less than 45 seconds

These standards are measurable and are caught quickly by test automation. They might not be stringent enough to ship with, but they are acceptable for the "magazine demo" quality releases.

Staying Within Technical and Asset Budgets Throughout the Project

The benefits of having the game run at shippable frame rates throughout development are vast. We get a much more true experience of the game emerging when it runs "within its means" at all times. However, there is an ongoing give-and-take between iterative discovery and incremental value. For example, developers may want to experiment with having 24 AI characters rush the player in an "AI wave" to find out whether it's fun. Do they have to optimize the entire AI system to handle 24 characters in the experiment? Of course not. If the experiment has shown that the feature *would* add a lot of value to the game, we have only improved our understanding, not the game. We have iterated to improve our knowledge, but we haven't yet incremented the value of the game.

Too often we'll add such a scene to the game without enough optimization. We have created a bit of debt that we have to pay back later. This payback cost could be large. It could be so large that we can't afford it and have to eliminate the mechanic altogether. This could occur for many reasons; here are some examples:

- The AI character models are too complex to afford 24 in the scene.
- Spawning a wave of 24 AI characters causes a one-second pause, which violates a first-party technical requirement (for example, TCR/TRC).

The list could go on. What can we do to reduce this debt and truly increment the value of the game? We need to do some spikes to determine the optimization debt and influence the product backlog to account for it. If a spike reveals these two problems, we could address them in the following ways:

- Plan for simple models with a smaller number of bones to populate characters in the wave.
- Implement an interleaved spawning system (like a round-robin) to spawn the characters one per frame over a second.

Both of these backlog items enable the product owner to measure the cost of the AI wave against the value we learned in the test. This enables cost and value to be their deciding factor rather than the need to ship a game on time.

There are many examples of this type of decision that need to be made early. When these decisions are not made, the optimization debt often becomes overwhelming. This requires an objective eye to watch out for. Too many times we view these features with the "developer's eye." We overlook the flaws that cause frustration to our stakeholders.

Summary

This chapter explored the XP practices of test-driven development and pair programming and the principles behind them. These practices support agility because they move programmers away from separate design, code, and test phases of development into iterative daily practices where these activities are mixed. They create code that matches emergent requirements, is more maintainable, and is of higher quality.

The next several chapters will explore the other game team disciplines and how their practices can be adapted for more agility as well.

Additional Reading

Beck, K. 2004. *Extreme Programming Explained, Second Edition*. Boston: Addison-Wesley.

Brooks, F. 1995. *Mythical Man Month, Second Edition*. Boston: Addison-Wesley.

McConnell, S. 2004. *Code Complete, Second Edition*. Redmond, WA: Microsoft Press.

Chapter 11

Agile Art and Audio

Computer-based artwork is dynamic and evolving. Art styles transform, and artists explore new meaning in what they create. The medium that they use has undergone as much change in the past few decades, with the advent of powerful and cheap computers, as it had since the caves in Lascaux, France, were painted 16,000 years ago.

Cell animation and pre-rendered computer graphics have enabled artists to add more motion to their work. This has made it possible for the wild imaginations of artists and storytellers to be more deeply shared such as in the movie *Fantasia*.

Video games have added a whole new dimension. Now art has to be interactive, which enables it to be used in ways its creators didn't imagine. The medium is complex and requires the artist to collaborate with designers and programmers to bring their work to life.

This chapter will explore the benefits, concerns, and common practices of artists on cross-discipline agile teams. This chapter covers principles and practices that cover many artistic disciplines including modeling, texturing, animation, audio, and so on. It refers to the members of every discipline as artists.

The Problems We Are Solving with Agile

> Why use agile for art? When Michelangelo painted the ceiling of the Sistine Chapel, he wasn't using agile. He had a plan to paint the entire ceiling.
>
> —A former artist co-worker

In reality, Michelangelo may have been better off using a more agile approach to painting the Sistine Chapel. There was a great deal of trial and error and false starts. He had no idea about how to paint images on a curved and segmented ceiling. He signed a fixed-price contract calling for 12 figures to be painted.

Four years later he had painted 300. It's no wonder he referred to it as one of the worst experiences of his life.

Video game artists face similar challenges. Translating their vision into reality runs headlong into the challenges of the medium, whether it is fresco or graphics processors. Overcoming these challenges and understanding the limitations of the medium before creating the final product are necessary.

The following are some of the main problems artists encounter:

- **Artists need to know whether they are creating the right thing and not wasting effort:** Parallel development of assets and technology that the assets depend on is a traditional source of wasted effort. Engine development is often started with optimistic feature sets, performance goals, and schedules. Unfortunately, projects fall short of these goals, and the assets created cannot be used as built and have to be rebuilt. Technical iteration requires an ongoing conversation and experimentation with what looks and works best. Every artist knows that the quality of a complex asset, such as a level, depends on a trade-off between polygon count, texture quality, lighting complexity, and the palette of effects available. None of these is independent of each other. Some levels require more effects than others and require trade-offs. We want to build the knowledge of these trade-offs during engine development before we commit to production. This requires frequent collaboration between the technology creators and the artists who leverage their work.
- **Artists need a stable, working build:** Nothing impacts progress more than a broken build. Graphical defects that impact visual quality prevent an artist from developing the best possible assets. Relying on a separate technology team to solve these problems adds delay. Cross-discipline teams are more likely to have a team member who quickly solves these problems or is able to communicate with someone who can help.
- **Artists need faster tools and pipelines:** Artists are often limited by slow iteration times and therefore can't iterate as much as they like. Less iteration translates to lower-quality art. A common problem is that programming team members, who have control over improving tools and pipelines, are not impacted by the same problems. They don't experience how slow it is to change a texture on a game. They are focused on the tasks that are important to

their team. Cross-discipline teams share common goals. Problems that impact individual progress impact the entire team. When this happens, then such problems receive the level of attention they deserve.

Concerns About Agile

Artists have several common concerns about agile and Scrum:

- **Scrum is for programmers:** Scrum is used to a great extent on software development projects, but it wasn't created for programmers. In fact, it purposefully has no specific practices for any one discipline. It's as applicable for artists as it is for any other discipline.
- **Art production runs on a schedule. We can't be iterative:** With video games, art and technology have to integrate with the gameplay mechanics to create a fun experience. Teams have to explore how all these components work together. Once they discover this, they can schedule the creation of ten to twelve hours of production content. Exploring in pre-production is necessary. Cross-discipline pre-production teams using by-the-book Scrum thrive. During production, many practices will change but remain agile. Production issues continue to create unexpected challenges. These challenges wreak havoc on the best-planned schedules. Artists creating assets still need rapid response to technical problems. They need to continually find ways to collaborate (see Chapter 7, "Video Game Project Planning").
- **Cross-discipline teams don't work:** On large projects, artists have traditionally been pooled with members of their own discipline, and they've learned to work that way. Once they try cross-discipline teams and experience day-to-day responsiveness from teammates who help them solve problems, they change their minds. Scrum doesn't prevent artists from communicating outside of a sprint. They can form communities of practice (see Chapter 8, "Teams") and still share ideas and practices with one another.

Like almost any developer, artists need to experience Scrum practices before they'll agree with the benefits. A sense of skepticism is healthy as long as it is paired with an openness to accept what works.

CONVINCING THE ARTISTS TO JOIN

When High Moon Studios started experimenting with Scrum, our artists were very skeptical of it. Some thought it was a "management fad" or a covert form of micromanagement. They wanted no part of it, and we didn't force it on them.

The programmers decided to try it and formed teams. Their daily scrums quickly identified impediments that impacted their progress. Many of these addressed the lack of proper assets to work with. The producers, recruited to be the ScrumMasters, spent much of their time pestering the artists to produce the assets the teams demanded.

Once the artists saw the producers focusing their effort on solving Scrum-raised impediments, they wanted to start using Scrum too.

Art Leadership

As with all leadership roles, agile shifts the responsibility of art leadership from daily command and control to mentoring and facilitation. The role of art leadership is to improve the quality of the art being created and to help artists improve their ability to create art. These two must constantly be balanced.

To improve the quality of art, the art lead (or art director) reviews new art in-game and provides feedback. This creates the opportunity to work with the artists directly within a sprint. This influences some of the daily practices. For example, art assets may need a sign-off or approval by a lead artist or art director, so some teams add a column on their task board called "Pending Approval" before the "Done" column to hold an art task to be approved before it is considered done.

A challenge for many agile game teams is how to avoid having art direction approval become a bottleneck for progress. Since art directors are usually not members of any one team, they do not have the same level of commitment to a sprint as teams who depend on their feedback. Delayed feedback is often a source of impediments for these teams. Studios develop unique practices, such as highly visible approval backlogs, to address this.

In addition to asset approval, art leaders must mentor less-experienced artists to improve their art creation workflow. Art cost is as critical as art quality. Without experience or familiarity with all the tools, new artists can waste a lot of time creating assets the hard way.

As the art lead works with artists to improve quality and reduce cost, they will see patterns for improvement that can be shared among all artists or opportunities for improvement that can be championed with the team that supports the pipeline and tools.

EXPERIENCE

In the mid-nineties, many 3D games were a mix of 2D and 3D. One (canceled) game I was working on at Angel Studios took place outdoors. In these outdoor levels, there were trees in the distance that, because of the limited rendering budgets, were tree pictures on billboards (2D cards that always rotate to face the player). One artist made beautiful tree billboards, but he was very slow in making them. This went on for a few months until the lead artist visited him and discovered that he was creating a full three-dimensional tree on the PC modeling tool, taking a picture of it, and using the picture for the billboard! That practice was changed.

Art on a Cross-Discipline Team

An artist on a cross-discipline team is faced with a number of challenges. Different vocabularies must be understood, and the artists must struggle to make themselves understood as well. They are reminded daily of how their art is used: how it leverages the strengths or exposes the weaknesses of the technology.

For a cross-discipline team that is measured by value added to a working game, the role of an artist shifts to that of a "game developer" who specializes in art. An artist doesn't simply create an asset for someone else to put in the game and make fun. The artist participates in the creation of an experience, where art has an equal value. By having a voice in the discussion about what is being created, the artist elevates the value of what they create and minimizes the cost of creating it.

Creative Tension

> When forced to work within a strict framework, the imagination is taxed to its utmost—and will produce the richest ideas. Given total freedom, the work is likely to sprawl.
>
> —T.S. Eliot

Creative tension exists between what we *can* do and what we *want to do* in a game. Creative tension is a good thing. It enables us to push the quality of an asset in the game while working within the bounds of technical limits, cost, and schedule. Creative tension puts pressure on our work processes, tools, and practices to find opportunities to eliminate waste.

Some of the best ideas are created from these limitations. When we were developing the game Midtown Madness, the shortage of level artists forced us to rely on a tool that procedurally created a city from a simple line map. This tool generated an entire city in an hour and allowed us to iterate hundreds of times whenever we discovered problems such as curb angles interfering with vehicle wheel physics. Had the entire city been modeled by hand, we could not have iterated as many times to improve the game.

Scrum compels teams to improve their performance every sprint. It forces creative tension to the surface where it belongs.

95-MILE-PER-HOUR ART

Game art has a function and a form. Its purpose guides its creation. Its function is less apparent when artists are separated from the game. During the development of Midnight Club, a city racing game, a group of artists created assets for the streets in a separate room. We were looking forward to seeing their work because we had a city filled with gray cubes. The day finally arrived when the new geometry was placed in the city. It was stunning. The city was truly coming to life. We started driving around and discovered a major problem. Much of the new detailed geometry was at the street level. The actual city we were modeling had a lot of this detail itself, but it was a terrible problem for a racing game. A staircase jutting out from a building could instantly stop a car using the sidewalk. Low planters became uncrossable barriers. Fun transformed into frustration.

Much of this detail had to be removed to eliminate the barriers at street level. From then on, the mantra repeated daily was "Create 95-mile-per-hour art." The art had to look good and function well for players in cars traveling past it at 95 miles per hour.

Art QA

Many problems are avoided when the entire team iterates on the game daily. Asset creation tasks aren't considered complete when they are exported but when they are verified in-game on the target platform. Verification not only includes seeing the asset in the game and ensuring that it functions well but also includes verifying that some of the less-apparent aspects of its use are correct. In-game asset verification tools aid in checking the construction of assets in the game in many ways:

- **Physics geometry view:** Does the collision geometry match the visible geometry? Is it aligned properly?
- **Texel density view:** Are the textures properly mapped? Are the textures the right size?

- **Wireframe view:** Is the out-of-view geometry being properly culled? Are the asset visibility flags set properly?
- **Sound volume view:** Are the sound min/max radii properly set? Are the proper sounds triggering at the right time?
- **Asset selection and highlight:** Is an asset lit properly in the game? It is visible to the player? How often is it instantiated? Rather than searching for an asset, this tool enables the artist to select it from a list and see it highlighted.

Artists need to have access to all the target platforms to test their work. Sometimes it is too expensive to equip every person on the team with platform development kits. In those cases, small groups share a development kit in a location that they can all see and control from their own workstation.

When QA is the responsibility of everyone on the team, then everyone needs to examine how assets are being used and make sure that they adhere to the budget requirements.

Building Art Knowledge

A goal of pre-production is to create knowledge. We want to know how fun the game is, how content will be produced, and how much it is going to cost. Creating this knowledge requires iteration. Unfortunately, teams often focus too much on core mechanics or the fun of the game and not enough on production costs. This result is that many projects exceed their production budgets or schedules. They need to explore production costs more in pre-production.

Level production often costs 50% or more of the production budget. Project teams need to refine their understanding of the effort to build levels during pre-production to avoid mechanics that inflate production costs beyond the budget. For example, some shooters have a fantastic feature that makes it possible for every object in the environment to be destructible. Unfortunately, this feature can double level production costs since building destructible geometry requires far more effort. By knowing this cost impact in pre-production, the product owner can better judge the return on investment for this feature.

Learning about production cost is an iterative process. It begins with a range of estimates based on existing knowledge (perhaps from a previous title) and is iteratively refined during pre-production. Refinement occurs by iterating on mechanics and building a "vocabulary" of rooms or simpler levels that grow as the team learns more.

Building a shippable level before a vocabulary of mechanics is established is wasteful. This waste is seen on many milestone-driven projects. Teams feel compelled to show something that is polished to their publisher when the gameplay is still undetermined. These polished milestone levels are eventually thrown out or require a great deal of rework when the team learns more about the gameplay.

Overcoming the "Not Done Yet" Syndrome

Teams are often called upon to demonstrate the potential value of a mechanic in a low-cost way. This often requires that stand-in assets, such as low polygon models or roughly blended animations, be used instead of polished assets. These demonstrations are useful tracer bullets to indicate where the game is headed. Although the results might be thrown away, their purpose is to learn more about a feature before deciding to invest more time in it.

> **TIP**
>
> Often level designers create a set of basic level shapes they refer to as **Lego bricks** that allow them to "snap together" a large level very quickly. These levels give a sense of scale for production levels that take many times more effort to create.

Artists often resist showing stand-in assets to the world and want to add more polish for a prototype. There is nothing wrong with doing this as long as it doesn't negatively impact the goal. For example, one project team discovered that their prototype level was running extremely slowly. After exploring the problem, it was discovered that hundreds of the props placed in the level were dynamically lit. The artists had done this since they didn't have enough time to properly prelight the level and wanted everything to look good.

Iteration often requires showing proof-of-concept work to demonstrate knowledge gained. Stand-in assets are fine to use, but care should be taken to make it obvious they are temporary. Candy-stripe textures or characters that look like "crash-test dummies" allow stakeholders to look beyond the test assets and judge the results.

> **EXPERIENCE**
>
> Be careful of using reference assets. Since they look good, they are often forgotten until there is a problem, such as the time an artist pasted in the eyeball of a character with a photo that was a megabyte in size! Another time, on Midtown Madness 2, an artist textured a garbage can with a picture from a real garbage can. The company, whose logo was on that can, successfully sued for its illegal use!

Budgets

One of the most frustrating things for an artist is seeing their work go to waste. It's not unusual to review the assets created for a game and realize that enough of them were created and discarded to complete *two games*. The majority of the team often consists of artists, so wasting 50% of their effort is a tremendous burden.

Much of the waste comes from assets being created when not enough about their requirements and budgets are known. Because a game artist's creation tools are often separate from the game itself, they "get ahead" of the rest of the project and create assets that are based more on speculation rather than the constraints of the emergent game. This is usually driven by schedule and resource allocation plans. A schedule might stipulate a certain number of assets created by a specific date, which in turn drives staffing on a project that may not be ready for it.

For example, a project plan and schedule may forecast a date when a set of characters is complete. As a result, a group of character modelers and animators join the project months before this date to start producing the character assets. At this point it's expected that the project has proven character requirements and budgets such as the following:

- The skeletal budgets, such as how many bones are required, and so on
- The model polygon requirements, such as how many characters are on the screen at any one time
- An identified set of behaviors to derive the animation sets
- Character motion needs, such as whether all the animations are identified for characters to "look good" while moving

If character mechanics are not sufficiently developed to the point where these things are known, it leads to waste. The character artists would have to guess about these requirements and, because they have to keep busy, start building assets with them. This usually results in character assets that need a great deal of rework or, worse, have to be used as is.

Cross-discipline teams iterate and refine specific asset budgets and requirements as part of the goal of finding the fun and the cost. As pre-production moves forward, budgets and production tool requirements need to become part of the definition of *done* for asset classes. When these elements become "out of sync," the team identifies it quickly and corrects the problem (such as altering team membership or future sprint goals).

Audio at the "End of the Chain"

Adding audio to an otherwise completed asset or mechanic is often the "last step" in a chain of steps (see Chapter 7), even in pre-production. This can lead to audio designers or composers with little to do at the start of a sprint and then too much to do at the end. Scrum teams often change the assumptions about handing off work and find ways to interleave work on multiple assets and increase collaboration across disciplines. Chapter 16, "Launching Scrum," addresses this in more detail.

Collaboration in Production

In Chapter 7, we explored lean production practices and how cross-discipline teams work together to reduce waste while continually improving what they are creating and how they are creating it. A side effect of these practices is that role boundaries begin to blur. For example, as concept artists shift from handing off drawings to engaging in more collaborative daily conversations with level designers, both begin to learn each other's role and vocabulary. The level designer won't start drawing concept art and the concept artist will not start editing levels, but they learn more about each other's goals and methods. They use this knowledge to modify their practices to better accommodate one another. For example, when working on a racing game that took place in Paris, the concept artist learned about the layout, landmarks, and visual style of Paris, while the level designer focused on what the vehicle was able to do. The two worked closely together to find intersecting areas (landmarks and street styles of Paris that worked well with the vehicle dynamics), and the result improved quality and reduced waste.

EXPERIENCE

When I started creating tools for artists and designers, my understanding of the complete process of creating games grew by a magnitude. It altered my approach to how I developed code and later led teams. A wider view of other disciplines benefits every role and is a natural advantage of cross-discipline teams.

Summary

Artists face many challenges on game development teams. They are often at the mercy of uncertain technology and impossible schedules that end up forcing them to overproduce assets and compromise quality. As teams grow, these challenges will also grow.

As with the other disciplines, artists need to see themselves as game developers first and artists second. When they work on art teams in isolation, it creates communication barriers between the other disciplines. Players aren't buying just art; they're buying art that does something entertaining. This requires a cross-discipline approach to creating value, which is what Scrum promotes.

Additional Reading

Goldscheider, L. 1953. *Michelangelo: Paintings, Sculpture, Architecture*. London: Phaidon Press.

Chapter 12

Agile Design

When I first started working on games professionally in the early nineties, the role of designer was being instituted throughout the industry. Following the mold of prominent designers such as Shigeru Miyamoto and Sid Meier, designers were seen as directors of the game, or at least the people who came up with many of the ideas. The role required communication with the team on a daily basis but not much written documentation.

As technical complexity, team size, and project durations grew, the role of the designer became more delineated. Some projects had teams of designers who specialized in writing stories, scripting, tuning characters, or creating audio. Hierarchies emerged to include lead, senior, associate, or assistant designers, among others.

The overhead of communication with large teams and the cost of longer development efforts led to a demand for certainty from the stakeholders. Large detailed design documents attempted to create that certainty, but at best they only deferred its reckoning.

This chapter examines how agile can help reverse this trend.

VIEWPOINT

"Designers are the chief proponents for the player. This has not changed in 20 years of game development. Though titles and roles have changed, designers look out for gameplay and quality of the product from a player's perspective.

"When teams were small—with ten or less people—this could be done easily; it was a series of conversations while textures were created and code was written. The design was natural and organic as it emerged from the team. 'Horse swaps' could easily occur. For example, trading a very difficult-to-build mechanic for an easy one that still achieved the same gameplay vision was relatively simple.

"However, in the past ten years, teams have begun to balloon, first to the 30- to 50-person teams of the nineties and then finally to the occasional several-hundred-person monstrosities of the 2000s. A single designer could not have all the conversations that needed to happen (even several designers have problems). As a result, documentation began to surface that outlined the product as a whole, from the very high level to the very granular. Although this paints the initial vision of the title, it does away with one of the most important facets of any type of product development: the dialogue.

"Scrum addresses this. Five- to ten-person cross-discipline Scrum teams usually include a designer. Each of these designers is entrusted by the lead designer to understand the key vision elements and speak to the team."

—Rory McGuire, game designer

The Problems

What are some of the problems that face developers on large projects? The two most common problems are the creation of large documents at the start of a project and the rush at the end of the project to cobble something together to ship.

Designs Do Not Create Knowledge

Originally when designers were asked to write design documents, they rebelled. Writing a design document seemed like an exercise to placate a publisher or commit the designers to decisions they weren't ready to make. Over time this attitude toward documentation has changed. Writing design documents has become the focus for many designers. It's felt that this is the easiest way to communicate vision to both the stakeholders and a large project team.

Designers need to create a vision, but design documents can go too far beyond this and speculate instead. Once, on a fantasy shooter game I worked on, the designers not only defined all the weapons in the design document but how many clips the player could hold and how many bullets each clip contained! This level of detail didn't help the team. In fact, for a while, it led them in the wrong direction.

The Game Emerges at the End

At the end of a typical game project, when all the features are being integrated, optimized, and debugged, life becomes complicated for the designer. This is the first time they experience a potentially shippable version of the game. At this point it typically bears little resemblance to what was defined in the design document, but it's too late to dwell on that. Marketing and QA staffs are ramping up, and disc production and marketing campaigns are scheduled.

The true performance of the technology begins to emerge, and it's usually less than what was planned for during production. This requires that budgets be slashed. For example, waves of enemy characters become trickles, detailed textures are decimated, and props are thinned out.

Because of deadlines, key features that are "at 90%" are cut regardless of their value. As a result, the game that emerges at beta is a shadow of what was speculated in the design document. However, it's time to polish what remains for shipping.

Designing with Scrum

Successful designers collaborate across all disciplines. If an asset doesn't match the needs of a mechanic, they work with an artist to resolve the issue. If a tuning parameter does not exist, they work with a programmer to add it. They also accept that design ideas come from every member of the team at any time. This doesn't mean that every idea is valid. The designer is responsible for a consistent design vision, which requires them to filter or adapt these ideas.

COPS AND ROBBERS

In the late nineties, while we were developing Midtown Madness, I was playing "capture the flag" after-hours in the game Team Fortress. One day it occurred to me that a version of "capture the flag" for our city racing game might be fun. I raised this idea with the game designer, and he suggested a creative variation called "cops and robbers." In it, one group of players are robbers, while the other group are cops. The robbers try to capture gold from a bank and race to return it to their hideout. The cops try to stop the robbers and return the gold. This feature was a big hit with online players and seemed to be even more popular than racing! Good ideas can come from anywhere!

A Designer for Every Team?

A designer should be part of every cross-discipline Scrum team working on a core gameplay mechanic. They should be selected on the basis of the mechanic and their skills. For example, a senior designer should be part of the team working on the shooting mechanic for a first-person shooter. If the team is responsible for the heads-up display (HUD), then a designer with a good sense of usability should join the team.

The Role of Documentation

When designers first start using Scrum, they'll often approach a sprint as a mini-waterfall project; they'll spend a quarter of the sprint creating a written plan for the work to be done during the remainder. Over time this behavior shifts to daily collaboration and conversation about the emerging goal. This is far more effective.

This doesn't mean that designers shouldn't think beyond a sprint and never write any documentation. A design document should limit itself to what is known about the game and identify, but not attempt to answer, the unknown. Documenting a design forces a designer to think through their vision before presenting it to the rest of the team. However, a working game is the best way to address the unknown.

A goal of a design document is to share the vision about the game with the team and stakeholders. Relying solely on a document for sharing vision has a number of weaknesses:

- **Documents aren't the best form of communication:** Much of the information between an author and reader is lost. Sometimes I've discovered that stakeholders don't read any documentation; it's merely a deliverable to be checked off!
- **Vision changes over time:** Documents are poor databases of change. Don't expect team members to revisit the design document to find modifications. Recall the story of the animal requirement for Smuggler's Run; that was a case of failed communication about changing vision.

Daily conversation, meaningful sprint and release planning, and reviews are all places to share vision. Finding the balance between design documentation and conversation and collaboration is the challenge for every designer on an agile team.

"STAY THE %#&$ OUT!"

One designer at High Moon Studios had a difficult time shifting his focus away from documentation when he joined his first Scrum team. At the start of every four-week sprint, he locked himself in an office for a week to write documentation for the sprint goal. The team didn't want to wait and pestered him with questions during this time. The constant interruptions led the designer to post a note on his door that read "Stay the %#&$ out! I'm writing documents!" Eventually, the team performed an "intervention" of sorts with the designer to get him to kick the documentation habit!

Parts on the Garage Floor

Agile planning practices create a prioritized feature backlog that can be revised as the game emerges. The value of features added is evaluated every sprint. However, many core mechanics take more than a single sprint to demonstrate minimum marketable value. As a result, the team and product owner need a certain measure of faith that the vision for such mechanics will prove itself. However, too much faith invested in a vision will lead teams down long, uncertain paths, which results in a pile of functional "parts" that don't mesh well together. I call this the "parts on the garage floor" dysfunction.

We saw one such problem on a project called Bourne Conspiracy. In this third-person action-adventure game, the player had to occasionally prowl around areas populated with guards who raise an alarm if they spot the player. This usually resulted in the player being killed. In these areas, the designers placed doors that the player had to open. At one point, a user story in the product backlog read as follows:

> As a player, I want the ability to pick locks to get through locked doors.

This is a well-constructed story. The problem was that there were no locked doors anywhere. This resulted in another story being created:

> As a level designer, I want to have the ability to make doors locked so the player can't use them without picking the lock.

This story is a little suspect. It represents value to a developer, but it doesn't communicate any ultimate value to the player. Such stories are common, but they can be a symptom of a debt of parts building up.

The parts continued to accumulate as sprints went by:

> As a player, I want to see a countdown timer on the HUD that represents how much time is remaining until the lock is picked.
>
> As a player, I want to hear lock-picking sounds while I am picking the lock.
>
> As a player, I want to see lock-picking animations on my character while I pick the lock.

This continued sprint after sprint; work was being added to the lock-picking mechanic. It was looking more polished every review.

All of these lock-picking stories were building the parts for a mechanic that was still months away from proving itself. The problem was that lock picking made no sense. The player had no choice but to pick the locks. Nothing in the game required the player to choose between picking a lock or taking a longer route. Ultimately, the vision was proven wrong, and lock picking was all but dropped from the game despite all the work dedicated to it.

Figure 12.1 illustrates this problem of "parts on the garage floor."

The figure shows many parts, developed over three sprints, finally coming together in the fourth. This represents a debt that could waste a lot of work if it doesn't pay off. It also prevents multiple iterations on the mechanic over a release cycle, because the parts are integrated only in the last sprint.

Ideally, each sprint iterates on a mechanic's value. Figure 12.2 shows the parts being integrated into a playable mechanic every sprint or two.

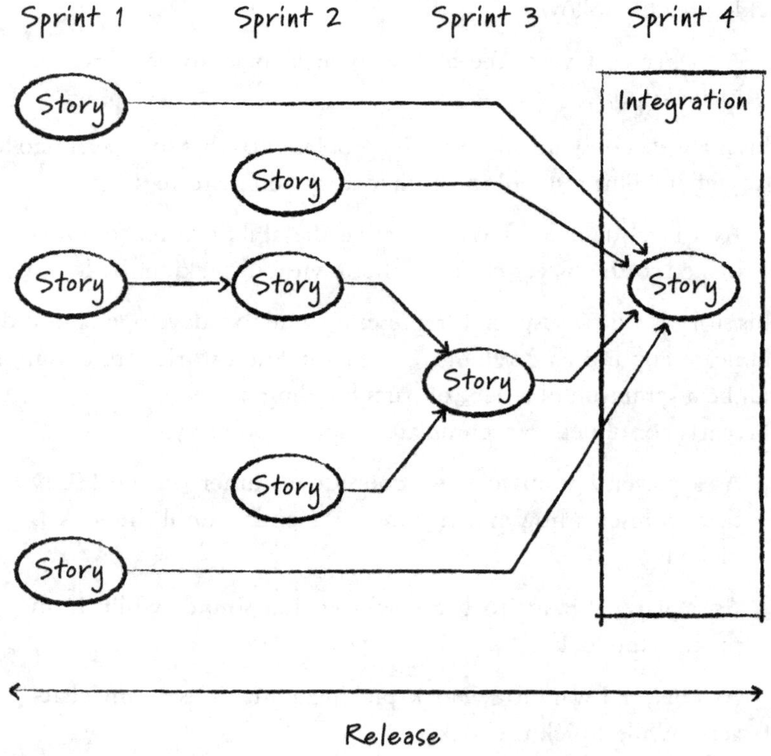

FIGURE 12.1 Integrating a mechanic at the end of a release

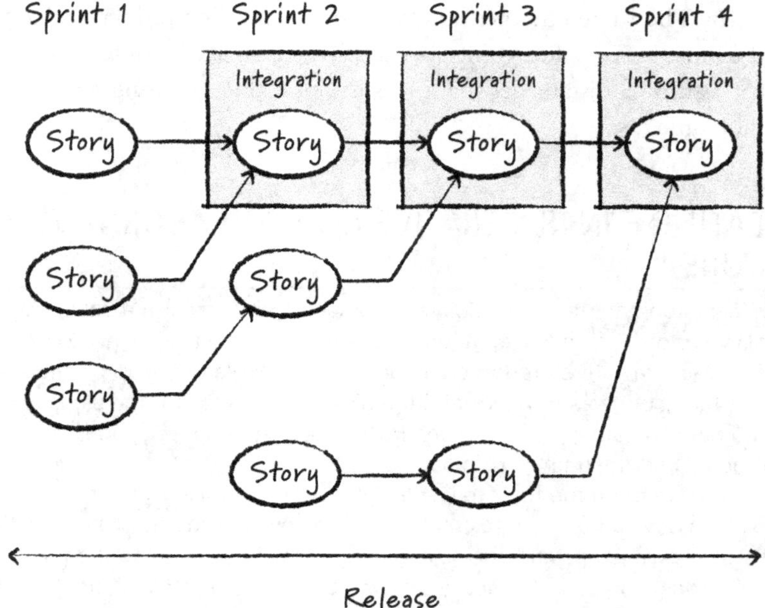

FIGURE 12.2 Integrating a mechanic every sprint

The approach changes the stories on the product backlog:

> As a designer, I want doors to have a delay before they open. These doors would delay the player by a tunable amount of time to simulate picking a lock while the danger of being seen increases.

Notice that this story expresses some fundamental value to the player, which communicates a vision to both stakeholders and developers.

> As a designer, I want to have guards simulating patrols past the locked doors on a regular basis so the timing opportunity for the player to pick the lock is narrow.
>
> As a player, I want to unlock doors in the time that exists between patrols of armed guards to gain access to areas I need to go.

The first few stories are infrastructure stories, but they describe where the game is headed. They build the experience for the player in increments and explain why. The value emerges quickly and enables the product backlog to be adapted to maximize value going forward. This is in stark contrast to building parts that assume a distant destination is the best one. Iterating against a fixed plan is not agile.

CREATING FUN IS ITERATIVE AND COLLABORATIVE BY NATURE

One year I took my family to Colorado to spend Christmas in a cabin. After a large snowstorm, my sons wanted to sled on the side of a small hill. So, I went to the local hardware store but could only find a couple of cheap plastic sleds. At first, the snow was too thick and the hill was too small for the sleds, so we packed down a path in the snow and built a starting ramp for speed. The sleds kept running off the track, so we packed snow on the sides. To increase speed, we poured water on the track to ice it—it began to look like a luge track!

After a few hours we had a great track. The boys would speed down on their sleds. They built jumps and curves and even a few branches into the track.

My oldest son said, "It's lucky that you bought the perfect sleds!" I hadn't done that, so we talked about it. The sleds weren't perfect; we had merely iterated on the track to match their characteristics. We added elements, such as the sides to the track, to overcome the sled's lack of control. We added other features, such as the ramp and track ice, to overcome the limitations of the thick snow and low hill. The sleds were the only thing that couldn't be changed.

I couldn't help comparing this to game development. We created an experience by iterating on things we had control over and adapted for things we didn't. In this case, design was entirely constrained to working with the level (the track) and not the player control (the sled), and we were still able to "find the fun"!

Set-Based Design

When a project begins, the game we imagine is astounding. Players will experience amazing gameplay and explore incredible worlds where every turn reveals a delightful surprise. However, as we develop the game, we start to compromise. Imagination hits the limits of technology, cost, skill, and time. It forces us to make painful decisions. This is a necessary part of creating any product.

Identifying and narrowing down the set of possibilities is part of planning. For example, when we plan to create a real-time strategy game, we eliminate many of the features seen in other genres from consideration (see Figure 12.3).

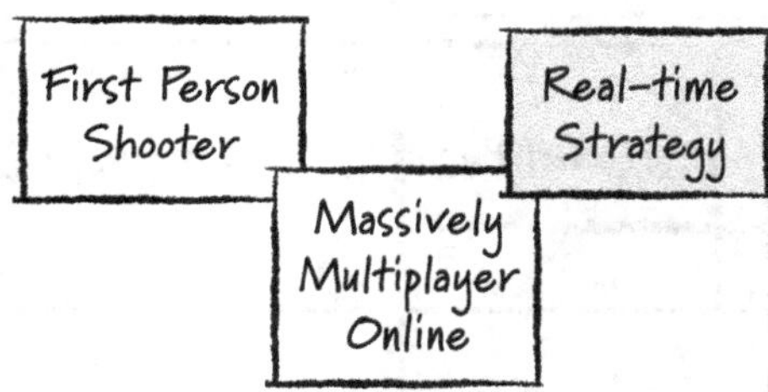

FIGURE 12.3 Narrowing the game to a specific genre

Planning continues to narrow down the set of possible features. Following a high-level design, many developers refine discipline-centric designs. Designers plan the game design possibilities, programmers plan the technical design possibilities, and artists plan the art design possibilities. These possibilities do not perfectly overlap. For example, the designers may want large cities full of thousands of people, but the technology budget may only allow a dozen characters in linear levels. Figure 12.4 shows how the union of design, art, and technical possibilities overlap to create a set of features that all disciplines agree upon.

As mentioned earlier, the project starts with an area quite large in scope. As time goes by, the project staff gains more knowledge of what is possible, and the range of possibilities shrink, as shown in Figure 12.5.

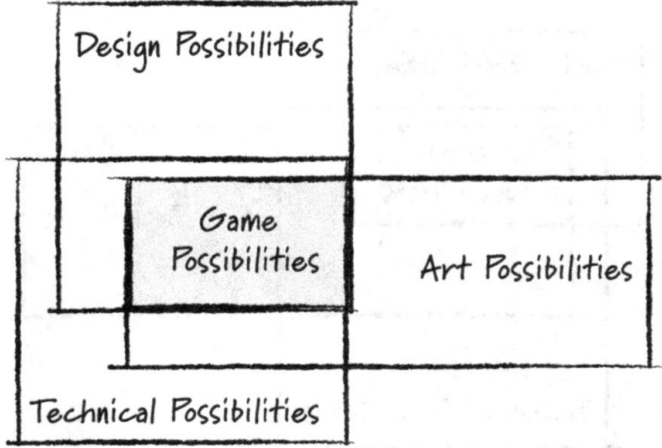

FIGURE 12.4 The set of possibilities at the start of a project

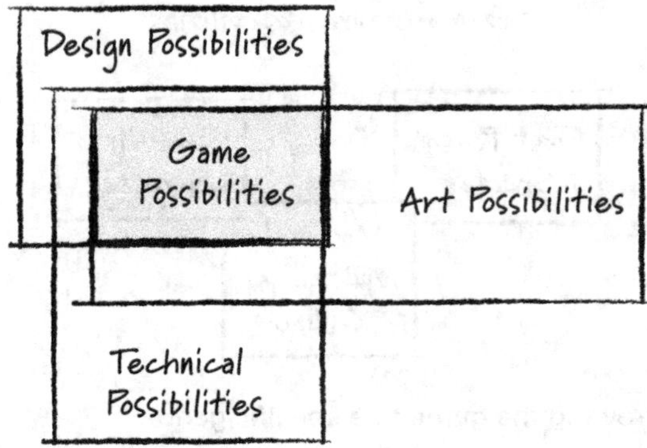

FIGURE 12.5 The set of possibilities as the project progresses

This refinement of scope slowly happens through iteration and discovery. It requires cross-discipline collaboration to find a common ground so that effort is spent on a rich set of features possible for everyone to succeed.

Problems occur when the disciplines branch off from one another and plan in isolation. If the disciplines refine their set of possibilities too early or in isolation, then it greatly reduces the set of overlapping options for the game. This approach is called **point-based design** in which a single discipline design is refined in isolation (usually the game design). The set of design options have been narrowed so much that the overlapping game feature set has been vastly reduced, as shown in Figure 12.6.

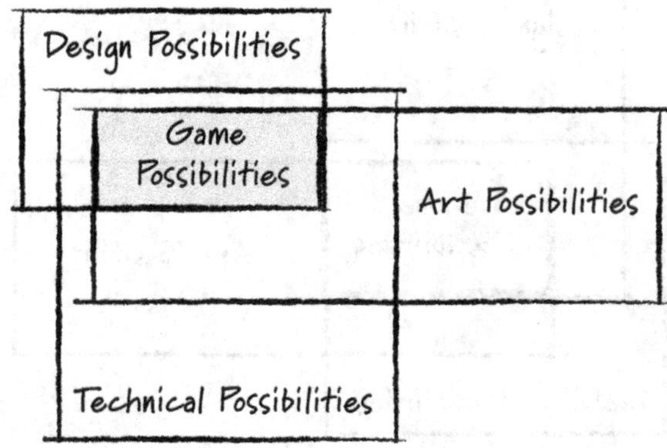

FIGURE 12.6 Narrowing game design too soon

This is the reason for cross-discipline planning. It keeps options open and the union of all sets as large as possible, so when more is learned, the project has a wider range of options.

An example of the problem with a point-based design was with a level-streaming decision made early on a game called Darkwatch. Early in development the designers decided that contiguous sections of levels had to be streamed off the game disc in the background during gameplay so that the player felt the game was taking place in one large world. The decision was made although no technical or art tool solutions for such streaming existed.

Entire level designs were created based on the assumption that the technology and tool set would be created and that artists would be able to author the streaming levels efficiently. Unfortunately, these assumptions were proven false. The effort required to implement the full streaming technology left no time to create the tools necessary for the artists to manipulate the levels. As a result, the levels were "chopped up" into small segments, and these segments were loaded while the player waited. The gameplay experience suffered greatly from this.

Another approach to narrowing multidiscipline designs, called **set-based design**, is used to keep design options alive as a number of solutions are explored and the best design is converged upon. Set-based design has been shown to produce the best solutions in the shortest possible time (Poppendieck and Poppendieck 2003).

A set-based design approach to such a problem as the streaming level example is different from a typical point-based design. Instead, a number of options are explored:

- A full level-streaming solution
- A solution that streams portions of the levels (props and textures)
- No streaming at all

As each option matures, knowledge is built to enable a better decision to be made before level production. Potential solutions are dropped as soon as enough is learned about cost, risk, and value to show that they weren't viable. Although developing three solutions sounds more expensive, it is the best way to reduce cost over the course of the project.

Making decisions too early is a source of many costly mistakes. This is difficult to combat since such decisions are often equated with reducing risk or uncertainty. In point of fact, early decisions do not reduce risk or uncertainty. The delay of the level design decision in the set-based design approach is an example of postponing a decision as long as it can be delayed and no longer. This is an essential part of set-based design.

Lead Designer Role

The lead designer's role is similar to other lead roles; they mentor less-experienced designers and ensure that the design role is consistent across multiple Scrum teams. Lead designers meet with the other project designers on a regular basis (often once a week) to discuss design issues across all teams (see Chapter 8, "Teams," to learn about communities of practice).

Scrum demonstrates—through sprint results—whether the project has enough designers. Scrum teams challenge designers who cannot communicate effectively. A benefit of Scrum is in exposing these problems so that a lead designer will step in to mentor less-experienced designers.

Designer as Product Owner?

Many game development studios using Scrum make the lead designer the product owner for a game. This is often a good fit since the product owner role creates vision, and when we think of visionaries, we often think of successful designers such as Miyamoto, Shafer, Wright, and Meier. Lead designers make excellent product owners for the following reasons:

- Designers represent the player more than any other discipline.
- The product vision is driven primarily by design.
- Design is highly collaborative. Experienced designers should be experienced in communicating vision to all disciplines.

On the other hand, designers often lack experience for some product owner responsibilities:

- **Responsible for the return on investment:** Most designers I've known often need to be reminded of the cost implications of their designs! A product owner needs to carefully evaluate costs against the value for each feature.
- **Project management experience:** Teams accomplish many, but not all, of the duties traditionally assigned to someone in a project manager role. Many requirements or resources that have long lead times require a long-term management view.
- **Avoiding a design bias:** Product owners need to understand the issues and limitations for all disciplines. They cannot assume that everything outside the realm of design "can be handled by others."

For these reasons, it's often beneficial to have a senior producer support the "designer as product owner." A producer can be a voice of reason and cost management.

Summary

Agile reverses the trend of isolation of disciplines. This trend sees designers turning more to long-term plans and documentation to communicate with teams that are ever increasing in size. Scrum practices require the designers to collaborate and communicate face-to-face on small, cross-discipline teams.

In reversing this trend, designers need to embrace the benefit of emergent design. No designer has a crystal ball about any mechanic. The limitations of what is possible prevent this. Instead, they need to ensure that their vision is communicated and open to all potential ideas.

Additional Reading

McGuire, R. 2006. *Paper burns: Game design with agile methodologies.* www.gamasutra.com/view/feature/2742/paper_burns_game_design_with_.php.

Chapter 13

Agile QA and Production

Part of the role definition for quality assurance and production is the ability to communicate with all disciplines. Since fostering a common language across all disciplines is a principle for agile game teams, QA and production have an advantage when agile is adopted.

At the same time, agile practices change the role of QA and production the most. Fortunately, the change is for the better. This chapter addresses those changes and how the QA and production roles fit into agile teams and organizations.

Agile QA

Every year I'm invited to my sons' school for parent career day. It's always fun. To the class, "video game developer" is the coolest career imaginable. I could be standing next to the "astronaut/secret agent" dad wearing his space suit, and the kids would climb over him to ask me questions.

An inevitable question is, "How can I be a game tester?" They dream that the role of a tester is eight hours a day of the same fun they experience playing games. What could be better than that? Unfortunately, I am forced to destroy this notion. I describe the long hours with games that crash. I describe how testers are often very frustrated because they have an understanding of what the game is and have very little influence over how it is developed. I don't want to discourage future generations of testers; I just don't want to give the impression that there is this wonderful job waiting for them because they are "good at playing games."

As you may guess, the QA role attracts people who are passionate about games. The sheer number of people applying for this role gives the industry the ability to choose from among the best. We need to leverage their passion and experience far more.

In this section, we'll learn how to do that. We'll explore the role of QA on a game development project, and we'll explore how it changes on an agile team.

The Problem with QA

Traditionally, quality assurance is largely performed at the end of the project by a dedicated QA team. Figure 13.1 shows the pattern where most bugs are discovered on such a project after alpha, when all features are considered complete but not debugged.

The reason for this is simple; testing is performed on a potentially shippable game. Since the typical game project does not achieve this state until post-production, most testing has to be compressed between the alpha and ship dates. As a result, armies of testers are hired in hopes of achieving a ship date with a working game. It is impossible to hire and properly train a small army quickly, so testers are minimally trained for each game.

This type of quality assurance doesn't always assure the highest quality. By alpha, the important decisions about the game have been made, and the job of QA is to find and report minor defects. Most major defects are rooted too deep in the design or architecture of the game to be properly addressed. For example, if level pacing isn't fun, it may be too late to correct it. This compromises the quality of the final game.

The other problem with traditional testing practices is that quality becomes the responsibility of remote[1] QA and not the developers. Studio cultures

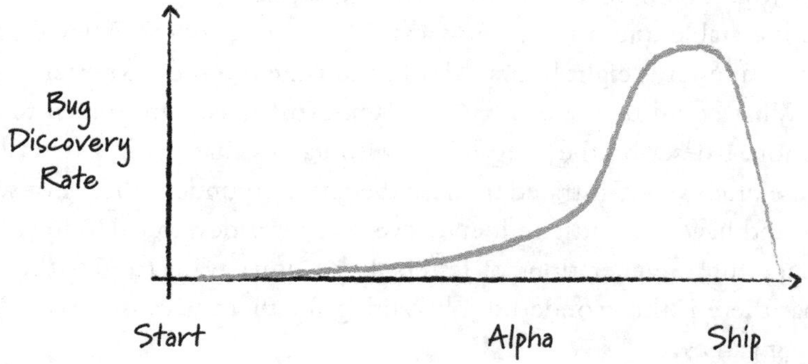

FIGURE 13.1 Bug discovery rate on a traditional project

1. Such as a publisher's QA department in another location or a QA service

encourage this by basing employee performance evaluations on the pace of feature implementation or asset creation. Bugs that do not stop progress are considered part of making the game and are tolerated before alpha. Adding QA practices during this time slows feature and asset creation in the short-term, so it is deferred.

BLACK BOX AND WHITE BOX TESTING

Testing can be divided into two types: black-box and white-box testing.

Black-box testing uses a player's perspective to test a game at the highest level. A tester is given a list of expected behaviors and the conditions or input for causing them. The tester then ensures that they occur. It's also meant to ensure the pacing and mechanics are fun and engaging (see the "Play-Testing" section later in this chapter).

White-box testing uses an internal perspective to test a game. The components of the game, from code to assets, are examined and tested for standards and functional compliance. This requires skill and experience in the discipline that created the code or asset to be tested.

Agile Testing Is Not a Phase

The approach to QA on an agile project is different from that of a traditional project in a number of ways:

- **Testing takes place on an agile project throughout its life cycle:** This is a major benefit of creating a potentially shippable version of the game every sprint. Defects are not deferred or tolerated.
- **Testing is white-box testing:** Testing focuses on the internal components of the game rather than the game as a whole. This requires more skilled "product analysts" who can specialize in areas such as code reviews and test automation.
- **QA is part of every role:** Each developer performs QA in their daily work. QA doesn't eliminate this need but catches problems that slip through and helps improve team practices so that similar problems are more likely to be caught by the developer in the future.

Although large testing groups are still built up in post-production, an agile project maintains a core QA group throughout the project. The goal is to catch most problems as they occur, well before alpha, as shown in Figure 13.2.

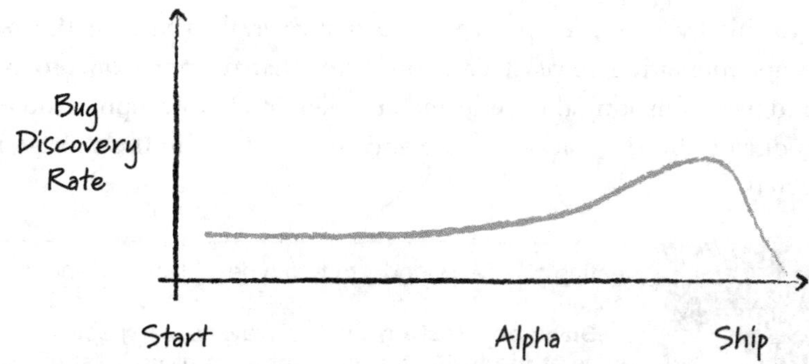

FIGURE 13.2 Bug discovery rate on an agile project

DEFINITION

The game industry traditionally refers to members of a QA group as **testers**. This title becomes obsolete as a studio adopts agile. Testing becomes part of everyone's job, and the QA function specializes and overlaps those of other disciplines. However, since everyone uses the term **testers**, I use it here along with **QA**, which defines the role more than the individual.

The Role of QA on an Agile Game Team

Compared to traditional approaches, agile projects extract more value from testing. Much of this value comes from each team's goal of delivering a playable and potentially shippable game every sprint. The QA role shifts to take advantage of this:

- Testers are members of teams, rather than gathered in separate QA pools. This increases the speed of feedback on defects to the developers.
- Stories require QA action for approval before they are considered done by the development team.[2] This creates a true pace of development, which should include fixing defects and reduces the cost and added risk of fixing them at a later date.
- QA's voice is heard throughout development, not just at the end. This allows their valuable feedback to influence the game.

2. The product owner has the final say, however.

QA's role on an agile team grows beyond its traditional role. It starts with QA's participation in sprint planning. As each story is discussed, QA needs to understand how that story will be approved, before tasks are estimated. This usually takes the form of how the story and the conditions of satisfaction (CoS) are written.

Consider, for example, the following story:

> As a player, when I hit the jump button, my character will jump.

The team discusses this story and may ask the following questions:

- Will the character have jump animation? Will it need smooth transitions?
- Can the character jump to a higher level?
- Can the character jump from a moving platform?
- Can the character jump while walking or running?

These questions help the team understand the tasks necessary to implement and test the story to ensure it is done. For example, the answers to the previous questions may define the following CoS:

- The character will have a simple stand-in animation that will not be blended.
- The character will jump up to a ledge or down to a lower level.
- The character is not expected to jump correctly from a moving platform.
- The character can jump from any starting motion, but its momentum will be ignored. It can jump only a fixed distance and height.

Using these CoS, both QA and the developers verify that the story is complete before the end of the sprint.

QA should also locate problems that are not part of specific CoS but are part of development. For example, if the test level is missing some physical geometry that enables the player to "fall through the world," QA should identify it as an impediment.

A tester should help to ensure that the team is not impacting other teams. This includes the following:

- **Performing regression tests on areas the team is working on that could break other areas of the game:** For example, if the team is working on character control for jumping, keep an eye on other character motions to ensure that some side effect of the team's changes is not breaking them. Another example would be if every time a player dies, their character assumes the jump pose, then the team working on jumping has probably broken something!

- **Testing tools and pipeline changes that a support team wants to release to the content creators:** This includes testing beta versions of a tool with the content creators to verify changes have not broken a workflow.
- **Finding ways to improve testing:** For example, if bad textures are frequently crashing the game, QA should raise a request to have the texture exporters improved to catch the problem.

Some of QA's time is spent verifying gameplay and offering advice on areas of improvement. This requires an ongoing dialogue with members of the team. Since QA is a voice for the consumer, they need to keep a "consumer eye" on the game. They should point out any issue that the consumer will notice (such as progression stoppers).

QA will be challenged in this new role. They are required to communicate with every discipline, understand the tools, and stand up and be heard. QA has traditionally been a "gateway role" for other roles in game development, so it's appropriate to develop these skills to grow their career in game development.

QA, Embedded or in Pools?

To what degree should testers be spread across teams or located in a QA pool that tests independently? There is no simple answer beyond "It depends." It depends on what the team and project need in order to ensure that quality is built into everything they are working on. It depends on the skill level of the testers and how much white-box testing they can accomplish. It depends on the testing tools, harnesses, and telemetry that are available.

When a game is in early development, the depth of gameplay and limited assets don't need as much separate testing; teams might share testers. As the project progresses, there is more to test. The game may need to run on several platforms. The growth of complexity requires not only more testing of the added features but more regression testing to ensure that previously added features have not been inadvertently broken. QA pools can even out this workflow, helping team testers in times of need. As a game approaches its ship date, QA may be concentrated in a single pool or in separate pools dedicated to each platform.

When a tester is embedded within a single team, they take on a more expanded role. They can assist the team in addressing impediments and completing tasks. For example, if an artist needs to test an asset on the PS3, an embedded tester can help them by creating a PS3 build, launching it, and calling the artist over when the asset is visible. Embedded testing encourages a tester to build their white-box testing skills and knowledge to overlap their work with the other developers on the team.

How Many Testers per Team?

A frequent question raised is, "How many testers does a Scrum team need, and when should they be added?" It's the same as asking how many animators or audio designers a team needs; the answer is "as many as you need!"

The number of testers depends on the testing needs of the team. This hinges on the following:

- **The definition of *done*:** As the definition of *done* for sprints approaches the final shippable state, more testing is required. For example, if a definition of *done* requires the game to be completely playable from start to finish without crashes on any platform, more testers are required than in early development when the game has to run on a development PC for a few minutes at a time.
- **Team testing practices:** If the team uses practices that support higher quality, such as TDD or thorough export testing, there will be fewer problems that QA is needed to find.
- **Test automation:** It depends on the coverage level of automated test utilities, ranging from simple smoke tests to complex scripting, that allow the game to "play itself" and offload manual testing.
- **Playability testing needs:** The game needs hands-on, in-depth testing from a player's perspective. QA needs to evaluate usability, pacing, and difficulty levels and provide feedback to the team.

Typically, one tester per team is enough for most of the project, but ultimately the team's needs are driven by sprint results. As the stakeholders raise the definition of *done*, it may put pressure on the team to recruit more testers to help them to meet their goals.

Using a Bug Database

As discussed in Chapter 7, "Video Game Project Planning," a debugging stage after the alpha date is unavoidable for many games. For these projects, the QA staff is expanded, and the entire game is tested from beginning to end.

It's dangerous for a project to rely too much on post-production testing and allow significant defects to remain undetected throughout production. When such defects are uncovered after alpha, they can invalidate a great deal of work. For example, discovering that the disc budget has been exceeded by 50% in post-production is very bad.

Ideally, post-production efforts should focus on tuning and polishing tasks that are identified and prioritized daily. Even without major flaws, tracking polishing, tuning, and minor bug-fix tasks can overwhelm a sprint task-board approach.

It's important that there be only one product backlog for the team. It's important for the product owner to prioritize a single list of work for the team to draw from every sprint. Before alpha, any bugs that are addressed must either come from the team during the sprint or come from the product backlog. If a bug database is maintained prior to alpha, then any bugs that are to be worked on are moved from there and placed on the product backlog to be prioritized by the product owner.

At alpha, all unimplemented stories on the product backlog are cleared off (they may become part of the product backlog for the next version of the game). From here out, only bug fixing and tuning work can be placed on the product backlog. The product backlog might even be replaced by the bug database.

The product owner manages the priority of bugs with QA through frequent triage sessions. As with hardening sprints, described in Chapter 6, "Agile Planning," the team draws a set of tasks to work on daily, without a specific sprint goal. The new goal is to burn down all the high-priority bug fixes and tuning work.

Play-Testing

A major benefit of producing a potentially shippable version of the game every sprint or release is that a game is tested early by potential consumers. **Play-testing** is a practice where consumers are lured in to play a game in development—often with the offer of free pizza—and provide useful feedback about the gameplay experience.

Play-testing can be as informal as a conversation. It can also take a more scientific approach by recording progress metrics or the answers to carefully designed surveys.

Play-testing has substantial, but limited, benefits:

- **It reinforces a definition of *done*:** Developers, who see a game every day, overlook flaws or shortcomings. Play-testing is often a shock when they observe how these problems impact real consumers. For example, that missing piece of collision geometry is always found by play-testers!
- **It won't produce any breakthrough ideas:** Don't expect the play-testers to provide original ideas. That's the developer's job. At best, they provide feedback that can improve backlog prioritization.
- **It teaches about usability and challenge:** Ever see a player simply run past a painstakingly scripted boss? It's a sobering thing to see. It's also very frustrating to see a player walk against a wall for two minutes until you realize that they are trying to make sense of a HUD map that is too vague!

EXPERIENCE

Play-testing is a tool for focusing a team on ***done***. We often scheduled play-testing sessions for the end of a sprint. This made the team look at the game with a different set of eyes and uncovered many polishing and tuning tasks that had previously been invisible to us.

Play-testing is often organized and run by QA or usability specialists. These duties include the following:

- **Recruiting play-testers:** Local universities and game retail shops are teeming with good play-test candidates. Be sure to enlist people who represent the full scale of demographics and skill levels. For example, a hard-core gamer won't provide the same feedback about the tutorial level as a casual gamer. Maintain a database of people, and invite the more valuable play-testers back.
- **Organizing and running the session:** A poorly organized and run session elicits inferior feedback from play-testers. Don't waste their time.
- **Including the developers:** It's very beneficial for the developers to see players interacting with their game in ways they did not anticipate. It can lead to improved interfaces and usability (see the sidebar "Damage Meter").

- **Letting play-testers meet the other developers:** Many testers are curious about game development and relish the opportunity to speak with the rest of the team at the end of the session. Encourage this. The conversations can be very fruitful!
- **Publishing the results:** QA's observations of how well the game was received provide many insights. However, care must be taken not to "overinterpret" the results to include subjective bias from QA. A simple compilation of the answers helps the team understand the results. Leave the conclusions to the readers or discuss them together.

Maintaining the playability of the game allows everyone to value the working game over the comprehensive design.

DAMAGE METER

During the development of Midtown Madness, we needed to find a way to communicate the level of damage to the player's car. This was important because if a car accumulated 100% damage, it stalled, and the player lost the race.

We first drew a meter that grew as damage increased. During play-testing, we found that half the players quickly and intuitively understood that a growing meter indicated growing damage, but the other half did not.

We then switched to a health meter that shrank as the car became more damaged and "lost its health." Once again, play-testing showed that half the testers understood it immediately, while the other half did not.

So, we went back to the drawing board. How could we communicate the car's damage level in a way that every player would immediately understand? Someone suggested we communicate a wider range of damage on the car's body. It was a great idea. We already had some body-damage effects, but it wasn't enough. So, we added wobbling tires, broken side mirrors, smashed windows, and smoke that darkened as the car approached destruction. At one point, we even added flames, but the vehicle licensees vetoed that effect!

At the next play-test session, all of the players understood the damage level of their cars!

The Future of QA

As the game industry continues to improve agile practices, the role of QA continues to transform. As testing becomes more white-box driven, testers require more knowledge about development disciplines, and testing specialties will grow. For example, test engineers in many industries focus on the quality of the code being produced by programmers. These specialists run code-quality scanner tools[3] and measure unit test coverage to ensure that coding practices are being held to a high standard. Is this a testing role or programming role? It's a bit of both, and it represents a typical evolution and blurring of roles in an agile environment.

The rising importance, skill level, and value of testers on an agile game project will improve the role and make it a truly desirable career.

Agile Production

Producers are the most open to adopting agile but usually with some trepidation. They are the first to foresee its benefits, but they are also concerned about the implications to their role on an agile game project. The main concern is that as teams become self-organizing and self-managing, then there will be no need for producers. In reality, producers are often the engines of ongoing agile adoption. As with the discipline lead roles, the production role is divested of many of the mundane tasks with agile, such as tracking hourly estimates and solving the myriads of small problems that cross-discipline teams handle themselves. Instead, an agile producer expands their focus on the big picture while helping teams achieve continual improvement in how they create games.

This section identifies the changes in responsibility for the traditional producer on a Scrum project and how they can assume the ScrumMaster, product owner, or product owner support role.

The Role of a Producer on an Agile Project

Producers are often seen as the person who makes sure everything gets done. This is not the case on an Scrum project. As Scrum teams take responsibility for what is done every sprint, they relieve the producer of some daily project management tasks:

- **Building and maintaining detailed schedules:** Scrum teams create and estimate their own tasks.
- **Tracking daily tasks for each member of the development staff:** This is managed in the daily scrums by the team.
- **Managing dependencies:** Cross-discipline teams manage dependencies daily and in sprint planning by selecting goals and team members who avoid external dependencies.

---

3. Such as PC-Lint

Instead, the producer should focus on the larger project management challenges:

- **Tracking external dependencies:** Will the outsourced cinematics be delivered on time?
- **Publisher collaboration:** Are the stakeholders playing the game if they can't attend a review?
- **Outsourcing support:** What does the outsourced level art team need to complete their work?
- **First-party (platform) support:** When are we scheduled for acceptance testing, and what are the requirements?
- **Risk management:** What are the external schedule and resource risks for obtaining licensee approval or assets?
- **Critical chain management:** What are the resource schedule needs for the production assets?

Most of these responsibilities are best described in a number of good game production books (see the "Additional Reading" section at the end of the chapter).

Producer as ScrumMaster

Many studios adopting agile struggle with identifying people to best fill the ScrumMaster role. It's often assumed that the producer is natural for the role, and many times this is true. There are benefits and potential drawbacks with a producer taking on the ScrumMaster role.

A benefit seen with producers in the ScrumMaster role is the ability to communicate equally well with all the disciplines. This is essential for a cross-discipline team. This allows them to remain unbiased toward issues or unconflicted about what they need to do. For example, programmers who become ScrumMasters often see issues through a filter that says most problems are best solved with code. This leaves the other disciplines feeling less supported.

Another benefit is that producers usually have fewer tasks to commit to every sprint. This prevents them from having to choose between completing critical tasks and supporting the team. Depending on the team, the ScrumMaster role can take anywhere from 33% to 100% of a person's time.

A common drawback with a producer taking the ScrumMaster role derives from their past duties on more preplanned projects. These duties required producers to lead individuals toward task completion. However, Scrum teams manage their own tasks to achieve a sprint goal as a team. The ScrumMaster does not interfere with the team by creating, estimating, assigning, and tracking tasks for them. Unfortunately, some producers assume, out of habit, that the ScrumMaster role continues to focus on tasks. This prevents teams from achieving all of the benefits associated with self-management.

Producer as Product Owner Support

On large game projects, the demands of a product owner's time has led to hierarchies of product owners (see Chapter 9, "Faster Iterations"). Similarly, the long-term demands of production planning, resource requirements, marketing, licensing, and first-party hardware support have led product owners to seek production support.

As a result, it is common to pair a product owner with a senior producer. The product owner manages vision while the senior producer attends to many project management details. This support enables the product owner to make better decisions based on license, franchise, budget, and schedule limitations.

License and franchise details are usually managed by the product owner, but there are details that need to be handled on a day-by-day basis. For example, providing sample assets or seeking approval on the use of brands or likenesses can be very time-consuming.

The most important schedule and budget limitations are those that define the production requirements and dates. Pre-production creates cost and schedule debt that is paid off in production. The product owner needs to monitor this debt to ensure it doesn't grow beyond the limits of schedule and cost defined by the stakeholders. For example, before defining the number of characters to produce, the cost for a single shippable character needs to be understood.

A product owner and senior producer make an effective pair to create the best game at the right cost and schedule.

Producer as Product Owner

Many successful games have been led by a senior producer who provides project management and vision for the game. As with lead designers who have strong project management skills, a senior producer with a strong vision of what the market wants is rare and invaluable.

When a studio has such a producer, the product owner role is ideal for them. The role leverages vision and project management strengths like no other (see Chapter 3, "Scrum").

The Future of Production

As the industry becomes more agile, the producer role will include specialized and team roles.

Teams no longer need the ubiquitous "gopher" but will need the support of the following specialists:

- Outsourcing/insourcing
- Licensing
- Franchise management
- Production planning and support
- Technical production (including first-party communication)

Producers can successfully assume the ScrumMaster and product owner roles as well. Production will not disappear from agile studios but flourish.

Summary

Agile QA and production will continue to draw people who have these primary strengths:

- A deep passion for video games
- Great organizational skills
- Great communication skills

These strengths are in demand in every industry, and the game industry has to compete for them like any other. By leveraging them, agile organizations reap major benefits from QA and production, while testers and producers receive greater challenges in which to rise.

Additional Reading

Chandler, H. 2008. *The Game Production Handbook, Second Edition*. Sudbury, MA: Jones and Bartlett Publishers.

Crispen, L., and J. Gregory. 2009. *Agile Testing: A Practical Guide for Testers and Agile Teams*. Boston: Addison-Wesley.

Hight, J., and J. Novak. 2007. *Game Development Essentials: Game Project Management*. Clifton Park, NY: Delmar Cengage Learning.

Irish, D. 2005. *The Game Producer's Handbook*. Boston: Course Technology PTR.

Isbister, K., and N. Schaffer. 2008. *Game Usability*. San Diego: Morgan Kaufmann.

Laramee, F. D. 2003. *Secrets of the Game Business*. Boston: Charles River Media.

Part V

Getting Started

Chapter 14

The Myths and Challenges of Scrum

A studio's development process is a reflection of its culture, and cultures change slowly. Change usually has to overcome resistance, but change happens—especially in the game industry—whether we like it or not.

Change requires commitment from a studio. It should avoid quick-fix solutions or ritual adherence to defined practices. With agile adoption, both of these extremes are often seen. Some fall in love with the values and principles and dive into adoption with full faith that the only possible outcome is success. Others sabotage agile adoption from the start. Saboteurs repeat "urban legends of agile failure" or label agile as "the latest management fad." This is referred to as spreading fear, uncertainty, and doubt and is addressed later in the chapter.

There is a kernel of truth to many of the myths. This chapter identifies the major ones about agile and Scrum. The purpose of this chapter is to look behind the myths and explore the truths and falsehoods that they rely upon. It will also explore many of the barriers to Scrum adoption. Exposing these facts enables a studio to better judge the value of agile because the best possible path for adopting it is to understand the reasons behind every practice and leave little to faith. This is the benefit of an empirical system: to base what we do on what we know rather than on theory or conjecture.

Silver Bullet Myths

Common to the tales of vampire slayers, silver bullets possess magical properties that give the hero an advantage when facing certain disaster.

Often the adoption of Scrum is motivated by a project disaster. A studio ships a game that is a financial failure or has a project canceled because of budget, schedule, or quality problems. During these times, studio management is more open to change. This isn't necessarily bad, but desperation often leads them to seek a project management silver bullet.

The problem is that Scrum doesn't work miracles. It has no magical properties. Improvements in development by using it require an understanding of the underlying principles, not blind faith. Scrum is a framework to build a process that supports talent, great teams, and leaders. It does not replace them.

By avoiding the following silver bullet myths, you avoid falling into the trap of thinking a process can solve all your problems.

Scrum Will Solve All of Your Problems for You

Sometimes we have grand assumptions about what a process can accomplish. Perhaps if we create enough rules, then everyone will follow them, and problems will disappear. The truth is that if there are underlying problems, Scrum will only expose those problems. It doesn't solve them.

EXPERIENCE

A former California studio adopted Scrum following another project failure. From the start, the daily scrums unleashed a flood of complaints about studio operations. Management quickly decided that Scrum was the source of these problems and immediately halted its use. As expected, the level of complaints fell off, and management felt that they had averted a disaster.

The best that can be asked of Scrum is to facilitate problem solving through transparency. What is done with this transparency depends on a studio's culture. This studio closed because they ignored the problems that existed for years.

Projects Using Scrum Can Always Ship on Time

Another myth is that Scrum teams always ship games on time. This is born out of desperation to avoid delays from impossible schedules, but Scrum won't accomplish miracles.

Many projects attempt to fix budget, schedule, and scope simultaneously. A benefit of Scrum is that you measure velocity against the goal and know what is possible early on, make the right decisions and commitments, and then monitor and progressively refine those decisions.

Sometimes Scrum is blamed and abandoned when its empirical measures show that a goal is impossible. The goal was probably impossible to begin with, but Scrum reveals it sooner than a traditional project, which enables problems to be hidden.

Fear, Uncertainty, and Doubt

Some myths fall under the category of fear, uncertainty, and doubt (FUD).[1] FUD myths are like urban legends; they are exaggerated stories that have a kernel of truth that make them stick.

There are many reasons people use FUD to sabotage agile adoption. The main reason is that change alone creates FUD. Change threatens the status quo and therefore a person's security in their position. Sometimes the memory of past successes creates the belief that the practices used then will continue to apply equally as well in the future. Problems are seen not with the process, which has proven itself, but with the developers using it now.

This section addresses some of the common FUD myths about agile. Chapter 15, "Working with a Publisher," will address strategies of overcoming the status quo, which can be the greatest obstacle to adopting agile.

Endless Development

> Agile teams never plan. They just iterate without a goal.

Sometimes a team new to Scrum assumes that being agile means they don't need to plan. They start by iterating to discover the game that emerges. Eventually the urgency to ship intrudes, and the team has to scramble, often with enforced overtime, to finish something. This isn't agile. It's an iterative and incremental death march. It's a danger for agile teams that don't sufficiently plan.

It is also essential to have a shared vision for any project, whether it is agile or not. If the product owner on a Scrum team does not provide a vision, the team cannot be sure that their work creates the greatest stakeholder value.

EXPERIENCE

I once knew a team that had no product owner. They were working on a first-person shooter. The product backlog was prioritized by the lead programmer. Since he was focused on physics, each sprint would show increasingly impressive physical effects. After their first release, buoyant rag-doll bodies were seen floating down a stream in front of the player. When we asked to see how enemies were shot and fell into the stream, we were told that shooting wasn't implemented yet.

A few months later the stakeholders canceled the project.

---

1. http://en.wikipedia.org/wiki/Fear,_uncertainty_and_doubt

Management Fad

> Scrum is just another management fad. It will be replaced by something else next month.

Someone investigating agile will encounter labels such as Scrum, Extreme Programming, Evo, RUP, Scrum-#, Scrum Type-C, lean, feature-driven development, kanban, and so on. It's a confusing process landscape. This was one motivation behind the agile manifesto. Decades of discovery about how people best work together to create new products are embodied in its simple values and principles. It is an umbrella "brand" name for any number of processes and frameworks that embrace them.

The expanding list of labels represents the various practices that are constantly emerging as agile becomes more common and accepted. This book has described numerous practices for game development that lie outside the core definition of Scrum. We could label them (perhaps *Scrum-G*), but the point is for each studio to evolve and adopt their own practices to best fit their needs. There will never be a single template for game development that applies to even a majority of game types or studios!

Scrum is a great starting place. For almost a decade, people such as Mike Cohn and Ken Schwaber have fought to keep it a simple framework for each team to adapt for the needs of their products:

> Agile will go away, but it will most likely go away in the same way discussing the merits of object-oriented development went away. Agile will eventually become the accepted way of doing things, and it will just be what we do. In the same way no one says, "Gotta run, I'm late for the object-oriented design meeting" (they just say "design meeting"), we will stop talking about agile development but only after it is the norm.
>
> —Mike Cohn

The Double Standard

> We hear one of two things about Scrum. Either Scrum was successful, or if the project using it failed, it did so because they weren't using Scrum correctly.

Scrum can't be blamed for failure or even credited with success. Teams succeed or fail because of many factors: technology, capability, vision, communication, collaboration, talent, or even the underlying idea of the game. Scrum creates transparency into how well these elements are working, often in a measurable way, but that's all. It doesn't prescribe what to do when sprints repeatedly show the game isn't fun or the velocity of the team is low.

Change Is Bad

> Our process has worked in the past. If we change things, we'll fail.

Studios have a certain level of resistance to change in the process they use to create games. This is not necessarily a bad thing. A studio's process evolves over many years. It's reinforced by its strengths and successes.

However, processes also embed cultural weaknesses. For example, many studios institute a one- or two-week "lockdown" before a milestone date. The lockdown ensures that no new features are allowed into the build that can destabilize it while the build is debugged and polished. This is a concession to a development culture that allows too many defects into the game during development.

Lockdowns slow development because the cost of fixing bugs increases the longer you wait. Also, the entire project staff is usually not engaged in bug fixing during a lockdown, and therefore they have to find other things to do. Lockdowns also end up becoming a dumping ground for checking in bug-ridden code or unpolished assets under the assumption that they will be fixed later. This creates a vicious cycle that can inflate the duration of future lockdowns!

Changing core practices, such as introducing unit testing to improve code quality, is more challenging than adding a quick fix, such as a lockdown. The problem is that quick-fix practices become a normal part of a development.

Over months and years, such quick fixes build up. Each of them adds a bit of drag to development. Resistance to change prevents corrections to the process until there is a catastrophic failure (such as a project cancellation over high cost or slow progress).

NORMALIZATION OF DEVIANCE

Two examples of how ignoring problems can lead to tragedy are the Challenger and Columbia space shuttle disasters that took the lives of 14 astronauts. Both incidents involved problems that were well known and documented with the shuttle system. These problems had occurred frequently but had not resulted in the loss of a shuttle. As a result, they became an acceptable part of operations until there was an accident.

Following the Challenger accident review, the phrase ***normalization of deviance*** was coined (Vaughan 1996) to describe how the attitude toward defects in the shuttle system resulted in its loss. Unfortunately, identifying this problem with NASA's culture was not enough to prevent it from contributing to the loss of the Columbia years later.

Endless Meetings

Scrum consists of nothing but meetings!

As previously described, the meetings defined by Scrum within a sprint cycle are as follows:

- Daily scrum
- Sprint review
- Sprint planning
- Sprint retrospective

All of these meetings, except for the daily scrum, occur once a sprint. Many teams find that for a four-week sprint, these once-a-sprint meetings can be conducted in a single day. This represents one day of meetings for a 20-working-day sprint, or 5% of the available time. The daily scrum meeting is a 15-minute, timeboxed daily meeting. This uses about 3% of the working day. Totaling these percentages results in 8% of a team's time, or a little more than three hours of meetings each week average.

Scrum meetings are optimized to create the highest bandwidth of necessary communication. A 15-minute daily scrum will often identify issues that are easily solved within a day. If not identified, the issue might grow to waste days and require hours of meetings to address weeks later.

The details in this book will help teams run these meetings as effectively as possible without losing their benefits. If any of these meetings do not engage everyone attending nearly 100% of the time, then there is room for improvement.

NOTE

Shorter sprints will use a greater percentage of time in meetings. For example, the sprint review, planning, and retrospectives might take six hours to complete for a two-week sprint rather than the eight that a four-week sprint might require. See Chapter 4, "Sprints."

CONSISTENCY AND MONKEYS

Consistency is a hard-coded survival trait. Change is resisted. It's a primal instinct. I never fully appreciated this fact until I read about the following experiment (Stephenson 1967).

Five monkeys were placed in a room with a banana tree at the center. Whenever a monkey attempted to climb the tree to pick a banana, a sprinkler system sprayed all the monkeys with water until the monkey retreated from the tree. They repeated this until all the monkeys learned to avoid the tree.

The next stage of the experiment involved replacing one of the monkeys with one who had never been sprayed with water. The new monkey soon approached the banana tree. However, before it could reach the tree, the other monkeys jumped into action and beat the new monkey until it drew back from the banana tree. This was repeated every time until the new monkey learned not to approach the tree.

The researchers continued to replace original monkeys who had been sprayed with water one by one with fresh monkeys. Eventually none of the monkeys in the room had ever been sprayed with water for climbing the banana tree. The monkeys still continued to beat up any monkey who approached the banana tree. None of them "knew why" they shouldn't approach the tree. They just knew that it was off-limits.

Sometimes we developers exhibit similar behavior. A company's culture becomes intertwined with "best practices" that aren't questioned and never replaced. Personally I did this for many years pursuing waterfall methodologies. I wrote big documents and schedules for projects that attempted to address every detail. Even after those projects shipped—following months of crunch and despair—I would start the next project the same way.

Scrum Challenges

> The only thing harder than starting something new is stopping something old.
>
> —Russell L. Ackoff

Scrum is not a "one-size-fits-all" solution for developers. A goal in adopting Scrum is to initiate a never-ending cycle of continual improvement customized to the needs of a studio's culture, people, and products. Before this goal can be realized, a studio or team has to start practicing the fundamentals and navigating early challenges. This section describes a few of these challenges and some of the ways of navigating them.

Scrum as a Tool for Process and Culture Change

Any process can be used to make games, but no process is perfect. Even if we were to identify a perfect process, the constant change in our industry would quickly make it obsolete. This is a major motive for using Scrum. Scrum is not a process; it's a framework for creating and evolving your own process. It can help any organization create transparency, which enables commonsense change.

Scrum will influence every part of your studio. Scrum pressures managers to focus on mentoring and coaching. It involves buy-in from departments such as HR, which can resist the emphasis on team performance. It demands people take ownership in areas in which they had no ownership and give up ownership in areas they once ruled over. It challenges marketing to participate with development far earlier in a project. It even puts pressure on facilities to provide open team areas and wall space.

Scrum adoption starts with creating transparency to expose cultural weaknesses and strengths. An example of this was a studio dominated by technology; games were seen as platforms to demonstrate technical achievement. Tools and pipelines to improve productivity for artists and designers were lower on the list of priorities because the programmers were always trying to accomplish nearly impossible challenges. The build was rarely working because of all the bugs left along the way, so the time it took to iterate on an asset change was very long.

How did Scrum influence change? First, it made the high iteration costs visible. Requiring a potentially shippable version of the game every two to three weeks exposed a lot of problems. At first, the teams spent half their sprints trying to cobble together a working build. Since velocity was measured by the value of the features working in the game, their initial velocity was low.

This simple measurement of velocity is important. Teams need clear performance measurements to evaluate themselves and make changes to improve that measurement. Our example team did this. They started to come up with ways to improve the reliability of the build. Because velocity derives from what is seen in the game, which includes art and design, they formed cross-discipline teams. They colocated to reduce the overhead of communication. Programmers focused on improving tools and pipelines. All of these things improved their velocity.

Before they adopted Scrum, they would have thought that such change was only possible through great technical effort. Scrum allowed cultural change, which resulted in huge performance gains.

EXPERIENCE

"After research into methodologies, we were drawn to the advantages of agile software development and decided to adopt Scrum. Within the first few months of Brütal Legend development, the team was practicing Scrum, and the initial payoffs were impressive. Because of Scrum's emphasis on features over systems, on rapid prototyping and iteration, on cross-disciplinary teams, on people over process, and on the creation of a potentially shippable piece of software, every sprint/milestone made the game playable at a very early stage in development."

—Caroline Esmurdoc, executive producer and COO,
Double Fine Productions, Inc.

Scrum Is About Adding Value, Not Task Tracking

Running a daily scrum is easy. Prioritizing a list of features to be implemented is straightforward. Creating a task board and burndown chart takes minutes. So, why do some teams struggle adopting Scrum?

One reason is that many studios that adopt Scrum come from a task-centric culture. Progress is measured against how well individuals complete their work against estimates. Task tracking is an important tool in Scrum, but value creation takes precedence. If value isn't maximized, then the tasks were wrong.

Have you ever heard someone report "All of the tasks for feature X are completed" only to see that feature X is nowhere near being done? In Scrum, the conversation shifts to discuss a feature's emerging value and the impact on the tasks for that feature. If this shift doesn't occur, then the value of Scrum practices is greatly diminished. For example, in a task-centric culture, the daily scrum is seen as a task-reporting meeting that is easily replaced. In a culture focused on value and team commitment, the daily scrum takes on greater importance.

Cultural change is hard. The status quo will often fight tooth and nail against it. Scrum is a framework for this change, but it comes from real leadership, not from a book or a fixed set of practices.

EXPERIENCE

"One of the first things I did when starting to work with my current team was this: 'We're going to try this Scrum thing. We're going to start with Scrum, but our goal is to end up with a process that fits this team and the work it does. I will never say no to a change proposed by the team, but I insist on one thing. We will try Scrum by the book for at least two sprints (one to learn the process and one to figure out what you don't like about it) before we start making adjustments.' From day one, it was ***their*** process. We were just starting from a template called Scrum."

—Bruce Rennie, independent developer

Status Quo versus Continual Improvement

Building a culture of "continual improvement" is one of the ultimate goals of Scrum. Scrum practitioners use empirical measures to assess benefits of all practices. If, for example, a practice change improves velocity, then it's a beneficial change.

This is a simple idea to introduce, but it can be challenging to embed. The status quo, or groundless resistance to change, is often a tremendous barrier to continual improvement.

Fear of change is not always baseless. Management fears that introducing profound change gambles a studio's future. Introducing change requires bravery. For example, changing a process that may have worked for a PlayStation 2 game paints a big target on the person who changed the process for a PlayStation 3 game. There is enough risk in changing platforms alone to cause someone to hesitate over changing one more variable.

This is why it often takes utter project failure and crisis to usher in significant change. This isn't ideal either since it often leads to the "silver bullet" adoption pattern described previously. Ideally, any method for introducing change needs to do it in ways that

- Make small, reversible steps
- Are measurable to ensure that any perceived improvement is real

Scrum supports change in this manner. At worst, a change in practices will impact a single sprint of two to four weeks. Metrics, such as task burndown slope, user story point velocity, or any number of metrics that the team has introduced, provide frequent measurement of the value of changes.

This change of culture can't happen only from the bottom up. It has to be supported by company leadership. Management needs to understand the tools that Scrum provides them to ensure that teams are making progress and that leadership, vision, and commitment exist.

Lack of management commitment to Scrum and agile principles is a major challenge for studios attempting to adopt Scrum. Under pressure, a manager might find it easier to alter a team's goal midsprint rather than fight to preserve the team's commitment to the sprint goal. Educating management about the benefits of Scrum—especially for them—is an ongoing effort.

EXPERIENCE: "SCRUM IS HARD"

"Traditional project management seems a little backward to me. First you hire a team's worth of really smart, highly diverse people. Then you try to tell them what to do. As far as I'm concerned, you may as well try to stuff an octopus into a string bag. At least that would be easier.

"Because of my belief that the power lies with the people, I searched for a solution that would give it to them. The agile manifesto, and Scrum in particular, provided what I was looking for.

"That doesn't mean that I walked out the door; it means that my role changed to one where I work with the team rather than for the team. Has it always worked? No. Scrum is difficult. Some people only see the framework, the steps to follow; they do not understand that it requires self-reflection, hard work, trust, dedication, and thorough thought."

—Senta Jakobsen, COO, EA DICE

Cargo Cult Scrum

When teams first start using Scrum, they are encouraged to follow the practices "out of the book." This enables them to become accustomed to the practices while the principles sink in. Once the team experiences the initial benefits, they begin altering practices to improve upon those benefits, but it's important that changes to the practices still preserve the principles behind them.

However, some teams stick to the "out-of-the-book" practices and resist changing anything. These teams end up practicing what I call **Cargo Cult Scrum**. This refers to the infamous cargo cults of the Pacific.

Until World War II, many Pacific Islanders were never exposed to Westerners or their technology. This changed drastically during the war when the Navy arrived to occupy the islands and construct airfields. When the airfields were complete, cargo planes would land and bring in supplies. These planes carried many things including simple trinkets that were shared with the islanders to promote goodwill. The islanders loved these objects (such as steel knives and mirrors) and gathered around the airfield every time a large aircraft landed seeking further gifts.

When the war ended, most of these airfields were abandoned, and the cargo planes stopped coming. The islanders once again found themselves isolated from the Western world, but they did not forget the cargo planes and their treasures. They wanted them to return. Out of desperation, they tried to draw the cargo planes back by replicating the practices they saw at airfields during the war.

They constructed bamboo towers and manned them with natives wearing coconut headphones who spoke into pineapple microphones. They built bamboo mock-ups of small planes, lit fires next to the runway, and waved flags of cloth in the air. But the cargo planes did not return. The practices weren't enough to bring them back.

This approach is similar to what is done on Cargo Cult Scrum teams. Following the practices isn't enough to bring the full benefits of highly productive teams. Teams need to understand the principles behind the practices and improve those practices to best fit their product, people, and culture.

Scrum Is Not for Everyone

One of the challenges of Scrum adoption is that Scrum is not for everyone. The initial challenge will be that some people refuse to work in an agile environment and leave. Some of these people will be valuable. They leave because they are not comfortable with the change in their position.

Some developers reject participation in any team activity (such as a daily scrum). Some have grown comfortable from a career of working in relative isolation and being called upon to be heroes during crunch times. Others find a niche in a lax management environment where they are given a great deal of freedom to create technology or assets on their own. Joining a Scrum team and making daily commitments to a team of peers limits these individual freedoms.

Most studios find ways to accommodate these individuals, perhaps creating special "R&D" roles for them, but in many cases they eventually leave. The transparency Scrum introduces to a studio makes such positions stand out and not easily justifiable.

The benefits greatly outweigh the losses. Scrum grows leaders and outstanding contributors at a far greater rate than those who are lost.

Overtime

Scrum doesn't limit teams to working 40-hour weeks. Its practices enable teams to find a sustainable pace of work. This pace is discovered as they commit to sprint goals and learn how much they can achieve sprint after sprint without overextending themselves.

NOTE

In everyday vocabulary, a sprint is something that isn't sustainable. Calling it a **jog** might have been more accurate but less appealing.

A sprint can have many uncertainties. Unanticipated problems or unforeseen work slows progress. When this happens, teams sometimes put in a bit of overtime to fulfill their goal.

How much overtime should a Scrum team work? It's up to them. If they find that they are working overtime too often, they need to address the problems that are causing it. Common examples for this are late commits or handoffs at the end of a sprint or committing to extra polishing and tuning work on the last sprint of a release.

When management doesn't tell teams to work overtime, their attitude about it changes. When a team decides to work overtime, they do it as a team. Occasionally working a few extra hours shoulder to shoulder with your teammates is a team-building experience.

EXPERIENCE: GETTING WORK DONE

"I have a little sticker on my monitor. It reminds me to move fast slowly. I believe that this is how Scrum needs to be practiced within the game industry. The industry has a serious addiction to running around with its hair on fire. There is a propensity to believe that only those with flaming hair are doing real work. This is simply not the case. Although it would be much easier to ignite my hair and start running, real work gets done when I take the time to figure out how to move quickly. The framework that Scrum provides helps to reinforce this."

—Senta Jakobsen, COO, EA DICE

Crunch

Extended periods of enforced overtime are called **crunch**. Many studios that are new to Scrum continue to practice it until the empirical measure of velocity demonstrates its futility.

Studies have shown the impact of crunch on productivity and quality of life.[2] For High Moon Studios, the proof came when management enforced companywide overtime early in our adoption of Scrum. The teams were told to work 10 hours a day for 6 days a week on a troubled project. The subsequent burndown charts told an interesting story. Figure 14.1 shows the hours the average team burned down per week from their sprint backlogs.

Week 1 was a normal workweek, before overtime. Weeks 2 to 5 were crunch weeks of 60 hours each. In the first week of crunch (week 2), velocity greatly increased; more work was being done because of the 50% overtime. However, as weeks passed, the velocity decreased until week 5, when the velocity was less than it was before crunch started!

How is this possible? The reasons are simple. People were tired. They made more mistakes. They lost their concentration.

This realization represented a huge benefit of Scrum for High Moon, providing simple empirical evidence about what works and what doesn't. This is why there is no rule about overtime in Scrum. There doesn't need to be a rule. If your teams are using Scrum to find the best way to work, they'll quickly discover that after several weeks of overtime, any benefit from it is lost. It becomes common sense to maintain a sustainable pace.

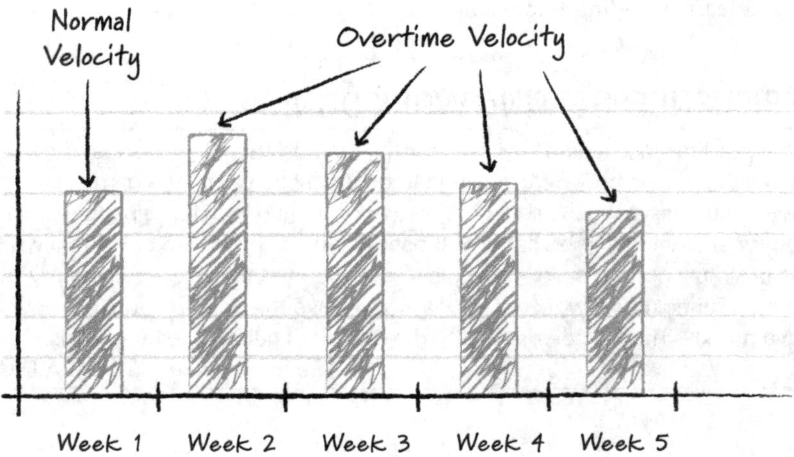

FIGURE 14.1 Burndown during crunch

2. www.igda.org/quality-life-white-paper-info

VELOCITY IN HOURS

Although the term ***velocity*** usually refers to the number of story points accomplished per sprint, the velocity, or change, in hours of work remaining in a sprint per day or week provides interesting, though less stable, feedback about a team.

EXPERIENCE: COUNTING CARS IN THE PARKING LOT

We first started using Scrum at Sammy Studios in 2003. Sammy was owned by a Japanese Pachinko manufacturing company called Sammy Corporation. Although we had gotten off to a slow start, Scrum was helping us get back on track and demonstrate good progress. However, good progress wasn't enough for Sammy Corporation. A source of concern from them was based on the opinion that American game developers don't dedicate as much overtime as Japanese developers. They felt the lack of crunch meant a lack of commitment to the success of the studio.

Sammy Corporation eventually merged with Sega to accelerate their transition into game development and publishing. During this time, they debated about whether to retain Sammy Studios. To help in the debate, they had someone drive past the studio late at night and count the number of cars in the parking lot. The count was low, which to them meant that our commitment to success was also low. Weeks later they informed us that they were closing the studio. Fortunately, our local management was able to acquire the studio, which was renamed as High Moon Studios.

Managers often confuse overtime with commitment. They think that forcing people to work overtime demonstrates commitment to the success of a project. In reality, this is like forcing someone to smile to prove they are happy. It just doesn't work that way.

Summary

The best way to adopt Scrum is to do it with eyes wide open. Establishing useful metrics such as velocity and establishing practices such as the daily scrum provide immediate demonstration of its value.

Scrum is a framework. It doesn't include practices to optimize code, create better art, or tune a mechanic. Those come from each studio's development practices and culture. In this light, there is less to fear about the change Scrum introduces.

Keep the myths and challenges from this chapter in mind as you read Chapter 16, "Launching Scrum." It will continue to introduce challenges and describe how to meet them and what to expect in a studio as Scrum principles take hold.

Additional Reading

Heath, C., and D. Heath. 2007. *Made to Stick: Why Some Ideas Survive and Others Die*. New York: Random House.

Pascale, R. T., M. Milleman, and L. Gioja. 2001. *Surfing the Edge of Chaos: The Laws of Nature and the New Laws of Business*. New York: Three Rivers Press.

Chapter 15

Working with a Publisher

As a member of the Nintendo Ultra-64[1] Dream Team in the mid-nineties, Angel Studios was exposed to a very collaborative publishing model. Nintendo and Angel discussed a game idea, and we were asked to "find the fun" with it. Nintendo funded the project for three months and then visited to see the results. Occasionally, the legendary Shigeru Miyamoto—creator of Mario, Donkey Kong, Legend of Zelda, Nintendogs, and many other hit games—visited as well!

Nintendo had no interest in any documents we'd prepared; they only wanted to see the game. If the game was making progress and demonstrating fun, Nintendo funded another three months and left us with the instructions to "find more fun." If not, the game was abandoned, and another idea was discussed.

This iterative approach, which gauges progress based on the game alone, is very agile, but few publishers pursue development in such an agile way. In fact, there's a polarization of views about agile approaches such as Scrum within the publishing community. Some have mandated that all their first-party developers use it, while others have banned it. Those that use Scrum have found challenges in establishing the best level of collaboration.

Establishing an agile relationship between publishers and developers is challenging. Publishers don't simply hand out money to developers who offer nothing more than a promise to try to "find the fun." There usually has to be a more formal arrangement. Outside of our industry, there are plenty of examples of agile contracts between stakeholders and developers that work and could form the model for the game industry.

This chapter examines the problems with the existing publisher/developer relationship, the challenges with establishing a more agile model, and a range of solutions to becoming more agile.

---

1. This was the code name for the Nintendo 64.

The Challenges

When I was working in the defense industry, documentation was king. For every week of actual development (writing code, testing, and so on), I spent two weeks writing documentation. Everyone's cubicle had an overhead shelf filled with binders that demonstrated the amount of documentation each of us had written for their current project. Our performance was measured primarily by the amount of documentation we generated.

The last defense industry project I was on was to design an avionics architecture for a new fighter jet. It represented hundreds of millions of dollars of work that our company was desperate to secure.

My job was to compile hundreds of various design documents into a single document to deliver to the Air Force within a few months. After a couple of weeks it became apparent to me that I could not create a comprehensive, organized, and readable document from all of these separate documents. I approached the project manager with my concern. "Oh, don't worry about that," he told me. "The Air Force just weighs these documents; they don't actually read them!"

I was shocked at this revelation. I finished compiling the master document with an eye toward maximizing the weight. When completed, the printed version weighed 20 pounds and filled one of those boxes that copier paper comes in. It was truly massive. The document was delivered, and I was given a pat on the back for a "job well done." Shortly after, I resigned.

One of the main reasons that game development has become less iterative is the increasing requirement for detailed, up-front plans from publishers. This has resulted from the rising cost of project failures. Publishers desire more certainty from developers and want to be sure they are "thinking things through" before creating code and assets. Publisher-side producers are encouraged to demand a detailed plan and schedule, tied to a contract, because it places much of the responsibility for project uncertainty in the hands of the developer.

Developers are encouraged to create these documents and schedules because the false sense of security they provide gives them time to explore the game, fund their studio, and (ideally) ensure that the publisher's long-term financial commitment is established.

Although design documents have not reached the size of those on major government weapons systems, most publishers and developers are realizing that there is no correlation between the size of the design documents and the success of a game. The illusion of certainty and the ulterior motives that drive these bad practices have to end. The business model won't support it for much longer.

Focus Comes Too Late

Most games demonstrate significant increases in gameplay value after alpha, when integration, debugging, optimization, and polishing begin in earnest. This is often a stressful time between the publisher and the developer because the publisher finally has a potentially shippable game to provide feedback on, but the definition of alpha usually means that all features are implemented and so it is too late to consider many of the suggestions.

The pressure to add these last-minute changes is often too much. Teams succumb to adding late features because they know the game needs them, and they don't want to ship a bad game after all the effort put into it. Unfortunately, the ship dates are not changed to reflect this added work, or if they are changed, it involves a performance penalty for the studio or damage to their relationship with the publisher.

Milestone Payments and Collaboration

Publishers usually hold the upper hand in a development agreement. Contracts often allow them to terminate a project at their convenience. Given this leverage, they can usually dictate new features, which result in "feature creep."

Milestone payment delays and threats of termination are blunt tools. The pressure they create results in milestone builds that lack fun and also lack consistency with and adherence to a vision. They might satisfy a milestone deliverable checklist, but they don't move the game toward market success as much as they should.

Contracts negotiated between a publisher and developer usually cover the full development cycle of the game from concept to gold master. Given this liability, publishers prefer to have some guarantees of performance. These typically take the form of milestone schedules linked to payments. Milestones usually occur every three months and have specific testable conditions in them such as the following:

- Three playable levels
- The AI characters navigate environments and attack the player.
- Players can join other players for online gameplay.

These seem like reasonable milestone deliverables, but they highlight a few problems:

- **Quality cannot be defined in a contract:** Development studios are highly dependent on milestone payments, so if the choice comes down to providing two great levels of gameplay or three mediocre levels, as defined by a milestone the developer may choose the latter simply to be paid. There is no way to contractually define a quality bar unless the developer allows the publisher to subjectively judge the quality of deliverables, which they would be negligent to allow.
- **Collaboration is discouraged:** In the event that a publisher or developer identifies a change to the game that alters future milestone deliverables, it's usually difficult to introduce such a change into the contract, especially if it impacts the budget or ship date. As a result, game-improving changes are inhibited at many levels.
- **Problems are hidden, and trust is destroyed:** Developers try to load as much of the development fees from a publisher into early milestones as possible and define the deliverables in a way that avoids exposing problems until late in the project (see the "Examples of Milestone Definitions That Hide Problems" sidebar), when the cost of cancellation is too high.
- **Developers don't want to expose problems to the publisher early because they think they will overreact and cancel a project:** Publishers think that developers won't openly share the bad news, so they end up assuming the worst. These attitudes destroy trust.

EXAMPLES OF MILESTONE DEFINITIONS THAT HIDE PROBLEMS

The following are milestone definitions I have seen in contracts, which help the developer avoid hard questions from the publisher after a milestone is delivered:

- **"The AI is 60% complete":** I have no idea what "60% complete" means. It could mean that everything is broken and the AI does nothing.
- **"First-pass at the main character model":** First out of how many passes? Two or one hundred?

Limited Iteration

Many publishers see the need to iterate planning and development. One common practice used is to allow "rolling milestone" definitions. These enable the detailed definition of a milestone to be fleshed out during the preceding one. Although this enables details to emerge, it doesn't permit changes to major deliverable dates or much flexibility within the milestone being worked on. Like an Oreo cookie, it sandwiches the flexible part between two inflexible lumps.

First-Party Problems

The issues of contracts and payments largely disappear when a studio—acquired by a publisher—becomes a first-party developer. This seems like a relief to a studio that has struggled to survive, but it raises different challenges.

When a publisher owns a studio, the publisher has more freedom to control it. For example, if a project is late, they might transfer developers from another project over to help, which rarely does (see the discussion of "Brook's Law" later in this chapter). They might decide that they don't trust some of the design decisions being made and dictate them remotely, which destroys morale.

Some studios with a track record of success erect barriers with their parent publisher to avoid these problems, going so far—in one case—as to bar them from entering the premises!

It doesn't help to keep the publisher entirely in the dark because they have a role to play in the success of a game. For example, this success depends not only on the quality of the game but also on the publisher's responsibility in marketing it. A talented marketing group can help the developers fine-tune the game to deliver what the market wants.

Portfolios Drive Dates

Market forces often compel publishers to promise ship dates and even projected sales figures for a game. The demands of large retail chains, licensing deadlines, long-term portfolio plans, and the desire to please shareholders pressure publishers to commit to very uncertain and optimistic product flow and ironclad ship dates.

This compels a publisher to ask the improbable of their developers, even after many failures demonstrate the futility of this. It's not that publishers are unaware of the development realities. They simply can't resist the pressure from retailers and shareholders.

Perhaps as the market changes and as new distribution channels appear, this problem may be alleviated, but it won't happen soon. One solution is to increase the level of collaboration between the publisher and the developer to make them partners in the goals of the game. This requires a higher level of trust that has to be slowly built to overcome long-established fears.

Building Trust, Allaying Fear

The common root of all these problems is a lack of trust and collaboration between a developer and publisher. Trust takes a long time to build. Building it through iteration, transparency, and collaboration are agile principles.

The first step is to deliver value regularly. When a publisher receives sprint builds with significant incremental improvements to the game, it builds confidence and trust.

The second step is welcoming change from the publisher. Observations from publishers contain valuable feedback about the marketable value of the game. When this feedback is reflected in the game within the next few sprints, it builds trust. Publishers and developers become true collaborators, rather than rivals trying to manipulate one another.

These steps lead to greater trust in the developer's ability and decision making. It enables honest discussions of project goals whenever scope, schedule, and cost start to conflict as they invariably do on most projects. By having these discussions earlier, when there are more options for addressing problems, the relationship and product benefit.

First, the fears that publishers have of releasing the "agile genie" must be overcome.

The Fears

Publishers have a great deal of fear about agile. Some of these fears are as follows:

- "We'd have no idea where the project is headed. They could iterate forever!"
- "If the scope is flexible, developers won't work very hard. We'll get half the game for our money!"

Developers have fears about an agile relationship with a publisher as well:

- "The publishers will micromanage the product backlog, and we'll have no creative control"
- "Allowing publishers to always change the scope will lead to a death march!"

These fears aren't groundless. A misunderstanding of agile or Scrum practices and principles make it possible for any of these problems to be realized.

Understanding Agile

Teams slowly absorb the principles of agile development as they iterate, deliver working builds that demonstrate value, and receive stakeholder and customer feedback. Publishers are not faced with the daily lessons of agile and can't absorb these principles as quickly. As a result, they may not understand the importance of Scrum practices and their role as a stakeholder, which leads to the following dysfunctions:

- Not playing sprint builds
- Not attending reviews or planning sessions
- Ignoring the product backlog
- Demanding detailed schedules and documents up front and ignoring the need to revisit them based on actual progress
- Making urgent requests in the middle of a sprint

These are typical actions of publishers who are accustomed to traditional projects that hide uncertainty and don't demonstrate real value until post-production. Agile developers need to reinforce the principles and benefits of agile development with their publishers. One method is to establish a publisher-side Scrum advocate or even a publisher-side product owner.

Publisher-Side Product Owners

A product owner is usually a member of the project development team. Video game product owners need to provide frequent and subjective feedback. Does the control of the player feel right? Is a mechanic fun enough? This feedback requires daily engagement with the team. They are the single voice for all the customers and stakeholders of the game.

Unfortunately, many stakeholders reside with a publisher who is based thousands of miles away. This challenges the product owner's capacity to create a shared vision with them. One solution is to delegate a portion of the product ownership role by creating a publisher-side product owner. This person represents the publisher-side stakeholders to the developer. Figure 15.1 shows the arrangement between both product owners.

The publisher-side product owner communicates with the developer-side product owner as frequently as necessary.

The publisher-side product owner has the following responsibilities:

- Review each sprint build
- Participate in as many sprint review and planning sessions as possible
- Attend the release planning and review meetings
- For first-party developers, ensure that the developer-side product owner is tracking ROI and general project cost dependencies
- Represent the developer-side product owner to publisher-side stakeholders such as executives, marketing, and sales groups
- Ensure that all the publisher-side stakeholders are aware of the current status of development

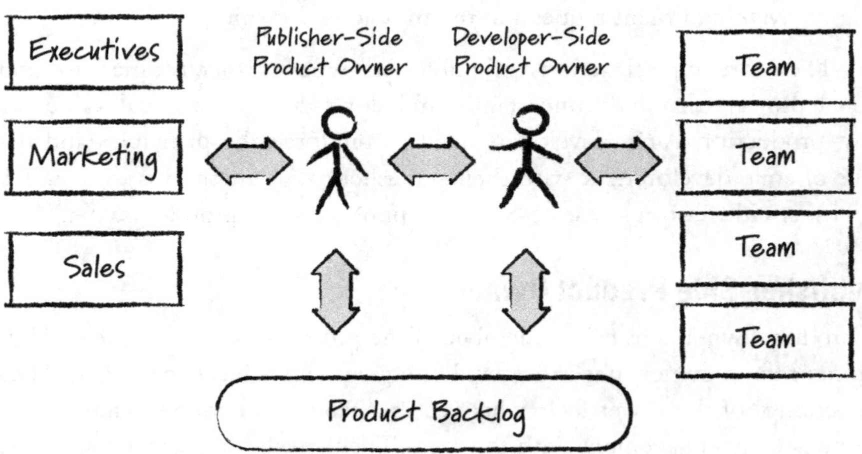

FIGURE 15.1 The product owner roles

The two product owners should communicate about every aspect of the game and clearly define the limits of ownership. For example, the publisher-side product owner might own the release goals (epic-level stories) while the developer-side product owner owns the release plan (the stories that fit within the release). This is different for every studio, publisher, and game. For example, some externally licensed games require strong publisher-side product ownership, while intellectual property being developed at the studio must have stronger developer-side product ownership.

Third-party (independent) developers usually maintain more ownership since they have sole responsibility for maintaining their own financial stability.

Together, the two product owners manage the product backlog. This includes discussing the addition, removal, and prioritization of features. The publisher-side product owner must understand that new features are always welcome on the product backlog, but the product backlog itself is not a promise of what will ship with the game. They need to understand what velocity means and how to use it to avoid feature creep and allow collaboration to exist between the publisher and developer.

Meeting Project Challenges Early

Scrum's empirical measure of development velocity and the transparency of the product backlog enable honest and continual discussions of scope and schedule. By developing a potentially shippable set of prioritized features every sprint, the team and publisher have the following controls over the project:

- **Control of the release date:** If the velocity of the features being introduced is different from predicted, the release date can be earlier or later than planned.
- **Control of the scope:** Scope is the easiest factor to manipulate as long as value emerges during development, rather than emerging all at once after alpha, which is often the case.
- **Control of the budget:** The product owner continually measures ROI based on value, velocity, and cost. This gives greater visibility into whether the budget being spent on the project is generating sufficient return in value seen.

Most publishers are used to waiting until after alpha for the state and quality of the game to emerge, which is usually too late to apply these controls without expensive consequences. Thus, they are not accustomed to having them available. Agile projects give more stakeholders more visibility and control.

As Chapter 6, "Agile Planning," described, these controls are similar to those applied during a cross-country drive. An experienced driver won't rely on a map, or plan, as the only source of information about the trip. They fine-tune the plan based on the reality emerging, such as miles driven per day or—if there is enough time—side trips taken to add value to the trip.

Managing the Production Plan

Chapter 7, "Video Game Project Planning," described how production debt is impacted by decisions made in pre-production and how the estimation of this debt is continually refined.

Production plans are critically important to publishers and developers. They represent major cost and resource obligations. The date that teams start production is a signal that the gameplay is more certain and that they are in the home stretch. Unfortunately, the desire to reach the state of production often overshadows the reality of whether the game and team are truly prepared to enter it. Often the date, or the need, to transition production resources takes precedence over whether the game is ready to enter production.

Developers and publishers need to clearly establish the goals a game must meet before it enters production. Metrics need to be established in pre-production that demonstrate the production plan is still viable. These metrics, such as the number of people-days to produce each level, continually measure the cost of completing assets in pre-production as they approach production quality. Without them, production schedules remain highly speculative and optimistic.

Production forecasts and metrics should be part of every release deliverable. Given these forecasts and metrics, the publisher and developer plan coming releases to ensure that production dates are met or to update planning to match reality.

Allaying the Fears

Given the tools described earlier, developers and publishers begin to allay the fears that were identified at the start of this section.

> We have no idea where the project is in development. Developers can iterate forever!

Agile methods require close participation between the stakeholders and the developers on a regular basis. Without a shared vision, a game easily strays off course and becomes something the publisher did not want.

With development projects that cost $20 million becoming common, publishers must have the games prove their value along the way, regardless of the methodology used. Scrum creates a framework for close collaboration and iteration that allows this.

> If the scope is flexible, developers won't work very hard. We'll get half the game for our money!

Publishers should be impressed with the velocity of features introduced by Scrum developers. If not, the project should be canceled. Agile contracts give both parties an opportunity to identify when a game idea is bad or a team is not a good match for a project. Neither party should wait two years or spend $20 million to discover that all the hard work won't provide a sufficient return on the investment.

> The publishers will micromanage the product backlog, and we'll have little creative control.

> Allowing publishers to change the scope will lead to a death march!

A first-party developer without a product owner owning the vision is in greatest danger of this happening. They need to establish the roles on both sides in terms of product ownership. The practices of Scrum reinforce this every sprint.

Agile Contracts

Outside the game development industry there are many examples of agile contracts that have evolved over time. Examples include such products as tax preparation software or airline reservation websites that slowly expand their features as business evolves and changes.

This model enables clients and developers to work with a series of contracts. Rather than committing to years of promised effort involving large sums of money, the smaller contracts each cover an incremental released version of the product, which provide much more certainty and far less risk. Although developers might prefer the security of a long-term contract, the reality is that the "termination for convenience" clause in most contracts allows a project to be canceled at any time, for any reason.

Most games don't have regular incremental versions. Many games have one "big-bang" release followed by a small number of patches. There is greater risk in funding these large projects, which leads to detailed, ironclad contracts.

Since agile game development provides a more incremental delivery of value, it gives publishers and studios the potential to build relationships where progress is measured on a regular basis to determine whether the project is worth pursuing further, much as Nintendo and Miyamoto did with Angel Studios.

The benefits of this approach are significant. Not all ideas result in great games. Some teams are not well matched to a game they are tasked to develop. It's better to abandon those efforts early than to spend years following a bad path.

While frightening to consider at first, it is actually a measure of success for projects to "fail early" rather than to "fail late." Failing early reduces the possibility of harming the relationship between a publisher and developer. On the other hand, spending $10 million for a game that never sees the shelf creates a lot of bad feelings and destroys careers. Besides, no one wants to spend years of their career working away on a mediocre game.

There is precedence for this type of contract in the game development industry. As more developers become agile, more publishers will find the benefit in pursuing agile contracts over traditional ones.

In the meantime, publishers and developers continue to explore more agile practices with traditional development agreements such as iterating against a plan or using the kill-gate model.

Iterating Against a Plan

Huge design documents and schedules are like a woolen security blanket in the rain; they give comfort for only a short amount of time. Despite up-front planning's poor track record, publishers and project managers demand it because the only alternative they see—no planning at all—leads to chaos and ruin. They're not wrong.

When faced with this, the challenge for agile developers is to gradually introduce agile planning practices and to find the cracks in the big bang process that always exist—such as rolling milestone definitions—and exploit them for the benefit of the project.

What does an agile team do when a publisher demands all-embracing design documents and schedules? The first thing is to determine how much flexibility exists within the publisher's process. It's rare to find a publisher that does not allow some form of rolling milestones described earlier. If these are allowed, such milestones are managed the same as releases. When the publisher requests an upcoming milestone definition, hold a release planning meeting for it, and invite a representative from the publisher who can make decisions.

Over time, a developer builds trust by allowing some change from the publisher. Care must be taken to not give them a blank check for changes. If a fixed scope list exists, rather than a backlog, each change must be accompanied by the deferral of other work from it.

Most long-term deliverables are tied to the minimum required feature set. As described in Chapter 7, the greatest threat to schedules and resources is an excessive amount of advance speculation about the details for these features. They paint teams into death-march corners.

If—in the worst case—no flexibility or trust exists and the developer cannot refuse the work, what can be done? Although the team benefits from some practices such as sprints and daily scrum meetings, they will be limited in how they may react to the emerging game. They should attempt to insert meetings in the schedule that require stakeholders to review progress and make decisions about the course of the project. Another useful tool is to enumerate all known and potential risks and identify how they will be addressed (see the "Experience" sidebar). Transparency is still encouraged; hiding problems only creates debt that the team pays back with a death march.

EXPERIENCE

For our first project to ship on the PS3, we drew upon the memory of all the problems we encountered with the PS2 and enumerated them as risks. These included broken tools, buggy libraries, poor documentation, and delayed test hardware. We highlighted all the potential impacts to the productivity and schedule that would occur if any of these problems were realized. As it turned out, all of them were. Although we couldn't mitigate the impact to the project, we worked together with the publisher to address the issues. As a result, they became partners in finding a solution, and this prevented us from being blamed for something we had little control over.

Fixed Ship Dates

A common impression about agile is that it does not allow games that use it to ship on a fixed schedule. The impression is based on the idea that agile teams don't plan but simply iterate with a very short horizon—they just don't know when the project will end!

Although most games have a ship date, many of these are considered "firm" rather than "fixed." Firm ship dates are established by publishers to fit portfolio or budget projections. A firm ship date will drive the project, but if it desperately needs another month or so of work to achieve far better results, it won't be a disaster to slip the date. Fixed ship dates, on the other hand, are critical for the success of some games. Examples of games with fixed ship dates are those that must ship simultaneously with a movie release or games like Madden Football that must be on shelves by the start of each NFL season. The penalty in lost sales for missing these dates is major.

How is a project with a fixed ship date managed differently from one that is not? Mainly, it is the way risk is handled. Risk is uncertainty about what a team is creating and how it is going to build it. For example, if we want to dedicate 20% of our project budget to creating a cooperative online death-match mode with AI opponents for our game, a few of the uncertainties might be the following:

- Will the AI work online?
- Is 20% of the budget enough to create a fun and complete experience?
- Will problems in other areas delay work or take people away?

The list can go on. Any one of these can threaten the project's schedule and result in the feature being dropped after almost 20% of the project's budget has been spent on it.

So, how is risk handled? Developers often try to plan and schedule their way out of risk by creating exceedingly detailed plans that attempt to identify the solution to every foreseeable problem. Unfortunately, since the danger lies in what a team does not know, it's certain that the tasks required to overcome risk will not be identified up front. The best way to handle risk is to focus on answering the unknown, in other words, creating knowledge.

Creating knowledge and value is important for any project, regardless of the ship date. For projects with fixed ship dates, the prioritization of work to reduce risk is a bit higher. For example, if a movie-based shooter game with a fixed ship date has to decide between shipping six months after the movie's release or dropping online gameplay, they will be more likely to drop online. A game that is not based on such a license, which instead has a firm ship date, is more likely to be delayed to ensure the feature is included.

So, let's return to the original question: Does agile aid or impede a project's ability to achieve a fixed ship date? Executed properly, an agile project has significant advantages over other methods. Two core principles are behind this advantage:

- **Prioritizing to create knowledge and reduce risk:** Focus on delivering high value and addressing risk early. Fixed ship dates only enable a project's staff or the scope to vary. Increasing the number of developers on a troubled project usually doesn't help. Brook's Law[2] says that "adding manpower to a late software project makes it later." The law also applies to game development. The best option is varying the scope, or feature set, of the project. Identifying the best features that fit within the schedule is critical to the success of a game with a fixed ship date.
- **Not postponing debt:** Frequent integration, immediate defect correction, and maintaining target performance (for example, keeping the game potentially shippable) will prevent late surprises that require rework and delay. When projects with fixed ship dates postpone critical work to post-production, they often meet with disastrous results.

Two tools for applying these principles are the product backlog and the definition of *done*. Stories that address schedule risk must often be prioritized over others on a project with a fixed ship date. An example of this is a spike to mock up a full level. This would create early knowledge about the level dimensions to better refine the production schedule and risk. Doing this constrains some of the options for emergent gameplay, but it might be necessary to know this information sooner than later.

Elevating the definition of *done* (see Chapter 5, "User Stories") enables risk to be addressed earlier. For example, if a game must ship on all platforms, a product owner might require stories to run on all the platforms earlier in the project than they normally would. Although this additional definition of *done* may slow teams down, especially if the platform technology isn't fully mature, it accelerates improvements and creates more knowledge about the risks of those platforms earlier.

As described in Chapter 7, agile methods don't attempt to plan away uncertainty with large documents, but they also don't ignore uncertainty. They simply tailor the practices to the different level of uncertainty over time. Planning for short-term goals, such as sprint goals, is done at a high level of

2. http://en.wikipedia.org/wiki/Brooks%27s_law

detail. Planning for medium-range goals, such as release plans, is less detailed but receives continual refinement. Long-range planning for things such as ship dates, production scheduling, and so on, is also continually refined and influences short-term planning. For example, an agile plan won't say "Production will start on September 14" a year in advance. It will refine a range of times over the course of pre-production. The reason is that not only will we gain knowledge about production in pre-production, but the debt itself will change. By acknowledging uncertainty and working to refine it, agile planning will increasingly match the reality that is emerging rather than drifting further away from the big document written at the start of a project.

Too many times fixed ship dates result in little innovation or a poor game that must be shipped before it has been properly polished. Games released along with the release of movies have long had a reputation for low quality. This doesn't need to be the case. Eliminating the waste of dropping features at the 11th hour after months of working on them is a good place to start.

Sometimes a fixed ship date is impossible to achieve. A risk-based approach for developing completed features will not work miracles, but it will expose the bad news sooner than later.

Agile Pre-Production

Publishers aren't deaf to the agile message. They understand that fun cannot be defined in a document. They've seen detailed plans and schedules fail projects again and again. However, most publishers exist as publicly traded companies that must be able to forecast budgets and ship dates for their games. As a compromise to this reality, publishers are more readily engaging developers to be more agile in pre-production alone. This involves small teams taking longer to iteratively explore potential features, creating knowledge about production costs, and defining the quality and fun of the game. Since production is more expensive and amenable to predictive schedules, this is a reasonable compromise.

> **NOTE**
> Chapter 7 described lean production and the benefit of agile thinking during production.

The Stage-Gate Model

With a "big-bang" release model, a contract that covers the entire development cycle is a rather large gamble, especially for an original idea. For these games, publishers may require decision points, called **green lights**, often at the juncture of two stages to decide whether to continue funding the game. Two of the most common green-light junctures are the following:

- **Concept green light:** The publisher decides whether to let a game enter the pre-production stage after reviewing project concepts, an initial plan, and a prototype.
- **Production green light:** The publisher decides whether to let a game enter the production stage after reviewing the gameplay, the production-representative assets, and the resource plan and schedule for production.

Publishers fund a number of game ideas and use green lights to funnel them down to a select a few of the best. This is called a **stage-gate model**. It gives a larger number of innovative ideas a chance to be proven.

Figure 15.2 shows a stage-gate being used to winnow four games down to the one that demonstrates the best value.

The stage-gate model creates a clear advantage for an agile developer. It aligns the principles of agile with the goals of the model: to judge the game itself rather than the plan for it.

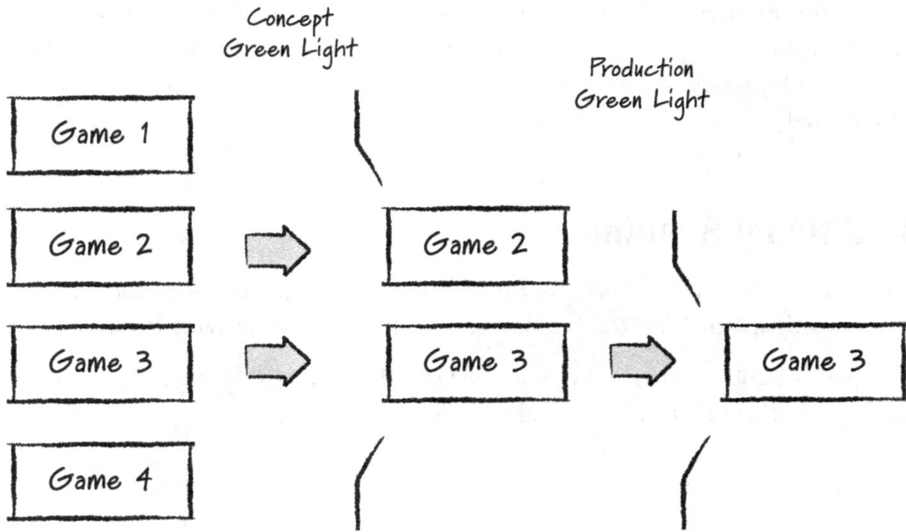

FIGURE 15.2 A stage-gate in action

EXPERIENCE

I've found that teams facing the "do-or-die" barrier of a green light become very focused on the actual game, rather than the plan. Although no one wants to have their project canceled, it's far less painful to be on a project canceled early than one canceled a year later.

The stage-gate model can also establish the boundary between a longer pre-production stage that is largely exploratory and the production stage that is far more predictable.

NOTE Mark Cerny's method (2002) is an example of a stage-gate process that focuses on proving game value before entering production.

Summary

Although publishers may not consider themselves agile and may even recoil in fear at the term, they have been trying to find ways to be more agile for more than a decade. Iterative practices have been creeping into the way business is done between them and developers. By continuing to build an agile vocabulary and trust through applying agile principles, this trend will continue and allow game development and publishing to remain a viable and even lucrative business model.

Additional Reading

Cook, D. *Rockets, cars and gardens: Visualizing waterfall, agile and stage gate.* http://lostgarden.com/2007/02/rockets-cars-and-gardens-visualizing.html.

Cooper, R. 2001. *Winning at New Products: Accelerating the Process from Idea to Launch, Third Edition.* Cambridge, MA: Basic Books.

Chapter 16

Launching Scrum

Although Scrum practices are simple and easy to learn, its adoption challenges organizations, processes, and cultures. It can take years for those challenges to be overcome. This dichotomy is often referred to as the **Zen of Scrum**. Although each studio has their own pace of adoption and challenges, there are enough common ones to establish a rough road map.

The adoption of Scrum often takes the form of three stages. This chapter describes them and some strategies for introducing Scrum to your studio.

The Three Stages of Adoption

In the movie *The Karate Kid*, a boy wants to learn karate from an old master. The master agrees but only on the condition that the boy does whatever he is told. The master begins by having him wash and wax his cars, paint his fence, and sand his patio floor. The only constraint he imposes is that the boy use exact motions for each chore. For example, when waxing the car, wax is applied in a clockwise motion with the right hand and removed in a counterclockwise motion with the left hand.

After days of effort, the boy is exasperated. He expected to be taught karate, not perform chores. When he complains, the master has him repeat the motions he was taught for the chores as he throws punches and kicks. The motions used for the chores are the exact motions used to block such attacks; the chores were meant to teach them subconsciously.

The movie illustrates the first stage of martial arts competence: the apprentice stage. In the apprentice stage, the student is focused on the proper forms, in other words, learning the basics. The second stage is the journeyman stage. Here the student modifies the motions to leverage their strengths and offset their weaknesses. The third stage of martial arts competence is the master stage.

Masters create their own moves. They reinvent the art since they know the underlying principles.

NOTE In martial arts, this progression is known as Shu, Ha, and Ri.

A similar progression of stages is seen with teams adopting Scrum. Teams cannot master self-organization and continual improvement from the start. They need to establish muscle memory with basic practices in the apprentice stage; expand, add, and change them in the journeyman stage; and then take full control of how they organize and achieve their goals in the master stage.

Figure 16.1 shows the three stages of Scrum adoption.

NOTE Apprentice, journeyman, and master stages are not guidelines but convenient labels that help identify typical milestones of progress with Scrum. Different teams have different pacing and will improve in different orders than what is represented by the road map.

The Apprentice Stage

In the apprentice stage, teams become accustomed to iterating on features and committing to sprint goals. They are challenged to deliver an improved version of the game with a two- to four-week cadence that requires cross-discipline collaboration. They learn to step up every day as a member of a team

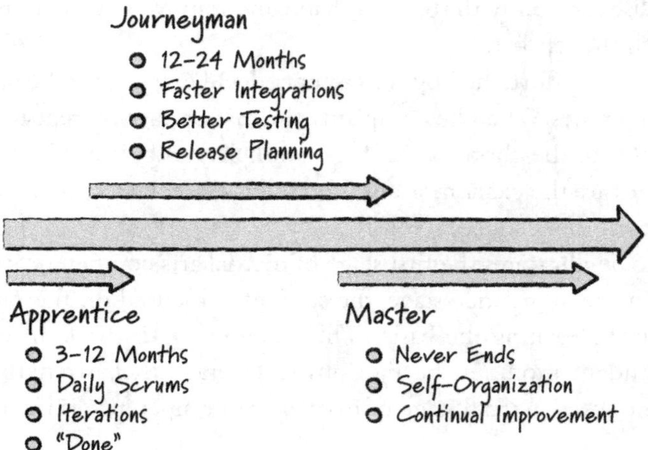

FIGURE 16.1 The road map of Scrum adoption

who is committed to their sprint goal and to report any impediments to their progress.

The team establishes a shared definition of *done* between themselves and the stakeholders. These challenges put pressure on the build process, pipelines, and development practices to improve. These improvements appear quickly and demonstrate the benefits of Scrum.

Adjusting to Sprint Pacing

Many traditional teams don't need to demonstrate their game to stakeholders very frequently. Often a demonstration is given every several months when a milestone is due. The work needed to integrate changes made since the last milestone, to fix errors, and to polish the game often requires the final few weeks before the milestone date.

When teams transition to Scrum, the pace of producing a working game for demonstration to the stakeholders is accelerated. Now they need to show something every two to four weeks. The immediate problem is that the process to produce a build now occupies a larger portion of time. Teams can spend 50% of their time maintaining a working build. This overhead puts pressure on the practices used to commit and test changes to the game. Rather than abandoning agile because integrating is costly, an agile team finds ways to drive down the cost of iterating. Chapter 9, "Faster Iterations," discusses this.

Defining Done

Traditional project management does not fully burden developers with the responsibility of judging when their work is done. They merely need to accomplish tasks assigned to them in a timely manner. Scrum requires teams and stakeholders to develop a definition of *done* that they agree upon and can be tested. Establishing this definition challenges the apprentice team.

At first, this definition might only require a game to run without crashing. Later, a feature may be expected to run on a target platform at 30 frames per second. The challenge with the definition of *done* is that it causes new tasks to emerge during a sprint. At first, the team might ignore these tasks; they think a successful sprint means that all the estimated tasks are completed at the end. It comes as a shock to them to learn that the working game is considered more important than task completion alone.

As the definition of *done* is refined and understood by the team, they will factor an amount of uncertainty into sprint planning. If past sprints required 20% additional time for work not reckoned for, the team will leave that much slack in future sprint planning.

Daily Scrum Challenges

The daily scrum is an essential practice of an effective Scrum team. Without it, teams would find it more difficult to manage their progress toward the best possible sprint result. The daily scrum is a brief discussion among teammates to ensure that they understand where the game is, with respect to their sprint goals, and where they are headed next.

Daily scrums are hard to get right from the start. Dysfunctions or misunderstandings about the purpose of this practice can prevent teams from achieving its full benefit. This section describes some of the common dysfunctions and ways to alleviate them.

Reporting to the ScrumMaster When the team members report to the ScrumMaster in a daily scrum, rather than the team, it indicates that they view the ScrumMaster as a manager. This creates a barrier to ownership and commitment. Team members may think it's the ScrumMaster's job to solve all their problems and tell them what to do. This is common with an apprentice team. The reason for this behavior is that people need to overcome a career history that allowed far less ownership. They don't yet fathom or trust that their team takes ownership of the sprint goal and controls the means to achieve it.

The ScrumMaster can subtly discourage this behavior through a number of practices. For example, they can avoid eye contact with the person speaking in the daily scrum. This encourages the person to address the entire team. The ScrumMaster should also pose key questions such as "What problems could we have with achieving our goal?" or "What do you think we should look at next?" These questions drive teams to come up with solutions they own.

TIP

Sometimes not talking at all is the ScrumMaster's best tool. A few moments of uncomfortable silence will often result in some creative ideas being offered. Silently counting to ten or more gives their minds something to do while waiting for the team.

The ScrumMaster can inadvertently reinforce this dysfunction. One way is by taking notes at the meeting. Excessive note taking creates the impression that the task information they are reporting is being recorded and tracked. This creates distrust and must be avoided. If the ScrumMaster needs to record task hours to produce the up-to-date burndown chart, they should explain this to the team.

Not Reporting Impediments Teams not reporting impediments either have none or don't have a sense of ownership or commitment to their sprint goal. The latter is more likely.

The ScrumMaster can do a few things to encourage problem reporting during the Scrum. One is to help the team understand that if they weren't able to achieve the progress they had set for themselves at the previous day's daily scrum, then they ought to report the impediments that caused this to the team.

Key questions help. For example, occasionally adding a fourth question such as "What threatens our achieving the sprint goal?" at the daily scrum can help. The team will begin to speak up, not for themselves, but for the team when they realize that their problems threaten the team's success and therefore belong to the team.

Lack of Focus on the Sprint Goal Sometimes teams focus too much on finishing the tasks they estimated in the planning meeting and not enough on the sprint goal itself. The result of this is that all the tasks are accomplished by the end of the sprint, but the value of what was added to the game is lacking. Progression stoppers are those that prevent the player from completing a level, annoying bugs that are not fixed, assets that are missing, and so on.

The main goal of a sprint is to add value to the game, but "finding the fun" can't always be predicted in sprint planning. A lot of trial and error occurs during a sprint. Tasks are volatile when the goal is as subjective as "finding the fun." For example, an initial sprint backlog based on a goal to allow the player to navigate a complex environment may not anticipate all the character control issues that will typically arise. That doesn't mean the team should avoid responsibility for them. Even if unforeseen work threatens lower-priority stories, they should add the emergent tasks that the definition of *done* requires.

ScrumMasters encourage this behavior in a number of ways. One example is to embolden the team to change the daily scrum to focus more on the goal. Instead of going around the room to answer the three questions, the team could visit each story on the task board and address the progress and issues for them. This focuses the work more on the stories themselves. Another useful practice is to conduct a short play-through of the game before a daily scrum. This focuses the team on the value being added to a running game rather than progress against the sprint backlog.

The team should be creative in exploring the practices of the daily scrum to improve their chances of achieving their sprint goal.

Replacing the Daily Scrum with a Tool I'm often asked by teams starting Scrum "Can we replace the daily scrum with a software tool?" My answer is always an emphatic "No!"

As described earlier, the daily scrum is not simply a meeting to update task hours. The daily scrum's purpose is for the team to inspect their progress and make commitments to each other about the work needed to achieve their shared sprint goal.

It takes a while for teams new to Scrum to understand the purpose of the daily scrum. In the past, tasks were likely estimated and assigned to them by managers. How the tasks came together to fulfill larger goals was not their responsibility. Scrum turns that upside down. Teams are given total responsibility for the tasks and how to accomplish the larger goal. This requires a different mind-set for the new Scrum team. It's not a simple challenge; years of muscle memory must be overcome. This is why the daily scrum might seem wasteful at first. New teams think it's all about the tasks and their estimates.

Tasks and estimates are critically important, but experienced Scrum teams don't focus entirely on them. Their daily scrum is a beehive of activity that focuses on what everyone is doing to achieve *done* and the emergent challenges to their shared goal.

EXPERIENCE

"iPhone development using agile is unlike most other games. You can literally work for two weeks and 'ship' what you have as a finished product on the iPhone. So, knowing when to ship is the most important thing.

"Our main focus is on making smart decisions on scope, technical decisions, gameplay, and marketing trade-offs. This is the most critical aspect of our product development and requires the focus of the whole company. We need to be efficient, yet our business plan calls for us to create original games that are differentiated from the thousands of game apps in the marketplace, so there is always a tension between doing what we know how to do and biting off an experimental feature.

"The vision of the game is communicated through a brutal process where we winnow down many ideas into one that the company is fully behind. That one idea is championed and led by a single person who has authority to be the final arbiter of trade-offs.

"***Done*** varies, but for the most part, every sprint's work runs on the target platform. Releases are always pushed to everyone's iPhone for testing and evaluation over the weekend. ***Done*** means potentially shippable, and we don't move on to new functionality until the previous functionality is shippable. We strive to avoid—at all costs—parts on the garage floor and always elect to ship 'better with less.'"

—Chris Ulm, CEO, Appy Entertainment

The Journeyman Stage

The journeyman stage of adoption occurs as teams improve how they iterate and deliver value. Sprints are no longer mini-waterfalls with a design phase at the start and a test-and-fix phase at the end. These activities take place on a daily basis.

Journeyman teams take more ownership of their practices and process, identifying and solving impediments and examining the underlying assumptions of how disciplines work together. These changes focus on improving their craft and team velocity.

An example of such an improvement was with a team that created characters. The last stage of creating a character was to supply sounds at particular animation trigger points, such as a footstep sound during the walk cycle. One problem was that the animators were checking in all their animations to revision control late in the sprint, which caused the composers to rush their changes in so the team could achieve its sprint goal. This rush didn't lead to the best sounds being added. The solution the team originally applied in their apprentice stage was to create a cutoff rule that all animations had to be checked in five days before the end of the sprint. This allowed plenty of time to add the triggered audio, but it forced the animators to work on animations that might be needed for the next sprint after the cutoff. Although this solved the immediate problem, it was a resource-based solution that didn't improve velocity.

As the team's experience with Scrum increased, they found a better solution. This required the animators to deliver each unpolished animation as it was created to the composers and then polish the animation after the composer attached audio. Although this might seem like a simple fix, it violated a deep-rooted artistic preference to not share an asset until it is completed. In this case, and in many others like it, a discipline's bias was overcome to improve the team's velocity. Journeyman teams build cross-disciplined trust and find ways of optimizing the entire cycle of development rather than parts of it.

EXPERIENCE

Apprentice teams often create work to prepare for future sprints such as writing small design documents or creating partial assets. Journeyman teams eliminate most of this by reducing handoffs and by chopping work into smaller batches. These changes arise as the barriers between disciplines are broken down.

Journeyman teams also use more long-term agile estimating and planning practices such as release planning and story point estimation as described in Chapters 5 through 7. They also introduce change to discipline practices, such as test-driven development as described in Part IV, "Agile Discipline."

Release Cycles

Journeyman teams improve how releases are planned and executed. As an apprentice team, they were challenged by the sprint cycle or may have had releases that didn't use velocity. Journeyman teams are accustomed to the pace of sprints. They work with the product owner to plan and monitor releases through story point estimation (see Chapter 6, "Agile Planning"). This gives them the tool of velocity measurement, which is necessary for them to quantify a plan's size and their pace of implementing it.

Team Colocation

Agile principles emphasize face-to-face communication whenever possible. The benefits of this are demonstrated best at the team level. When a team is spread across a studio, the overhead and problems that arise from a lack of easy communication are seen daily. Studies have shown that when teams reduce the physical distance between themselves, their performance increases in many ways (Van Den Bulte and Moenaert 1998). Eventually teams realize this and rearrange themselves to improve communication.

Physical Arrangement Teams that want to colocate often have limited options. Sometimes an office is arranged with small cubicles that cannot easily be removed because of power and data wiring limitations. Team rooms or "bullpens" are less expensive to create than cubicle farms or separate office spaces, so teams lucky enough to influence the initial office space build-out can create an ideal location for themselves. Otherwise, they may need to slowly adapt their current space though remodeling. Usually it's best to have one team colocate to judge the cost and benefit before a studio will allow all of them to colocate.

What makes an ideal team space? There is no single solution. Sometimes teams can't even agree among themselves about what makes the best space. On a cross-discipline team, the programmers might want windows while the artists don't want light from the outside. It's up to the team to work this out. These are some of the other issues teams need to consider when defining their area:

- Is there enough wall space for a task board, information radiators (see the note "Information Radiators"), and whiteboards? Teams can never have enough wall space!
- Is there enough "slack" in the space so that developers can pair up or gather around a monitor? For example, can a programmer sit with an artist to discuss a problem?

- Is there space for meetings, such as the daily scrum or a play-through? Is there a development station available to conduct a play-through with the entire team?
- Is the room off the beaten path? Will traffic through the area from people outside the team create disruption?
- Are there rooms where people can have private conversations, conduct interviews, or read their e-mail?

What kind of furniture is best? My opinion is that mobile, modular, and adjustable furniture like that built by Anthro[1] is best. Teams change and improve over time. The ability to regularly rearrange their space creates a big benefit.

INFORMATION RADIATORS

An **information radiator** displays information in a place where those passing by can see it. With information radiators, those passing by do not need to ask questions; the information simply hits them as they pass.[2]

Concerns Before teams colocate, members often raise concerns about the potential problems of colocation. Two of the more common concerns are run down in this section.

> Programmers (artists, designers, and so on) need to work in quiet isolation to focus and be effective. We can't do this in a noisy team room with constant interruptions.

There are certainly more interruptions in a team room. Most of these are the point of the team room. When individual developers are trying to achieve individual goals, such as writing some code or creating an asset, interruptions often impede them from achieving that goal as quickly. However, Scrum emphasizes the delivery of value integrated into the game, not the value of finishing "parts" that should join flawlessly because a document or Gantt chart states they will.

When a team is focused on achieving a common goal that requires everyone's participation, fast access to other team members who can help progress is

---

1. www.anthro.com
2. Cockburn, A. 2007. *Agile Software Development: The Cooperative Game*. Boston: Addison-Wesley. Reproduced by permission of Pearson Education, Inc.

essential. For example, it doesn't make sense to have an animation programmer building an animation system apart from the animators. They should be solving the problem together.

Noise and interruptions from outside the team are usually a source of unnecessary interruptions. Teams should strive to eliminate things that distract them from their goals, such as public-address systems (DeMarco and Lister 1999).

EXPERIENCE Every team that I have seen colocate doesn't want to return to isolation.

> If I am not sitting with a group from the same discipline, then I won't learn and collaborate with them as much.

This argument creates a barrier for teams who want to collocate. It has some validity. One example of this was in a large studio where half a dozen AI programmers spread out across three teams. This led to three incompatible AI solutions, each duplicating the effort of the others. Although it was beneficial to have an AI programmer close to the designers and animators, there still needed to be communication that occurred with the other AI programmers. Communities of practice, described in Chapter 8, "Teams," enabled this to occur. The AI community of practice met as frequently as necessary to share knowledge that benefited all their teams needing AI.

Release Dysfunctions

Teams can encounter some common dysfunctions as they start using releases, rather than sprints alone. These are usually caused by the longer time frame and the difference between the definition of *done* for a sprint and the more demanding definition of *done* for a release. Also, the release cycle can bring out vestigial waterfall behaviors that cause problems.

This section identifies symptoms of release dysfunctions and identifies ways to help the team cure them.

Hardening Sprint Used as a Dumping Ground Hardening sprints, described in Chapter 6, are a practice that teams should strive to minimize or even eliminate. The danger from hardening sprints is that they become a dumping ground for work that should be completed during normal sprints. Left undone, this unfinished work interferes with progress and reduces team velocity.

Here are some warning signs that hardening sprints are being abused:

- Artists are postponing asset completion and leaving too many stand-in or missing assets in the game each sprint.
- Programmers are deferring bug fixes.
- Designers are not tuning features for gameplay value.

Every sprint should achieve a level of *done* that includes much of this work. If this isn't happening, then the definition of *done* needs to be improved to include it.

TIP Frequent play-throughs during the sprint can help the team focus on making sure their work is done.

Postponed Value Apprentice teams often divide sprints into phases, treating them like mini-waterfall projects. A similar problem can affect teams during releases. Early sprints are considered "design sprints," while later sprints are focused on debugging, tuning, and polishing for the release.

Velocity is used to measure the progress of a release and forecast its completion (see Chapter 6). This forecast assumes that the velocity trend will be a straight line through the remainder of the release. However, teams might experience a velocity drop-off toward the end. This is often accompanied by overtime, as teams compel themselves to achieve their goals. Teams are working harder, yet velocity seems to be dropping!

Figure 16.2 illustrates this happening over a four-sprint release. The solid line shows the total story points accomplished during the release. The dotted line shows a subjective value of the game (the fun) from the product owner's perspective (there's no practical or easy way to measure this…it's meant to illustrate a point).

Ideally, value and story points both grow at a steady pace. In the figure, story point velocity (slope of the dark line) grows quickly at first and then slows down at the end of the release. Value grows slowly at first—there isn't much "fun" being added to the game in the first few sprints—but the game becomes a great deal more fun in the last few sprints.

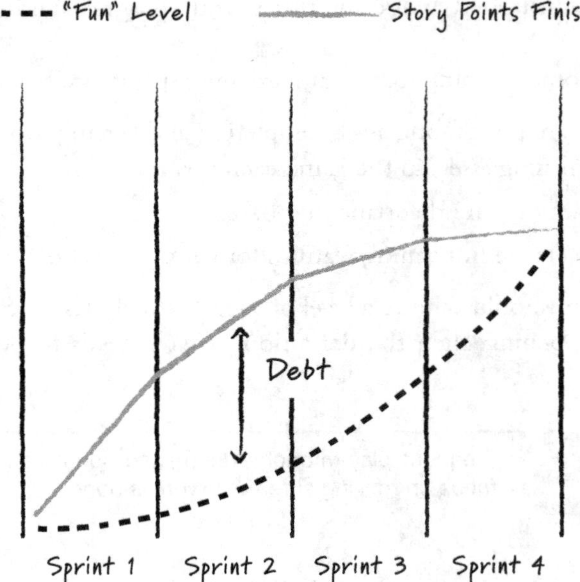

FIGURE 16.2 Velocity and fun in a release

What happened is that the team used a waterfall approach in the release, treating it as a single phased iteration of the game with integration, debugging, and polishing at the end. This builds up unfinished work in the release, called **debt**.

Debt consists of the following:

- Polish or tuning work
- Assets that are left out or built before the team knows what works best
- Bugs that aren't fixed
- Developing large assets in parallel

Debt postpones the actualization of value toward the end of the release much like a waterfall project defers it until post-production. Teams need to prevent this debt from growing so as to build value continually.

For example, consider a team with a release plan of creating a level that explores various mechanics. This level has many rooms that are each meant to offer different challenges to the player. A team might build the entire level using a phased approach. In the first sprint, untextured modular parts are used to create the level. In the second sprint, design places the AI and triggered events. In the third sprint, detailed geometry is created. Polishing, debugging, and sound design are done in the final sprint.

By creating a large level this way, the team is building a debt of work that has to be "paid off" by the end of the release. If any of these steps take too long, then the deadline drives the team to rush completion of the entire level or delay the release. This often leads to stressed teams and concerned stakeholders. Another drawback is that a polished experience won't exist until the end of the release, so the value is not seen until the end. This allows for almost no gameplay iteration on the polished level.

A better approach is to create a polished and tuned section of the level every sprint. If there are four sprints in the release, each sprint goal might attempt to complete a quarter of the level each sprint. For example, if your level has a medieval village, castle, forest, and fair, your team would finish one of them every sprint. If the level is too large for the release, the team would discover it in the first sprint, and the product owner could either reduce the scope of the level or delay the release date. Another benefit of this approach is that polished and tuned gameplay can be iterated on for almost the entire release.

Existing gameplay, tool technology, or rendering technology might not support an approach of vertical slices every sprint, but this is a further argument for not risking an entire release to such uncertainties.

Improving Iteration

Journeyman teams begin to accelerate the cycle of continuous improvement by altering practices. To do this, they must measure their velocity and focus on improving it.

Journeyman teams will introduce significant new practices such as test-driven development to improve the quality of code or continuous integration, which allows change to be propagated more safely and quickly (see Chapter 10, "Agile Technology"). The team will seek to improve iteration times in every area of development, through automated testing, improved tools, or team practices that move QA closer to the developers (see Chapter 9 and Chapter 13, "Agile QA and Production").

Measuring velocity is critical for this to occur. Velocity and other measures of value create the empirical control system at the core of Scrum. Without empiricism, a process is like some alchemy, where teams try to transmute work into success through paradoxical practices.

The Master Stage

The master stage is the final stage of Scrum adoption and is the goal of every Scrum team to achieve. Such teams do the following:

- **Self-organize:** Master teams work well together. Great teams are based on chemistry and motivation. They trust one another and achieve a high level of communication. The team decides who joins or leaves.
- **Drive continual improvement:** They take control of the rules. Management merely has to support their needs. These teams take ownership of their own performance.
- **Enjoy their work immensely:** Work is a commitment to their teammates. They are all in it together, and everyone's contribution and creativity are valued and leveraged.
- **Deliver the highest level of value:** Master teams are often referred to as **great teams** (see Chapter 8), far outpacing other teams.

EXPERIENCE

Developers on great teams have referred to their experience as a highlight of their career. I've been on two such teams in 20 years and have always sought to return to that state.

Master teams are hard to define but easy to recognize. There is no formula to create them, but I have observed the following:

- **Independence and a sense of ownership:** The team needs to feel that they contribute creatively and have control over how they work.
- **Leadership:** There is often a natural leader on the team who communicates a vision between the team and the stakeholders and helps keep the team focused. This isn't a lead position defined by a role but by actions.
- **A core expert:** Not everyone on the team needs to be an expert, but on a master team there is often at least one core expert. This person supports the vision with brilliance that the team can rally around with confidence.

- **Team collaboration:** Teams grow great organically and evolve together based on chemistry and experience.
- **Proper studio culture:** Studio cultures can either nourish such teams or prevent them from taking root or flourishing. Sometimes great teams will form in a highly dysfunctional culture, but they don't last.

Great teams form independent of process. However, Scrum assists them based on the mastery of its principles. Team self-organization, sprint goal ownership, commitment, and a daily dose of visibility cultivate them.

Team Organization and Membership

Collaboration is a necessary element for master teams. A team of highly skilled developers who cannot collaborate cannot assume success.

Teams need to form carefully and have the ability to adjust their membership to enable them to improve collaboration and chances of success. At first, teams can't do this on their own. Team formation needs to be facilitated by studio leadership early on. They mentor and encourage the team to slowly take control and make the best decisions for themselves. Eventually these teams become self-organizing and make decisions on their own.

Let's examine how self-organizing teams adjust their membership.

Teams don't change membership midsprint. They hold off on such changes until after the sprint review but before sprint planning. There are two reasons for changing members. The first is to match the team to its goals. For example, if a team needs animation support for a coming sprint but does not have an animator, they need to have one join the team before they plan the sprint.

The second reason for changing membership is to improve collaboration and commitment. This involves adding or removing a member to make it easier for the team to work effectively. Removing team members is challenging but sometimes necessary. Often it's simple lack of chemistry, or there is a personality conflict.

If a member of the team is becoming an impediment, it needs to be addressed. If the team cannot address the problem, the ScrumMaster assists through observation and inquiry. This includes discussion in the retrospective and coaching the team member in question. Often they are not even aware of the problem, and the discussion alone is enough to fix it.

If the team is unable to fix the problem internally, they may have no choice but to remove the teammate. Studio leadership must support this (see the sidebar "Experience").

EXPERIENCE

Chapter 8 described how teams could request the removal of teammates that are not working out. I'm often asked how management handles these situations. Because I was the CTO at High Moon, occasionally a team came to me and requested that a programmer be removed from their team. I'd then speak with the team and the programmer about the issues that led to this and what was needed to avoid them in the future. If I thought the situation warranted it, I would approve the change. I then approached the other teams and told them that this programmer was free to join their team if needed. I'd explain the issues that led to their removal from the last team. Most of the time, another team agreed to take the programmer onto their team. On rare occasions, no other team would take them. This was almost always because of the individual being ejected from numerous teams in the past; the person suffered from a reputation of causing problems. At this point, it became a human resources issue, and the programmer was dismissed. It was a sad occasion, but it had to happen for the benefit of the studio.

At the start of a new release, a master team might substantially change their membership to accomplish a specific release goal. Usually these teams will retain a core of individuals. It's far more difficult and rewarding to build a chemistry of personalities that are effective together than to simply gather individuals with the necessary skills. Once a working chemistry is found, it should be protected and supported.

Major Practice Change

A characteristic of master teams is the ability to abandon or modify any practice, while preserving the underlying principles of Scrum and agile development. Some master teams have varied their practices so much that what they are doing is barely recognizable as Scrum on the surface.

An example of this is the introduction of lean practices as described in Chapter 7, "Video Game Project Planning." These practices eliminate sprint planning and sprint goals for teams creating production assets. These may seem like a gross violation of Scrum rules, but they aren't. The Scrum principles of empiricism, emergence, timeboxing, prioritization, and self-organization described in Chapter 3, "Scrum," still hold true.

Master teams make these changes relying on empirical measures, a sense of ownership, freedom, and a deeply embedded understanding of what the Scrum and agile principles mean.

Adoption Strategies

The strategy for rolling out Scrum to your project or studio has to be carefully considered. Transitioning an entire project to Scrum is challenging. A bottom-up or beachhead approach proves that Scrum introduces beneficial change with less risk. However, this approach takes more time.

This section addresses strategies and specific tools and practices for studios to use to manage adoption.

Beachhead Teams

During World War I, the major combatants fought battles on vast front lines. Offensives were launched along these fronts in massive attacks. Because of the ever-increasing lethality of 20th-century weaponry, these attacks were often ineffectual and resulted in nothing more than heavy losses in the attacking force. The war became a series of deadly stalemates and attrition. Eventual victory came to the side that could withstand more losses than the other.

Battles in World War II were different. They were often marked by the penetration of a small area of the front by a focused attack. Large units poured into the breach, taking advantage of the confusion and disarray of the opposing army. Offensives such as the Battle of France and D-Day are examples of this strategy.

A similar approach of introducing Scrum provides an effective way of overcoming the well-founded concern about large-scale change. Small teams first experiment with Scrum to increase studio knowledge about its benefits before it is rolled out to a larger group. These teams are often referred to as **beachhead teams**. If a beachhead team is able to establish a foothold and find success with Scrum, it encourages other teams to adopt it.

Beachhead teams have an improved chance of success with Scrum for a number of reasons:

- They can be staffed with people who are open-minded about trying it.
- One team is more easily coached than a dozen. Teams new to Scrum will have many questions.
- They can take on noncritical features at first, which puts less pressure on them to get it perfect the first time.

This seems like stacking the deck in Scrum's favor, and it is. It's similar to planting a seed in a garden; its germination period is when it is most vulnerable. Conditions have to be carefully monitored during this time. Even if everything is done right, the plant might not grow. If the soil is the wrong type or if there is not enough sunlight or moisture, no amount of care will allow it to grow.

The same idea applies to the beachhead effort. Scrum may not "take" in the studio. The soil (culture, management style, and so on) might not be fertile for it. In this case, it's better to see the experiment fail with one team than a dozen.

If a beachhead team is successful employing Scrum and the studio wants to increase its use, there are three methods to use: split and seed, split and reform, or cross-team coaching.

Split and Seed

In the **split-and-seed** method, a successful beachhead team is split up to "seed" other teams that are starting Scrum. This enables the most rapid deployment of Scrum experience throughout the studio. About eight teams can be seeded this way. Figure 16.3 shows what this looks like.

The drawback of this approach is that a successful team is broken up. Breaking up such a team is likely discouraging to the members. When random people are grouped, it takes time for them to form a strong team, if it happens at all. The other disadvantage is that not all the members of the original team will be effective coaches for the newly formed teams.

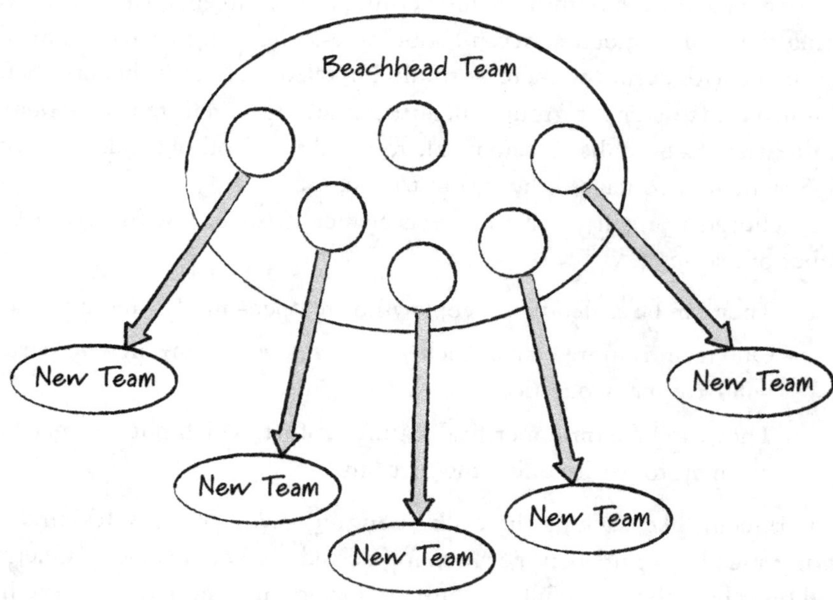

FIGURE 16.3 Split and seed strategy

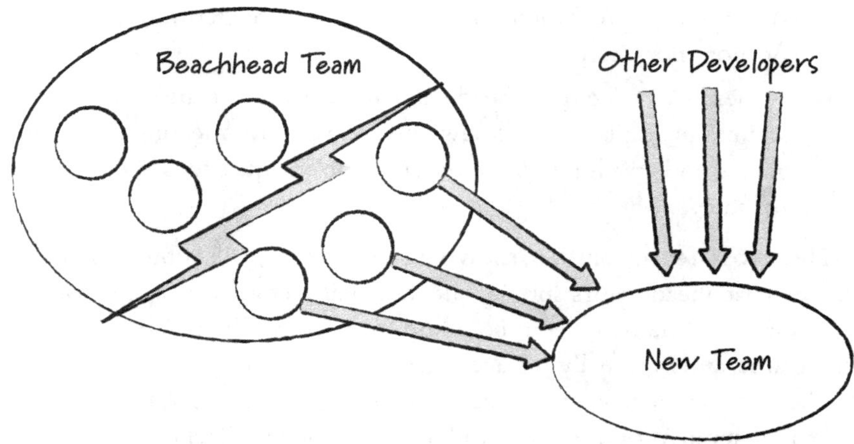

FIGURE 16.4 Splitting the beachhead team into two teams

As a result, a good team might be replaced by half a dozen or more that aren't nearly as effective. It can make the beachhead result look like a fluke. Therefore, this approach is not recommended if a more gradual adoption of Scrum is possible.

Split and Reform

In the **split-and-reform** strategy, the beachhead team splits into two, and each team brings in new members. This results in a slower adoption speed than the split-and-seed approach, but it enables each half of the original team to stay together.

This strategy, shown in Figure 16.4, is a compromise between the number of teams created and the desire to allow teams to remain together.

Although not as traumatic as split and seed, this approach still splits up a successful team and can result in dysfunctional teams. The old guard from the original beachhead team might exert more ownership of the process, which inhibits ownership and commitment from the new recruits."

Cross-Team Coaching

A third solution is to leave the beachhead team in place and have them coach other teams transitioning in a number of ways:

- A member of the beachhead team serves as a part-time member of a new team. They commit 50% or less of their time to each team.

- A member of the beachhead team becomes the ScrumMaster on one or more new teams.
- A member of the beachhead team attends a new team's daily scrum, sprint planning, review, and retrospective meetings, offering advice and coaching whenever the team has questions about Scrum practices.

This **cross-team** solution, shown in Figure 16.5, will subtract some time from the beachhead team's sprints, but they will recover it over the following several sprints as the new teams come up to speed on the practices, needs less of their time, and eventually replaces them.

The number of new teams transitioned to Scrum this way is limited to how many members of the beachhead team are suitable coaches and how much time they can spare.

In most cases, cross-team coaching is the best method of deploying multiple Scrum teams from the beachhead team. It enables them to retain a successful team and deploys Scrum quickly throughout a project or studio.

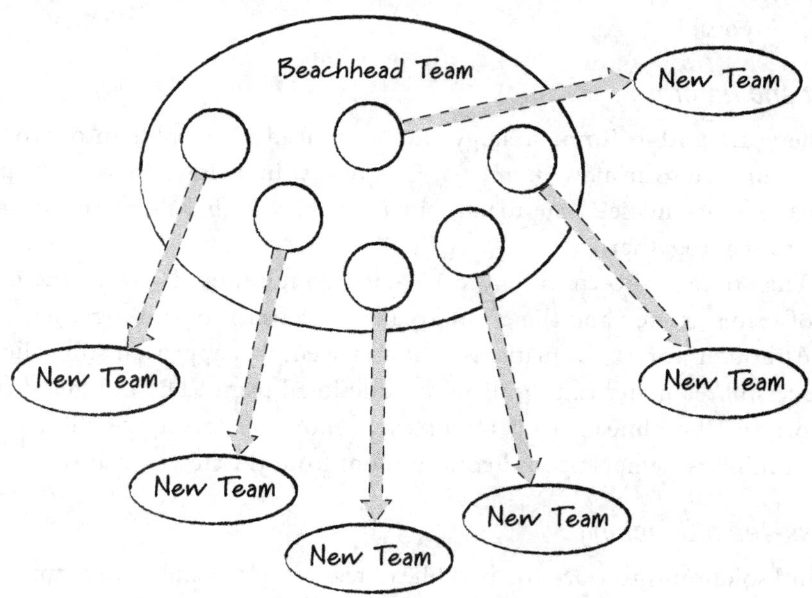

FIGURE 16.5 Cross-team coaching

Full-Scale Deployment

Some studios desire a companywide or projectwide deployment of Scrum. This presents more risk to the studio, as any major process change would, but if done properly is the fastest way to roll out Scrum. This section will discuss the areas of risk and an overall strategy to reduce it.

Transition Planning

Full-scale deployment has to be planned more carefully than the beachhead team experiment. The larger the number of people transitioning, the more challenging it is to communicate and sustain the vision for why change is taking place and to create the conditions that enable them to start using Scrum quickly. This is the goal of transition planning.

NOTE Transition planning is also needed after a beachhead team has proven successful and a larger number of teams are deployed from them.

The first step is to have at least one person become a Certified ScrumMaster (CSM).[3] This provides an exposure to Scrum practices and principles to ensure the team starts on the right path.

The next step is to establish roles and definitions. This is best done in a meeting with all the executives, stakeholders, ScrumMasters, and project leads that form the transition team that is responsible for the transition. The CSM or a Scrum coach facilitates this meeting.

NOTE A **Scrum coach** is someone with years of experience shipping games using Scrum and coaching teams. The Scrum Alliance recognizes and certifies such coaches.

The product owner and stakeholders for the project and ScrumMasters for the teams are identified. They must all be well versed in the duties and responsibilities of the product owner role.

NOTE The product owner should be considered full-time on any project of three or more Scrum teams. Ideally they should attend a Certified Product Owner (CPO) course.

3. www.ScrumAlliance.org

Next the studio executives discuss their expectations and roles with the group. They must be aware of the principle that teams are committed to work during the sprint and that all changes in priorities to the project should occur outside the sprints themselves.

The transition team should help the product owner create an initial definition of *done* (see Chapter 5, "User Stories"). Does it mean that each story must run at a minimum frame rate on the target platform? Does it have to run on the development platform? The transition team will need to establish the baseline definition with the expectation that it will improve over time.

The next step is to create an initial release plan that will allow a product backlog to emerge and the teams to quickly begin working.

The First Release and Sprint

The next step for full-scale Scrum deployment is to prepare for the first release for each project. This begins with establishing release goals and a release plan created in a release-planning meeting (see Chapter 6). This meeting is conducted by the transition team or with the entire project staff, if it's not too large.

Once a release plan is ready, the transition team will meet with the entire project staff to discuss the goals of the release. Leading up to this there should be a number of meetings with the teams to educate them about the practices and goals of Scrum.

The goals of the first sprint should be modest to establish a cycle of success. The first sprint will reveal a lot of problems with the existing studio practices and the team's adoption of Scrum.

TIP

Management should be careful not to go too far promoting Scrum. The team will be sold by the results. Overselling Scrum will turn some developers off. The best thing for management to do during a sprint is to support the teams by helping them address every impediment they can't solve themselves. There will be many at first. Once the teams see management being facilitative, it will sell them on Scrum more than any entreaty about its benefits.

The following are the principles and practices that the team needs to understand in preparing them for their first sprint:

- They are committing to the goals of the sprint as a team, not as individuals committing to their own tasks. The entire team will succeed or fail on this basis. Overcommitting is not a great danger, since they can renegotiate with the product owner during the sprint. Teams new to Scrum are more likely to underestimate their work.

- Commitment is reciprocal. Management will not change their goals or the sprint review date without a sprint reset.
- The definition of *done* must be clearly understood between the team and the product owner. The functionality delivered at the end of the sprint must reflect this definition.
- The rules of the daily scrum are understood.
- The purpose and utility of the burndown chart are understood.

EXPERIENCE

Iterating on ***any*** change within two to four weeks is challenge enough for some teams!

Following the first sprint, the ScrumMasters will need to set aside several hours to run retrospectives for the teams and then meet with the transition team to discuss the results.

Establishing the Product Backlog

A goal for the first release should be to refine the product backlog. This usually includes the following:

- Discussions with the publisher and license holders to establish a vision for the game
- Concept and design work to refine the vision
- Infrastructure work and risk identification

All of these elements are used to create a backlog and prioritize the stories within it.

TIP

It's easy to go too far and create a product backlog that is too finely detailed and unwieldy. The product backlog should be large enough to support several releases of stories, with detail decreasing with priority, yet not so large that the burden of maintaining it is too great. For a console game, 300 to 500 stories on the product backlog is a good target. For an iPhone game, probably 100 to 200 stories are enough, but your mileage may vary.

Summary

Every studio that adopts Scrum has a unique experience. The path from apprentice through journeyman to master is different. Some take a few years, others stall. The goal is to shift studio culture to one that emphasizes continual improvement, which assumes that change needs to occur, improvements need to be found, and there is no limit to learning. Culture usually resists change. It has inertia, and it trumps process every time. That's the challenge!

Additional Reading

Cockburn, A. 2007. *Agile Software Development: The Cooperative Game*. Boston: Addison-Wesley.

Cohn, M. 2009. *Succeeding with Agile*. Boston: Addison-Wesley.

Hackman, J. R. 2002. *Leading Teams: Setting the Stage for Great Performances*. Boston: Harvard Business School Press.

Conclusion

The practices and experiences of agile game development are real. Many studios are using them now. As new platforms and business models emerge, new practices, tools, and ways for creative people to make better games less expensively will evolve. This is what makes agile so well suited for developing games. The goal is not to find the "perfect" methodology but to embrace change.

This is a very unique and challenging time for game developers. Games are becoming more mainstream, and we are discovering different platforms on which to release games and new markets for them. Even "serious games" for education, health care, defense, city planning, and so on, are emerging as a significant market. At the same time, massive layoffs and lawsuits over unfair working conditions threaten careers and cause talented people to leave the industry.

The overhead, drudgery, and suffering that many game developers endure to make something "fun" impacts game quality. We should share the practices that help us reduce the waste involved in making games—waste such as waiting around, losing work to crashes, spending time on unworkable solutions, and communication problems. We need only compete on the basis of our creativity and talent. Doing this, we can raise the bar for the entire market and grow it.

We need to return to the state where most of us started when making games in our spare time: we need to love making games.

Bibliography

Beck, K. 2000. *Extreme Programming Explained.* Boston: Addison-Wesley.

Boehm, B. 1981. *Software Engineering Economics.* Englewood Cliffs, NJ: Prentice Hall.

Cerny, M. 2002. *Blog on the Cerny method.* www.methodgames.com/methodblog/files/category-3.html.

Cockburn, A. 2007. *Agile Software Development: The Cooperative Game.* Boston: Addison-Wesley.

Cohn, M. 2004. *User Stories Applied: For Agile Software Development.* Boston: Addison-Wesley.

———. 2006. *Agile Estimating and Planning.* Upper Saddle River, NJ: Prentice Hall.

———. 2008. Slides from Certified Scrum Master course.

———. 2009. *Succeeding with Agile: Software Development Using Scrum.* Boston: Addison-Wesley.

DeGrace, P., and L.H. Stahl. 1990. *Wicked Problems, Righteous Solutions: A Catalogue of Modern Software Engineering Paradigms.* New York: Yourdon Press.

DeMarco, T., and T. Lister. 1999. *Peopleware.* New York: Dorset House Pub.

Grenning, J. 2002. *Planning poker.* www.objectmentor.com/resources/articles/PlanningPoker.zip.

Jeffries, R., and G. Melnik. 2007. TDD: the art of fearless programming. *IEEE Software* May/June: 24–30.

Kent, S. 2001. *The Ultimate History of Video Games.* Roseville, CA: Prima.

Lakos, J. 1996. *Large-Scale C++ Software Design.* Reading, MA: Addison-Wesley.

Laramee, F. D. 2005. *Secrets of the Game Business.* Hingham, MA: Charles River Media.

Larman, C., and B.Vodde. 2009. *Scaling Lean and Agile Development: Thinking and Organizational Tools for Large-Scale Scrum*. Boston: Addison-Wesley.

Poppendieck, M., and T. Poppendieck. 2003. *Lean Software Development*. Boston: Addison-Wesley.

Schwaber, K. 2004. *Agile Project Management with Scrum*. Redmond: Microsoft Press.

Schwaber, K., and M. Beedle. 2002. *Agile Software Development with Scrum*. Upper Saddle River, NJ: Prentice Hall.

Steiner, I.D. 1972. *Group Process and Productivity*. New York: Academic Press.

Stephenson, G. R. 1967. Cultural acquisition of a specific learned response among rhesus monkeys. In: Starek, D., R. Schneider, and H. J. Kuhn (eds.). *Progress in Primatology*. Stuttgart, Germany: Fischer.

Sutherland, J. 2004. *Agile development: lessons learned from the first scrum*. http://jeffsutherland.com/scrum/FirstScrum2004.pdf.

Takeuchi, H., and I. Nonaka. 1986. The new new product development game. *Harvard Business Review* January: 137–146.

Taylor, F.W. 1911. *The Principles of Scientific Management*. New York: Harper Bros.

Van Den Bulte, C., R. K. Moenaert. 1998. The effects of R&D team co-location on communication patterns among R&D, marketing, and manufacturing. *Management Science*, v.44 n.11 Pt.2, p.1–18.

Vaughan, D. 1996. *The Challenger Launch Decision*. Chicago: University of Chicago Press.

Wake, W., and M. Cohn. 2003. *INVEST in good stories and SMART tasks*. www.xp123.com.

Index

C

D

E

F

G

H

I

J

K

L

U

V

W

informIT.com THE TRUSTED TECHNOLOGY LEARNING SOURCE PEARSON

Addison-Wesley Cisco Press EXAM/CRAM IBM Press. QUE PRENTICE HALL SAMS | Safari Books Online